IHSAN

THE THIRD AND SPIRITUAL BRANCH OF ISLAM

(SUFISM)

MYSA ELSHEIKH

IHSAN
THE THIRD AND SPIRITUAL BRANCH OF ISLAM
(Sufism)
Copyright © 2023 by MYSA ELSHEIKH
Published by MUSK STANDARD
www.muskstandard.com

info@muskstandard.com

All rights reserved. No part of this book may be reproduced, translated or transmitted in any form or by any means, electronic or mechanical, including photocopying, recording or by any information storage and retrieval system, without written permission from the author and/or publisher.

ISBN: 978-0-9566719-6-7 (Paperback)
978-0-9566719-7-4 (Hardback)
978-0-9566719-8-1 (Ebook)

CONTENTS

Introduction	i
1. What is Ihsan?	1
2. The Practice of Ihsan	17
3. Witness of God in Ihsan	35
4. The Ego	41
5. Monotheism in Ihsan	47
6. The Great Struggle	49
7. The Absent Ego	55
8. The Spirit	57
9. Purification of The Spirit	63
10. Diseases of The Heart	67
11. Cure of The Heart	81
12. Stages of Ihsan	99
13. The Lesser Ihsan	107
14. The Greater Ihsan	125
15. The Truth of God	127
16. Knowledge of God	131
17. The Great Character	135
18. The Love of The Prophet (Pbuh)	139
19. The Love of God	147
20. The Scholar of Ihsan	155
21. The Student of Ihsan	167
22. The Spiritual Contract	169
23. The Optional Worship	181
24. The Mention of God	187

25 The Responding Spirit	201
26 Spiritual Openings	207
27 The Ascension of The Spirit	217
28 The Presence of God	241
29 The Vision of God	243
30 The Pleasure of The Vision of God	261
31 After The Vision of God	263
32 Sainthood in Islam	269
About The Author	273

God Help us from the Evil of the Devil

In the Name of God, the Most Compassionate, the Most Merciful

God's Prayers of Peace and Blessings be upon the Prophet Muhammed (PBUH), his Family and Companions

INTRODUCTION

The Quran is the Holy Book of Islam. All Muslims believe the Quran to be God's Speech, and last message sent to humanity, through God's Prophet and Messenger Muhammed (Peace Be Upon Him). In the Quran God addresses humans, and refers to them using four terms. Each of these four terms refer to a specific aspect of the nature of humanity. These terms are *insan*, *basher*, *bani adam* and *nafs*. The word *insan* comes from a word meaning 'forgets'. This is a reference to the known limitation of the human cognitive component of memory. The inability for people to maintain knowledge and remembrance of all that it knows, at all times. This act of the mind's negligence in forgetfulness is considered to be benign and useful. The secret behind the mind's capability to consider a completely different second subject after it overlooks the first, by ignoring it in forgetfulness. This heedlessness of forgetting, requires the human mind to be constantly reminded of what is important to remember, such as God and religion. About this change in mind, God says in the Quran **"when they slipped from the religion, God slipped their hearts"** (61:5). This forgetfulness also places the importance of reminders to people of religion, God says **"they should remind of religion, for religious reminders benefit the believers"** (51:55). God says in the Quran, **"God does not make for a man two hearts in his one body"** (33:4), and that's why there is a need for movement of the mind from one topic to another, through the negligence of the topic to another considered more important. The Quran says the heart is one, and fluent attention is placed on only one topic at one time. The wisdom in one heart is to make the man's knowledge of the unity of the self, and so to know the meaning of that God is one.

Basher is derived from the Arabic word for skin, *beshra,* and it means creatures with skin, instead of fur or feathers. The human skin is one of many prominent visual differences that distinguish the human's body from that of other creatures and animals. This is a point from which one of the names for humans was formed in the Arabic language. It is a word used to emphasise the human from the perspective of their physical form, such as God says in the Quran about the angel appearing to Mary (To Her Peace) during the birth of Jesus that **"God sent to Mary an angel who came in the form of a proper human"** (19:17). To give emphasis the angel is described to have come in physical human form by use of the word *basher* in the original Arabic Quran. And the Angel said to Mary **"to eat and drink and be comforted, and if she meets any human to say she is fasting from speech, and cannot speak this day to any human"**(19:26), since speaking is done using the lips which are part of the physical human, again in this verse God uses the word *basher*. In the Quran its use is acceptable and relevant in association to the presence of commands to physical acts of worship that require the body as well as its manipulation and movement.

Bani adam meaning children of Adam is used by God in the Quran to remind us of our spiritual heritage as the children of Adam (as). Adam was the first human created, the first prophet in Islam, and the angels prostrated to him in honour of his spiritual position as Caliph of God. This is an origin accepted by most people. This meant that when speaking of dignity God used this term, for example, **"God bestowed to the children of Adam clothes to cover their shame, and feathers to wear for beauty"**(7:26). These terms which exist in the Quran, mention only three dimensions of the human; its body, mind and spirit. However, it is the spirit and the fourth term mentioned in the Quran, *nafs*, which is of most importance and central to understanding of the third branch of Islam, which is the topic of this book.

The human being has this compounded structure as it consists of three main things: a body (*jism*), mind (*aql*) and spirit (*ruh*), and the three are under the control of the *nafs* (the ego). As the ego rules over the three, it depends on the state of the ego to determine how much benefit or harm the person brings to their body, mind and soul. The Prophet Mohammed (peace be upon him) said in a Hadith in the authoritative Bukhari **"In the person there is a part when it is good, the whole person is good, and when it is bad, the whole person is bad, and that is the heart"**. The word 'heart' in this Hadith refers to the ego (*nafs*). However, the word *nafs* is mainly used to mean when the ego is in a negative religious state, when the person isn't practicing the religion, and the word heart can be used for both when the ego is in a positive or negative spiritual state. The word *nafs* gained this negative connotation as it is based on the word breath, and it's a classic act of animals to increase their breathing when in a state of anger or greed; classic ego's commands when the ego is in its abhorrent state. The Quran counts this as a harm to ask God to help from, God says **"God's help from the witches blowing on knots for magic"**(113:4), in other words from those who create fraudulent ways of magic due to their '*nafathat*' (much breathing), that are caused by their overwhelm in desire. This is why as well as meaning person, the word *nafs* also means intense desire in Arabic. The word heart (*galb*), literally means to flip, so to change, and thus carries a neutral meaning of this change going either way to what is good or bad. The ego and its diverse states means a fourth category of words exists in the Quran for humans. They are however names of religious spiritual states, such as *mutageen* (pious), *sidiqeen* (righteous), *shuhada* (martyrs), and *Awliya* (saints). They express the level of *nafs* people reached to achieve these noble spiritual stations.

This multidimensional form of the human requires an efficient religion to be one that demands worship in all these different levels. The Quran explains this, and even mentions that there will be separate judgment by God on the different dimensions of the human. God says **"the hearing and seeing and heart are all people will be responsible for on the Day of Judgement"** (17:36). God, upon recognising that His religion of Islam does meet the reality of the human, said He accepts to give it to people as a final religion, only once it has completed religious teachings on all human dimensions. In the Quran, God says in one of the last verses revealed **"this day, God completed the religion of Islam, and completed His favour and grace, and God accepts the religion of Islam for all people"** (5:3). However, it is the Hadith that explains to us this religion parts called branches, which are intended to meet the different parts of the human. This is part of Muhammed's (PBUH) role of prophecy, which is not only to provide the message of God, but to also explain what it means to the people. Muhammed's success in practice of the religion to demonstrate it in human form, that he was described as **"his character was the Quran"** (Ibn Hajar).

The religion of Islam, which is the message from God to His creation is a comprehensive guidance that acknowledges all dimensions of the human being. Therefore, it is a religion with aspects intended for the different dimensions of the human being. One of the names of the Holy Quran mentioned in the Quran itself is *Al-Ziker* (The Reminder). Seeing as it is a reminder of God, His worship and the Hereafter, and consequently, its regular recital in prayer acts as a constant reminder of God. The commandments of the Quran and the teachings of God's Prophet which instruct to physical acts of worship and legitimate certain actions are intended as guidance for our benefit, and their strict prohibitions act as preservers for our physical bodies from harm. As all humans are the children of Adam (as) a prophet of God in Islam, this validates the term *bani adam*. This is reflected in that as humans our worship which is a command from God is also inherent in our nature, and therefore, the human need and right to spirituality.

The religion of Islam is considered to consist of three main branches; they are Islam, Iman and Ihsan. The fourth and completing branch of the religion is the branch of Zaman. This is based on the authoritative Hadith of Umar Ibn Al-Khattab (raa) in which he says "**One day, while we were sitting with the Prophet Muhammed (pbuh), a man came to our presence. His clothes were sparkling white; his hair the darkest black. No signs of travel appeared on him. None of us recognised him. He went to the Prophet (pbuh) and sat in front of him, placing his knees before the Prophet's knees and he placed his hands upon the Prophet's thighs, saying 'Muhammed, What is Islam?' The Prophet (pbuh), replied 'Islam is to verbally testify that there is no deity but Allah and that Muhammed is the Messenger of Allah; to establish *salah* (daily prayer); to give *zakah* (obligatory charity); to fast Ramadan; and, to visit Allah's House as a pilgrim, if you are able.' The stranger said, 'You speak the truth.' Umar said 'We were amazed that he would ask him a question and then to tell him he was truthful!' The stranger then asked 'Muhammed, what is *Iman* (belief)?' The Prophet (pbuh) replied, saying '*Iman* is to believe in Allah, His angels, His Books, His Messengers, the Last Day, and to believe in *qadar* (God's Decree) accepting what reaches you of its good and bad. 'The stranger said 'You speak the truth.' Then, he asked 'What is *Ihsan*?' He (pbuh) replied, '*Ihsan* is to worship Allah as though you see Him, but if you see Him not, then to worship Him knowing He sees you.' The stranger said 'You speak the truth.' Then, he asked 'Can you inform me about the Last Hour?' He (pbuh) replied, 'The questioned knows no more about it than the questioner.' The stranger said, 'Then tell me of its signs.' The Prophet (pbuh) answered 'Among its signs are that the slave woman shall give birth to her mistress, and that the poor, naked and barefoot, the herders of sheep, shall compete in raising tall buildings.' The** stranger then left and I remained. The Prophet (pbuh) then asked me 'Umar, do you know who was the questioner?' I replied that Allah and His Messenger knew more. The Prophet (pbuh) said 'This was angel Gabriel. He came to teach you your religion." (Muslim)

In this Hadith reported by the great companion Umar (raa) who was the second Caliph of Islam, the angel Gabriel asked four questions, and Prophet Muhammed (pbuh) answered. The scholars consider that the answer to each of these questions outlines a branch of the religion of Islam. This Hadith also gives the totality of what the religion of Islam is, as in the end of the Hadith the Prophet said this was a recap from the angel on the religion. This function has made it one to the most important words uttered by Muhammed (PBUH) that it is nicknamed the Mother of the Sunnah, just as the first chapter of the Quran, the chapter of the Opened, which is recited obligatorily in every prayer, is called the Mother of the Book.

God said about the religion being complete **"this day, God completed the religion of Islam, and completed His favour and grace, and God accepts the religion of Islam for all people"** (5:3), meaning anything other than this will not be accepted as Islam. It also means only the totality is Islam, and must all be practiced. God says **"do people believe in a part of the revelation of God and disbelieve in other part? The punishment of those who do this is disappointment in this world, and on the day of judgement are taken to a strong punishment"** (2:85). God also says in regards to complete practice of Islam **"they were commanded to worship God sincerely in complete practice of the religion, with a pure belief about God, and to establish prayer and give in charity and that is the best religion"** (98:5).

God says **"those who accept other than Islam as religion, God does not accept their religion, and in the afterlife they will be among the losers"** (3:85). This is because the only religion that God now accepts is Islam, **"the acceptable religion to God is Islam"** (3:19). This means only what is mentioned in this Hadith or related to it can be considered the religion of Islam. Therefore, this Hadith is an outline of the religion in its most concise form, its skeleton in a way. It does this by fragmenting the religion into four branches. The four branches of Islam are called Islam, Iman, Ihsan and Zaman. This is based on the fact that these were the four main questions the Angel asked in these specific words, and the Prophet gave answers on.

This Hadith gives the structure of the religion, as it being made of different parts each with a name and basic description, making this Hadith important in describing the anatomy of the religion. The description the Prophet gave to each part after being questioned by the Angel, is merely concise of the tenets of each branch, however each branch while pivoting in what he mentioned, spreads to material much greater in amount found in the Quran and Hadith.

The Hadith of Gabriel (as) mentioned previously gave us the basic skeleton of the religion. The companions of the Prophet and the scholars who came after them built upon this skeleton by bringing together the knowledge spread in the Quran and Sunnah about each branch, and elaborated on their meaning giving us a correct understanding of our religion. However, the branch of Ihsan is unique from the other two in that it is about gaining specific religious spiritual states, and thus is not completely understood nor fulfilled except through personal experience and practice of the religion. Moreover, while there are some parts of the branch that can be practiced by the person on their own, other parts require the knowledge and guidance of a scholar of the branch of Ihsan.

The three main branches of the religion of Islam are called Islam (like the name of the religion), Iman and Ihsan, and each deals with the rectification of a certain aspect of the person. In the same way that the branch of Islam (*Fiqh*) deals with rectifying the physical worship (of the body), and the branch of Iman (*Aqida*) deals with rectifying beliefs (of the mind), the branch of Ihsan deals with rectifying the 'ego' (*nafs*) to gain in spirituality. The Prophet (pbuh) described the ego as "**yourself that lies between your two shoulders**" (Ibn Rajab). As the body, mind, and spirit are under the control of the ego, when the person rectifies the state of their ego, all their dimensions are rectified. The reverse is also right since the ego is rectified by correcting the body, mind and soul, through the sincere worship of God and the correct practice of the religion. The human is not a uniform entity like a piece of rock, a drop of rain or a clump of snow but made of different parts that are integrated into a body with mind and spirit and controlled by an ego. As this is the case, it is acceptable to assume bridging and inter-influence between these parts, so that the body can be influenced though mental means. In fact, traditionally, the Arabs who believed firmly in the unity of the diverse parts of the human, used the *rugya* (lit. Improvement), mantras of natural facts, such as stone is hard and star is bright, intended to pass through the mind to cure spiritual and bodily diseases.

The religion of Islam is based on and is considered a continuation of the religion of prophet Abraham (as) who built the four sided house of God in Mecca, and thus it is no surprise that it is also made of four branches. The number four is thus significant in Islam, and they argue that God chose to build a four-sided House instead of a circle, as are some of the traditional homes, due to its stability as a shape and sharp edges to signify the strength of His majesty. Perhaps, the four sided house was an early prompt from God about the Prophethood of Muhammed (pbuh) to come who is the greatest and last prophet of Abraham's (as) bloodline of divine revelation, that includes the distant cousins of Muhammed (pbuh); Moses the prophet of Judaism and Jesus the Lord of Christians. God says **"God gave the family of Abraham the holy books, religious wisdom and a mighty kingship"(4:54).**

The religion of Islam consists of four branches; Islam, Iman, Ihsan and Zaman. They each can be thought to represent a side of the House of God. Islam is to *verbally* say 'There is no God but Allah'. Iman is to *believe* that 'There is no God but Allah', and Ihsan is to *witness* that 'There is no God but Allah'. The branch of Zaman is to *recognise* that we are living in the End of Times, and that 'All will perish except for Allah' at the Last Hour. Zaman is about making sure the Muslim is well oriented in time and space. When in this world (*dunya*), they are emphasised to the fact that this is *dunya*, and to appreciate its shortcomings, and when in *barzakh* the intermediary world between this world and the next they are aware of this, and when it's Judgment Day they recognise its reality, until they reach their eternal place in hell or Heaven. This is to make sure, while in *dunya* they do not mistake it to be Heaven, and sit in leisure ignoring worship and with each stage they are well adapted to its needs. It is a branch of recognising to differentiate time, to know when it is temporal such as *dunya*, and when permanent such as the hereafter. This is to recognise that God is eternal without beginning and end, an important tenet in the belief about God in Islam.

To differentiate between the three branches of the religion is important. The verse says **"they believe not but to say they have submitted to Islam, until belief enters their heart"** (49:14), showing that God himself was not accepting for people to claim to be at a level of practicing a certain branch when they were not. In fact, historical problems that ensued among Muslims was caused by lack of understanding the different branches, the early of these being the khawarij who considered the two branches of Islam and Iman to be one. Many Muslims were killed as they were considered disbelievers for not reaching belief and did not practice aspects in the branch of Islam. In modern times, some Bedouins again clumped this time Islam with Ihsan, saying the branch of Ihsan is merely strong vigilances of God during worship, so that through a prayer in which you are aware of God watching you, you fulfil Ihsan. To claim this is a rejection of the existence of the ego, which is a rejection of free choice and thus accountability itself. However, in reality each branch is a separate unit, and while individual lack of paying of *zakah* (obligatory charity) doesn't make a person a disbeliever as it's part of Islam branch and not Iman, collective refusal of paying of zakah to the ruler as it happened in the time of Abu Bakr (raa) is a group rebellion against God and the authority, and that was the reason it was considered anarchistic heresy that required the control by troops. Their refusal to pay the *zakah* in masses was passive murder of the poor Muslims who usually received it, and thus the army was used to fight them in war.

The religion itself is called Islam after the branch of Islam, and in the Arabic language, it is possible to call the whole using the name for a part of it, such as the Prophet (pbuh) once called Ali (raa) Abu Turaba (Sanded man) for having sand on his clothes from reclining on the mosque's floor. This is to highlight its importance and essentiality to the whole. In this Hadith, it is the angel of revelation who named the different branches of Islam, but the overall name came from God. The religion is called Islam, named by God in a verse of the Quran. God says **"God accepts the religion of Islam for all people."** (5:3). Likewise, God sent in a dream inspiration to his mother to call His Prophet and her son Muhammed. Whilst pregnant Amna Bint Wahab, the Prophet's mother, saw in a dream a call to name her unborn baby Muhammed. The branch of Islam is significant in that it is the branch that deals with physical worship, of the body's obligations towards God, which is the most serious human expression. The *salah* (daily prayer), the fasting, the moving of the hand to give charity, and the walking to pilgrim to Mecca. This is the reason the whole religion came to be called Islam in honour of this great method of worship. While they are a hardship to the body, it is not considered that God wishes to destroy His creation in placing such demands of worship. The intention of God is to use it to identify the sincere believers and worshipers **"God tests people as to who will be perfect in worship"** (11:7). God says **'God wants for the believers ease, and does not wish upon them hardship"** (2:185) and God refused to accept pain and unnecessary punishment on his creation he says **"God has no need to punish people if they are grateful to God, and believe in God"** (4:147). It is people who chose their own destruction when they refuse to commit to the manual of life God revealed in the religion, and instead wear out their bodies in leisure and futile activities. God says **"God is not unjust to them but they are unjust to themselves"** (3:117). Thus the branch of Islam considers the human body and then gives guidance in restricting, controlling and organising this dimension. It does this by giving detailed instructions of different worship activities, such as the steps in making ablution the pre-prayer wash, and in praying such as the different body positions the person does while glorifying God in reciting a portion of the Quran.

The second branch is the branch of Iman. Iman (belief) lies in the heart, but the subject of belief is contained in the mind (*aql*). For example, two people can have equal amounts of belief, yet the belief itself can be different: one can believe that Jesus (as) was the son of God, while the other can believe with the same intensity that he was only a great prophet of God. The Quran says emphasising this difference between belief and objects of belief **"it is horrendous what their belief in the divinity of the bull has done to them, if it is even worthy to consider worship of a bull religion"** (2:93) proving that Iman can be on an incorrect state if the subject of belief itself is wrong and criticises those with faulty Iman as their belief state encouraging them to do evil. The Prophet in a Hadith pointed to his chest and said '**here lies *iman***' to mean it is in the heart. However the object of belief lies in the mind, and the tenets of belief of Islam, its creed is called *aqida* from the word *aql* (mind), and this refers to it being in the mind, and specifically the sane mind, for the word *aql* is only used in Arabic for sane minds. Thus naming after this word is to establish that the teachings of Islam were rational and acceptable to the sane minds. The word *aql* means knot, and refers to the mind serving as a tie between the person and the world, one who is sane and grounded in reality. Through this firm grip, they are good at navigating and surviving the world. But on the other hand, one of psychosis, one who becomes disconnected from reality when the rope between him and the mind is severed may end up dead. This use of the word *Aqida* is thus loyal to this meaning that faith is a rope between the believer and the greater reality of God. The Quran says **"God has touched them with humility**

wherever they may be, except with a rope from God and a rope from the people" (3:112). The rope of men means, the rope of the world. In praise of Islamic creed, Sheikh Busairy a scholar of Ihsan said in his famous Burdah poem, 'the Prophet came to us with a belief that doesn't corrode our minds'. The Quran says **"God revealed it an Arabic Quran, so that it can be easily understood"** (12:2), a language developed to be spoken in the dangerous desert environment and thus most suitable to give religious safety instruction about the danger of hellfire. God expressed that His intention in choosing the Arabic language was to better our intellect, and not their offence nor destruction.

To believe that the branch of Ihsan is merely to perform worship in the basic states of reverence mentioned in the Hadith of Gabriel (as) or is limited to these two states, would be like to mistake that the only obligations of the religion are the five mentioned to describe the branch of Islam known commonly as the Pillars of Islam, or that the tenets of belief a Muslim must believe in are the few mentioned in describing the branch of Iman. There are details to each branch that were not mentioned but are not less important or essential to each branch. There are obligations in the branch of Islam not counted, such as inheritance, marriage, and just governance. In the branch of Iman, the existence of jinn (spirits), miracles of the Prophets and the belief in hell and Heaven are not mentioned but they are just as valid as the others that were mentioned. Those that were mentioned are considered the minimum the person must practice of each branch. Similarly, it is not correct to think that the branch of Ihsan is limited to those two states in the description of Ihsan, or that those mentioned spiritual states could be easily learnt or directly practiced like the command for *salah* (physical prayer) or fast. There is a process to gaining these states, and there are details to the branch other than those mentioned in the Hadith. This is what this book aims to do: explain this process and act as a comprehensive manual to the branch of Ihsan, bringing together its details spread in the Quran and the Sunnah.

About the fourth branch of Zaman (Time), God says **"all will perish except His face"** (28:88). In the Last Hour of the world, the Prophet (pbuh) said all will be destroyed, even the angels who carry out the destruction will be asked to perish themselves. This branch explains that we are living in the End of Times and that this started on the day of the start of Muhammed's Prophethood as he is considered the Prophet of the last days. The message of his religion thus preaches minimalism, and lack of attachment to this world, merely as it is not right to attach to a thing about to be destroyed.

It is the practice of the religion that a Muslim does not neglect a branch of their religion, nor concentrates on one branch and overlooks the others. The correct way, for someone who wishes to learn the religion, is to start with the branch of Islam, then Iman and finish with Ihsan. This was the way the Messenger (PBUH) introduced the religion to the Companions and advised them to follow when inviting them to Islam. To the companion sent to invite Yemen to Islam, the Prophet said **'start with inviting them to testify to God, if they accept that, then teach them prayer, if they accept that, then tell them to fast, and if that is done they should pay their religious tax to the poor'** (Bukhari). Those who are already Muslim would be required to practice all branches of the religion simultaneously. Nevertheless, there is a natural spiritual advancement in the order of the branches of Islam.

It is possible that when the companions used to ask how to fulfil this noble branch of Ihsan, the response was that it was as simple as performing whatever God commands in the best way possible. Overtime this phrase wasn't sufficient, and people wanted to know how, for they felt their egos got in the way of implementing the teachings of the religion. They also wanted to know how to overcome their egos and desires, as well as the best way to do this and explanations to the changes and spiritual states that happen when they actually did what God commands. This led to the expansion of the knowledge of this branch, as well as its practice over the centuries, when scholars started to answer these subsidiary questions on the branch. This book hopes to collect the different teachings of this branch to make it accessible for its practitioners, and those who seek to become informed about this honourable branch in the religion of Islam.

In conclusion, the human is made of four different parts: a body, mind spirit, and ego, and Islam preserves this notion in being multi-branched by there being worship reaching each part of the human. Ritualistic physical worship for the body, beliefs and specified faith dogmas for the mind, and sincerity of devotion and rejecting following of the ego for the spirit. In this book, it is the worship of the spirit in practice of the branch of Ihsan that is to be described and explained in detail. The branch of Ihsan, which deals with this, is the third and spiritual branch of Islam and this book is aimed to be a comprehensive collection of its knowledge and a guide to its practice based on proof from the Quran and Hadith.

CHAPTER ONE

WHAT IS IHSAN?

Ihsan in Arabic literally means beauty, excellence and perfection. In Islam, the word Ihsan is used to mean spiritual improvement, charity and beautiful worship. In fulfilling the branch of Islam the person gets a mark of 'pass' in their religion, and by fulfilling the branch of Iman they receive a 'good pass', then by fulfilling the branch of Ihsan they achieve 'excellent' in their religion. The religion of Islam believes in a perfect God, so it is no surprise that it also believes in perfection of worship taught in Ihsan. The Hadith says '**God has commanded there to be perfection in all things**' (Muslim). This is to say all things must be done to perfection, and it is no surprise that he didn't leave out the command to perfect the worship. This is to say it should be part of the plan when deciding to do anything for this world or the next, is to intend to do it with quality so that it is created perfectly. The most important of all though is the perfection of religion and this is dealt with in the branch of Ihsan. In another Hadith, the Prophet (pbuh) said "**perfect your actions, if you slaughter make sure your tools are sharp to quicken the cut for the animal**" (Abu Dawood). The Quran praises "**who is better in religion than a Muslim who submit themselves to God in perfect worship of Ihsan**" (4:125). Then God confirms "**whoever submits themselves to**

God in perfect worship of Ihsan, to them will be a reward from God and neither will they become fearful nor sad" (2:112). This indeed is affirming that Ihsan is excellence and there is no religious state higher nor better than it.

What's more, the Prophet (pbuh) said '**Religion is to do what is whole for the sake of God and His Messenger**' **(Abu Dawood)**. According to Muhammed religion as a concept is what is complete, including acts of good and wholeness while practicing the branch of Ihsan and maintaining continuously a state of completeness and perfection of worship in religion. God described being complete in the practice of the whole religion as the best worship, and this is achieved in fulfilling all the branches and parts of the religion. God says **"they were only commanded to worship God sincerely with a pure belief about God, and to establish prayer and give in charity and that is the best religion"** (98:5). In other words, God says in the verse, since religion is to do what is whole to God, the best religion a person can have is one fully practiced, done fully for God.

That religion in general is that people endeavour to do what is whole or good for the sake of God, and this is a beautiful definition of the phenomena of religion. This is because the idea of God is that He is *qudos* (Holy) and this is the concept of a thing being complete, and whole (hence the word holy from whole), and whatsoever possesses this attribute such as God deserves reverence and praise. Thus, contrary to recent claims of religion having a history of violence and war and injustice, religion in general motivates towards doing what is best and perfect, including socially such as in giving charity and acting in good character. This has been the traditional and historical view of religion in humanity.

Ihsan as the spiritual branch of Islam aims to direct the human spirit according to God's revelation. It assumes, rather it is adamant of the existence of a spirit to the Human. A concept not popular in our scientific age of fanatical material investigation, and interesting and useful manipulations of it in the form of modern technology. The spirit is the least subtle aspect of the human, the body is chunky and visible, and the mind is obvious when present. However, the spirit is intricate and delicate. Therefore, when the person's worship reaches this level of the spirit it cannot be described as anything but perfect, for let alone the large movements of the body, even the subtle spirit has become directed towards God. God mentions that there is worship of the spirit, He says **"whoever finds great the symbols of God, it is from the piety of the heart"** (22:32). This is the piety of the heart and the word heart is commonly also used to mean spirit. This is because the spirit is assumed to be internal to the body, and it exists permanently in death. The word *galb* (heart) means the other side as it means that which turns, for if the physical body is a side, the internal is the other side, and therefore *galb* is used to mean what is internal. Traditionally scholars of Ihsan taught that the body is merely a shell, and that the spirit is the inner *lub* (kernel). The word *galb* (heart), is from the words '*gl* (word) *lb* (internal)', showing that the Arabs considered the spirit to be the internal words and experience of meanings, and spirituality is to make honest your words. That is because it is not completely honest to call yourself a Muslim if you are not fulfilling it to perfection. Then as the nature of the word inside them changed with life events, they named change after it '*galb*' -what flip turns, and as the flesh heart is the part of the body that beats the most, it is in a perpetual state of change, so they called it *galb* meaning the turner. This is also because the heart pumps blood turning it from going down to going upwards. The Quran frequently makes use of the term '*uli al albaab*' (people of insight –*lub*) to mean those of understanding and spiritual wisdom. In another verse God links having a spiritual heart with state of being people of witness, meaning presence of mind with events. God says **"in this is a reminder to those who have heart or lend their ear in a state of witness"** (50:37). In practicing Ihsan, which is the spiritual branch, the person is meant to become a person of witness, a seeker to witness the truth of the religion and the presence and sight of God.

The Quran differentiates between those in different branches of the religion as having different levels of religiosity. In one verse it differentiates between those who are still in the branch of Islam and those who reached the branch of Iman. God says **"the Beduins say they believe in religion, the Prophet should say they do not believe yet, but to say they submitted to Islam, until belief enters their hearts"** (49:14). This is to say that while the Bedouins claimed a state of belief (Iman), in reality they were still in a spiritual state of submission to God, meaning they still had not reached a state of complete belief to merit the title of Iman but were still on the first branch of Islam. This verse thus teaches honesty with the words that describe the person and their activity of spirituality, for in accurate words the spirit aligns with the body, and the person witnesses spiritual experiences of clarity and peace.

To reach a state of excellence in the religion, the person requires the basics; which are a correct *aqida* (belief - branch of Iman) and the correct following of *fiqh* (branch of Islam) after receiving knowledge of them both from qualified scholars. This is then followed by correcting the state of the ego (*nafs*) with the guidance of an expert in the branch of Ihsan to gain the spiritual states that fulfil the branch of Ihsan. Correcting the state of the ego is done mainly through *fard* (obligatory) and *nafila* (optional) worship, combined with a change in the person's character to the like of the Prophet Muhammed (pbuh). God says in the Quran **"they have in the messenger of God a good example for those who look forward to the meeting with God and the Last Day, and mention God much"** (33:21). This process of rectifying the ego is known as *Tazzkiya* (purification), and it is achieved through *Jihadul-nafs* (struggling against the ego) in order to reach the high spiritual states that define Ihsan. To confirm the idea that Ihsan is *Jihadul-nafs*, in the Quran God says **"those who fight in the way of God will be guided in the way of God, and God is with those who practice Ihsan"** (29:69). That those that struggle in the cause of God in acts of hardship are in a state of Ihsan.

This rectifying of the ego is to restrict it to that which is *halal* (permissible). It is what God permitted for it with Quranic permission to indulge in, compared to the lack of restriction of the ego in state of disobedience and disbelief. When a companion insulted another due to his ego commanded him to do so, the Prophet Muhammed (pbuh) said **'you are a person with *jahiliya* in them'** (Muslim) meaning you are a person whose ego is in a state of *jahiliya* (preislamic disbelief state) not one with stable belief in God. This is because one with faith controls themselves to only that which is allowed, while the disbeliever acts in any way they want without limit in wrongs.

In essence, the purpose of Ihsan is to guide the believer to spiritual states of experiencing the truthfulness of what the Messenger (pbuh) told us about God. This is what is meant by witnessing. This is so that we may come to worship Him out of a state of belief based on experience and not trust alone. Prophet Abraham (as) asked God to show him how He brought alive the dead. This was not out of disbelief, nor in mockery, but as he explained, 'to give him confidence', meaning to give him assurance and increase him in belief. The Quran says **"prophet Abraham prayed to God to show him how he gives life to the dead, and God asked if he believed, and Abraham said he believed but wanted to be certain in his heart"** (2:260). The Prophet Muhammed (pbuh) said commenting on this verse: **'We are of more need to ask God for proof than Abraham (as)?' (Bukhari)**. This is to encourage his followers to have faith in God with proof and to endeavour to seek it, as well as a form of humility to Abraham who was confident in knowing God's existence by publicly rejecting idol worship, and was to seek and search for God, a long journey that others have not experienced, thus more in need of the proof. Also Abraham was asking for proof from God Himself, while most people still need proof to reach God at all. The proof in the case of Abraham (as) was not for God's existence, as Abraham (as) was a believer and the proof for His existence is clear in the existence of His creation. It was a proof for God's attributes, and while Abraham (as) believed that God was able to raise the dead, he wanted to increase certainty. This certainty can only be reached by witnessing, and following this, the person then worships God in a state of perfection. The Prophet Muhammed (pbuh) encouraging us to ask for proof to reach certainty in belief so we may become aware of our level of belief and to endeavour to increase it, for he says if the great prophet of God Abraham (as) did this, then we are probably more in need of proof than Abraham. The Quran then says **"God said take four birds, and then cut them to peaces and put a part of their flesh on each of the four mountains, and then to call them to come and they will come fast flying"** (2:260). When Abraham (as) saw how the dead parts of the birds he placed in separate places came together and gained life, he was able to believe with certainty that God was capable of raising the dead. This is similar to the state of the pious man Azeer, who God raised his animal in his presence after it became bones. God said to Azeer **"look at the bones of the donkey, and see how God joined them again and clothed them with flesh. When it became clear to the man the power of God, the man said he believed that God is capable of all things"** (2:259). This knowledge of religion is then firmly based on experience, and can be used to promote perfected worship. The branch of Ihsan usually aims to give such levels of certainty to encourage sincere worship of God. Witnessing is not impossible as God is not shy to manifest Himself and the existence of His attributes, and the proof for this is the abundant creations that exist in the world that act as signs for His existence and Majesty. This means that to practice Ihsan, the person can be guaranteed God will give them spiritual experiences that when they witness will gain certainty of faith.

The Quran says **"if the Prophet is in doubt about what God revealed in the Quran to be from God, then to check with those given revelation in the past of the Jews and Christians. The truth has come to the Prophet from his Lord, and the Prophet and believers should not be of the doubtful"** (10:94). God encourages the seeking of knowledge to erase doubt, for in Islam it is not blind faith as with other religions, but it is supposed to be informed belief since the religion is true. This is because the religion acknowledges the important of truth and rationality as it respects the existence of minds in humans. In the case of the Prophet Muhammed (pbuh) God told him that revelation is possible and thus not to be in state of doubt as it is fact that there were books from God previously revealed and are followed by the People of the Book. This is an umbrella term to include Jews and Christians, who share belief in the Old Testament. In fact, the Quran is considered to be the fourth book revealed by God.

To the general believers God says in this verse that if they have doubt, they are to ask those who believed before them and have knowledge of the divine book. The Prophet had approached with his wife Khadija (raa) a sage called Waraqa Ibn Nofal, who was with knowledge of divine scriptures and he confirmed to the Prophet that it was possible to receive divine revelation and that the description of the revelation of the Quran is in mirror to the revelation of Moses (as) who received the Old testament, also known as the Torah. As Prophet Muhammed (pbuh) was the first believer in Islam, he was commanded to speak to the People of the Book. However, to the general Muslims it's a different interpretation of the verse, to mean those with knowledge on the Quran, for after God was sure Muhammed became reassured it was a real and genuine revelation from God, God considered him and his followers to be ready to receive miracles and proof that the Quran was from God and for them to no longer have to check with the People of the Book. The Quran says **"those who come after them say in prayer Lord to forgive them and their brothers who were before them in belief"** (59:10). Those with religious precedence are the scholars and the religious pious who explain why we should believe and to strengthen our faith using the proof God laid in the Quran.

In the branch of Islam, the person is demanded to submit (surrender to God), regardless if they believe in the religion or not, if they have faith or not as it is an emergency situation. This is expected due to the horrendous state of hell and great loss if the person didn't, thus it is called 'submission' (one of the meanings of Islam). When the soldiers in the lost side of battle submitted, they quickly threw their armour and fell to their knees to show they were submitting to the victor side so as not to be killed, for after one side gains prominence in war it is no longer a battle but a suicide to carry on fighting. This is because soldiers who have not clearly submitted were easily killed by the other side considering them a danger. God is in the greater side of life, He is with the power and the might, and the Majesty of controlling all that is around us of this world, which He created and owns, and submission is about telling Him you are on His side and recognise yourself to be the weak side that must submit for safety from hellfire. This means all that is required is a simple verbal utterance that the person believes in God and His Messenger, and the other physical acts of worship, like a failed soldier the Muslim sits on their knees on a prayer-matt to God five times a day showing they are still in a state of submission to God.

Therefore, the entering into the religion of Islam, and converting to it as well as the practice of the branch of Islam is a form of safety assurance and emergency practice from a danger of an eternal hellfire foretold. Just as with regular fire-alarm tests and people existing quickly outside, God requires all those who believe to show on a regular basis that they still have the idea of submission to Him and their safety in mind. In some Hadith the Prophet said when a slave who regularly offers worship stops due to illness, the Angels check on them, and when prophet Jonah (as) became trapped inside the whale, the Angels were curious about the dislocation of the voice of his praise of God, saying **'it's a familiar voice from an unfamiliar place'** (Al Haithami). This is to say if in a crowd a person screamed there was a lion approaching, or in a concrete building a fire alarm goes off, all sane people are expected to run, and not return to their belongings nor wait to investigate how true this fire is, for the loss is too great, there is a risk of death. Likewise, God expects the same after the Prophet (pbuh) had communicated the majesty of God and His command for us to worship Him, as well as the Quran pointing out to us to look and ponder into the world and to see His power of creating the world, its volcanos and its lions, and its large mountains and tall thunderous skies. This alone, along with the idea of us humans disliking pain and are weak to be easily burnt by fire, should mean that we would be quick to submit to God. Nevertheless, God doesn't want us to submit, and later in the hereafter and after death to discover if the religion is true or not. Hence the branch of Iman. A branch that specialises in affirming our faith in the existence of God and the hereafter. If while running once heard the fire alarm, the person is told to check and bring their awareness that the building is getting a bit hot, and a smell of plastic melting has spread, this would only make people more determined to leave the burning building. Likewise proof of the religion help people to make sure that they regularly perform their acts of submissions, with the zeal of one in the know that their worship is truly warding off harm and protecting them from the punishment of God.

In the religion these proofs are called *albayinat* the 'clarifiers', which clarify it is indeed the truth. God says **"is one who created the heavens and earth capable of creating like them again, indeed God can, and He creates with knowledge"** (36:81) and this is the main proof of the religion. Once having made contact with this world, and seen it, it is itself a proof that another world could be created. In fact it is legal poof used in business that if a factory creates a prototype or sample, they can form a contract expecting more to be created. However, it is insane once told of the hereafter and eternal hell to ask about proofs, but rather enter a state of submission, which God said to be by verbally and publicly declaring submission to God in the words 'there is no god but Allah and Muhammed is his Messenger'. The idea that as humans we could say what we do not know to be true to save ourselves, is considered sane and perfectly fine due to the importance of safety, and thus no one ever tells off a company or public building for its fire alarm going off when there is no fire. It is to survive in the case of worldly fire, but in the case of religion it is to prevent the eternal hellfire. This is like one who can hear telling a deaf person in sign language that the fire alarm has gone off, even though they themselves are not certain of the fire. The Quran said to the Bedouins 'you are not believers yet'. This is to say, that they are submitters, and still just people running out of a building not knowing if the fire is true or not, so as to preserve their lives. The station of belief, of coming to a state of faith in the truthfulness of the religion, is a higher station that only those who reached it could have the pleasure of claiming.

The Prophet Muhammed (pbuh) communicated the proofs and one of them is the Quran, which to the native Arabic speakers is so different to material written by man as a synthetic plastic pole is to a tree. The Quran main teaching of reminding the people of the wonder of the world, brought people's attention to nature; God's main exhibit to His claim of creating a hereafter. All prophets came with proofs of the truth of their divine claim, and act as revealers to the truth of God, and while theirs were temporal as were miracles, that only those who were present at the time saw them and benefited from them spiritually, the Quran is the eternal miracle of Muhammed (pbuh). Once the proofs are communicated, people have freedom of choice and some accept them, and others reject them **"that is because they are people who do not understand"** (59:14). In another verse God says **"the most evil of people are those who are deaf and dumb to religious teachings, and those who do not understand religion"** (8:22). Those who refuse to hear the argument of God and become deaf to them, and choose to be dumb and not utter to testify Him as God, and after understanding them rejecting them is their lack of reasoning. For whatever reason, they decide to continue to stay at their desks and enjoy the game in the computer than run with the crowd, and if told it is getting hot, they claim the hotness is due to the bodies of many moving and not proof of a fire. Thus, it has been the job of scholars to combat arguments of those '**with corrupt minds**', and scholars such as Al Razi (raa), Abu Hamid Al Gazali (raa), exposing their illogic and the incorrectness and incoherencies of the arguments of those of disbelief. The Quran and religion calls the event of people wanting to ignore their safety as '*fitan*' (confusion) as it disrupts the others in bringing them doubt and are a religious danger to the people. The scholars are the religious fire inspectors, people who would point out that the temperature has become very hot even before the alarm was heard.

That elementary the Muslim is a cautious person, is revealed in the second chapter of the Quran. In the second chapter God says **"a guidance to the pious worshipers who are cautious of the hellfire"** (2:2). That the Quran is a book revealed as a guidance to those of '*taqwa*' (those who are cautious of dangers). It is like a site plan to show us the way to exit a burning building, and the Quran describes the straight path to avoiding hellfire. The word *taqwa*, is from the word *quwa* (strength) and in the past those going to the wild would armer themselves to put themselves in a stronger state when facing danger, and this word then became to mean cautiousness in Arabic, and it used in the Quran to mean religious cautiousness or piety. This is as the case that by submitting to God the person becomes a Muslim, and thus forbidden to last in hell, meaning they will not have a punishment of eternal hell. However, to avoid hell altogether by going directly to Heaven, the person needs to get instructions, what the Quran calls '*huda*' (guidance). That makes the person practice the religion in a correct format and thus enter into a sincere state of worship of God, which leaves God to reward them with Heaven.

There is a flow in the practice of the different branches of the religion, and each branch prepares the person to the one after it. By the time the person reaches the branch of Ihsan, they have already perfected Islam and Iman. They have submitted in Islam to God, and when after a while of standing and bending and prostrating in prayer the person starts to question if this is all a waste and futile fatigue or if there is real danger of hell, this point marks their redirection to the branch of Iman, where they are taught the proofs for the truthfulness of the religion. Then a state of wonder enters their heart after recognising it is a true religion, but the level of worship and commitment they are doing isn't parallel to the level of truth of the religion and the existence of God and the coming hell and Heaven. It is this points that marks the beginning of the practice of the branch of Ihsan, where they rebalance this synchrony by learning to improve their worship to a level to reflect the firm belief they have of the religion. The branch of Zaman is merely a back turn, like the turned sewing of the edges of the fabric of a skirt, in that it is merely an emphasis to return the person to stabilise on the branch of Ihsan. That the world is futile to consider for it to be destroyed acts like a dead end wall that the walker walks back from and returns them to Ihsan to encourage them that it is better to maintain quality worship in a state of Ihsan.

The Messenger of God (pbuh) when was asked what Ihsan is, he said Ihsan is to '**worship Allah as if you see Him and if you see Him not, then to worship Him knowing He sees you.**' The Prophet (pbuh) did not say to worship Allah based on what he (pbuh) has told us, but he said '**as if *you* see him**' meaning coming from 'your' subjective state of experience of His existence. This means that the worship of God is no longer based on 'trust' that God exists, in either a state of submission or certainty of proof, but out of personally witnessing His presence. The wisdom of this is that the better knowledge of God gained by personal spiritual experience leads us to a better understanding of God, and a greater belief in His existence. This allows us to then worship God in a state of strong belief that is in a level of '**if you see Him**', even after we no longer see Him. A state of worship like that of the angels, who have seen too much proof for God to have doubt of His Existence.

The branch of Ihsan therefore leads to realising the presence of God and the truthfulness of His Names and Attributes that are revealed in the Quran and the Sunnah. This helps us realise and accept that we are His creations, and try to serve Him as slaves in complete submission to His laws and orders, giving us a better life and hereafter. This realisation of God by an increase in knowledge of Him and consciousness of His existence is called in Ihsan '*Marifa*' (realisation). This *Marifa* is achieved by purifying oneself from the ego and its diseases that hinder this realisation, so that the person comes to know their Lord and perform better worship of Him. This element of realisation of the truth of God's existence is essential in the learning and practice of the branch of Ihsan. It even allowed some scholars of Ihsan to call the branch of Ihsan *Ilm alhaqiqa* (the knowledge of Truth), and its people *Ahl Alhaqiqa* (the people of Truth). They are also called *Ahl Altahqiq* (the people of investigating), meaning the revealers of the truth about God. This witnessing of the reality of God and the religion, and what follows it with sincere worship, can cultivate to the sincerest and most pious of practitioners of Ihsan in entering the presence of God, and even having vision of God.

The first God experiment to establish the truth of God to be witnessed publicly was done by the Arabs when they left the House of God to be attacked by the African elephant army. Abdul Mutalib bin Hashim who was the Prophet's paternal grandfather and leader of Mecca at the time, merely evacuated Mecca and left God to prove that He was indeed the Lord of the House. He asked everyone to move out of the city into the adjacent highlands and declared 'we believe the House has a protective Lord'. Hence the Quran reminded Qurish of this saying **"do they not consider how God dealt with the elephant army"** (105:1). Therefore, the Meccan *kufar* (disbelievers) are considered to be worse in disbelief due to the fact that God showed them His signs and public proof before the coming of Prophet Muhammed (pubh), for this event happened on the year of Muhammed's birth. This increase in accountability is the price of proof, and likewise in the Quran Jesus said to his fellow diners that if they received a feast from the Heaven and still disbelieved after that, then they are in a worse spiritual level and their punishment would be greater.

This chapter of the elephant recalls the events of when the African people for the sake of widening their international business and increasing their riches, tried to steal Mecca's spotlight and fame, which was an international trade centre at the time, selling religious memorabilia and objects of worship. They proposed to do this by creating a second house of God elsewhere to get the clients of religion and open a souvenirs shop where the idols would be sold. Then when they built their new temple and marched to destroy the original one in Mecca, God attacked them with missiles from the sky, turning their strong muscular African bodies and the huge elephants into mincemeat. God sent an army of small birds carrying small stones in their peaks and feet and threw them over the army until they became like **"rotten eaten hay"**(105:5) reports the Quran. This is because the stones were hot, as were cooked mud pieces, and it left their flesh in dry small pieces, for the hotness of the stones dried the cut pieces of their flesh. In this way the burnt edges of the damaged flesh was sealed and the blood dried making it impossible for their bodies to heal whole again.

Fortunately, by the time the Prophet Muhammed (pbuh) grew up about forty years after the event, there was a new government in Africa. This time a king who the Prophet (pbuh) said was just, and none of the followers of Muhammed (pbuh) who immigrated to his land should expect injustice from him. He meant a new good king who respects God and His House. It seems after that incident Abyssinians started to take all religion seriously, and even gladly accepted the Muslims who emigrated from Mecca to Africa in fear of prosecution by the powerful disbelievers of Mecca. When the malicious Meccan disbelievers sent people to get the Muslims removed from Abyssinia the Abyssinian king asked to hear the Muslim's perspective first, and decreed the asylum seekers to be fine to stay in his land. However, the Africans whom God exterminated in Arabia, were fulfilling of Abdul Mutalib's hypothesis that if God existed, He would protect His house, and He did. This meant that by the time of the Prophet's revelation there was a strong revival in the belief in God. That even those who disbelieved in Muhammed's religion maintained that they believe in God and couldn't publicly reject His existence. The

Quran says about them **"and if are asked who created the Heavens and earth, they would say God"** (31:25).

Abraham asked for more proof from God, and God readily answered by telling him to divide birds and separate them into different mountains and watch them come back alive. This is the state of the true practitioners of Ihsan; God is willing to answer their prayers, the Prophet said **"There are worshipers of God who if swore for something to happen God answers their prayer"** (Bukhari). However, this is not the state of the general worshipers. A normal worshiper God does not give miracles, sometimes does not even answer their prayers in desperate situations. This is like a teacher being asked by a student who doesn't even do their basic work for extra lessons on advanced aspects of the subject – the teacher would refuse, saying they must first finish their daily work. However, in the case of a smart student she may be excited of their development and provide for them extra tuition. The very pious God gives attention to and answers their want to see more of the work of God, such as miracles, but those who neglect what already exists from normal existence of the seas, birds, and trees, God does not find right for them miracles, and this is the importance of sincere worship in Ihsan that then merits them miracles called '*karamat*' to happen. God promises those who perfect their worship and who are sincere in their devotion to God to get miracles, as He says **"to the saints of God is a foretelling of good in the life of this world and the afterlife. There is no change to the words of God and that is the great win"** (10:64). The Prophet Muhammed (pbuh) said in interpretation of this verse of the Quran that the glad tiding or foretelling are the true dreams experienced by the pious. This is to say that those who perfect their worship of God start to experience miracles of true dreams, which they see in the night and happen in the day.

The branch of Ihsan is commonly known as Sufism. This is said to have come from the word for wool (*sufi*) which the practitioners of Ihsan used to wear in rejecting this world and wanting God and the afterlife. Another origin of the word Sufism is from platform (*sufa*) which was near the Prophet's mosque where the devoted poor muslims used to live, and a third origin for the word Sufism is from a word meaning purity (*safa*), since the practitioners of this branch are dedicated to purifying the spirit in becoming near to God and gaining His vision.

CHAPTER TWO

THE PRACTICE OF IHSAN

The aim of the practice of Ihsan (Sufism) is to reach perfection in the practice of the religion. This is because by definition Ihsan is perfection, and the branch of Ihsan's practice trains its follower to become an ideal worshiper. Then when this is fulfilled the person has reached excellence in their religion. This greater success in religion through practicing Ihsan has encouraged and motivated the widespread practice of Ihsan in the Muslim people since the start of Islam. The Quran says **"who is better in religion than a Muslim who submit themselves to God in the perfect worship of Ihsan, and accepts the pure faith of Abraham, for God accepted Abraham as a close friend"** (4:125). There is none better in religion to those who submit themselves to God in practicing Ihsan. Therefore, the desire to practice it comes from a heart that realised the superiority of perfection in religion that Ihsan provides and seeks to gain it. This is because if the worshipers in other branches of the religion are amateur servants of God, then the person of Ihsan relative to them is a full-time professional. This is because an integral part of the practice of Ihsan is to remove the ego and its hinderances, which then allows the person to engage without hassle in the worship of God. This process is no different to a chef cutting short their finger nails to be better at making the dough. When the believer annihilates their ego in Ihsan it allows them to be better able to worship God at a higher standard.

The command to practice Ihsan comes from appreciating the place of Ihsan as an essential branch of the religion. Part of claiming to practice the whole religion for instance is to count oneself as a follower of it, and requires fulfilling all its branches – including the practice of the branch of Ihsan. To be fully in worship to God, a state of utmost piety and sincere devotion, means involving all parts of the human in worship and the practice of Ihsan includes even the human spirit to submit in worship to God. For this reason, the practice of Ihsan is a perquisite to being labelled a saint, and all Muslim saints have been either practitioners of Ihsan or for some of them like Abdul Qadir Al Jailani (raa), a scholar and pioneer of the branch of Ihsan. In the Quran God emphasises that his request upon mankind in terms of worship is complete devotion in religion, and in some verses God commands to this religious state. This was taken by the early practitioners of Ihsan to be firm evidence in including Ihsan as an important part of the religion and for Ihsan to be included in the definition of complete devotion. The Quran says **"they were only commanded to worship God sincerely with a pure belief about God, and to establish prayer and give in charity, and that is the best religion"** (98:5). The Quran also says **"call God in prayer with sincerity in religion even if detest the disbelievers"** (40:14) and **"God commands to justice, and for people to be upright in praying in the mosque, and for people to worship God sincerely. As God created them they will return to God in the end"** (7:29). This last verse even adds a reason to the totalitarian worship of Islam, explaining that it is not selfish of God to require worship at every human dimension, but rather it is only just since God created our whole person that He receives a complete worship and this is only possible through the practice of Ihsan. The command to sincere devotion set out in these verses of the Quran is merely asking a state of completion in religion that is achieved in the spiritual worship of Ihsan.

Success in practice of Ihsan comes in removal of the ego. There is only one way of rectifying the ego (*nafs*), and that is through *Jihadul-nafs* (fighting the ego). This is also referred to as *tazzkiya* (purification) as it includes purifying the person from their sins and sinful habits as well as gaining praiseworthy character and better worship that leads them to increase in spiritual purity. In fact, one of the reasons the Messenger (pbuh) was sent with revelation was to purify the believers. This was in answer to the prayer Prophet Abraham (as) made to God. Abraham (as) prayed **"to send among them a Prophet, who will recite God's verses to the people, and to teach them the book of revelation, and wisdom and purity, for God is the dignified and wise"**(2:129). In this verse Abraham called for the three branches of Islam to be included in the religion to come, that they shall receive revelation to confirm their state of Iman, wisdom of judgment in practice of physical devotion to confirm correct practice of the branch of Islam and purification of the spirit to fulfil the branch of Ihsan. Indeed God heard the prayer of Abraham, and Islam was revealed in the sections and description requested by Abraham for all to practice.

The Prophet (pbuh) said '**your worst enemy is your *nafs* (ego) that lies between your two shoulders**' (Ibn Rajab) and added in the Farewell Pilgrimage '**The *mujahid* (Holy Solider) is he who makes *jihad* against his *nafs* (fights and struggles against their ego) for the sake of obeying Allah**' (Tirmizi). This struggling against the ego, is to liberate the person from their ego's control and power, in commanding the person to its false and even sinful desires that are against the commandments of God. God says in the Quran **"consider the one who takes their desires as a god worshiped, the Prophet cannot be for them a guardian"** (25:43). The Prophet (pbuh) said '**there is no false god greater in evil in the sight of Allah than a followed desire of the ego**' (Abu Naim). It is based on such teachings of the religion, that the scholars of Ihsan became absolute rejecters of the ego and categorised holding an ego as a lesser form of disbelief and called having an ego *Alshirk alkhafi* (The Hidden Polytheism). The Prophet (pbuh) was first to hold a strong opposing stand against the ego, and said '**The hidden polytheism is to act in worship with human desire and aim**' (Ibn Udy).

A person with an ego follows the command of their ego as well as God's, or even more inclined to the first, but as it's an inner god it is *invisible* to the public. This is why it came to be called hidden disbelief. The state of *reya;* another sinful state of worship of performing worship for ostentation is called the small *shirk* (polytheism). Moreover, *reya* is merely a part of the invisible hidden polytheism. They are polytheism, as the acts of worships are no longer directed towards a unified One God, but rather for the pleasure of the ego in Hidden Polytheism or God, and the impressing of the masses in *reya* which is publicising worship – the Ostentation (small) Polytheism. This is because the motivation and intention of the worship is the desire of the ego to be ostentatious, and to gain other people's attention and admiration rather than pleasing God. This is a dangerous religious state as God does not give reward to worship done for any purpose other than Him, as it is in *reya or Hidden Polytheism*. This is because God considers the pleasure of pleasing others in informing them of worship or obeying the commands of the ego beyond that of God as a sufficient reward to their performers.

The Quran says **"consider the one who takes their desires as a god worshiped, the Prophet cannot be for them a guardian"** (25:43). This verse from the Quran describes such people as taking their ego's desires as gods, by submitting to them in obedience and holding greater respect and reverence to their own selves, meaning whatever their egos command them they do even when this is against God's commandments, and in this way, they give their egos an authority that should only be to God. Islam sees giving the right of worship or command to other than God as to give that thing a state of divinity beside God, i.e. polytheism. This is completely unacceptable in Islam and God says **"God does not forgive worship of other deities beside God, and forgives other sins to whom He chooses. Those who worship other deities beside God are fraudulent in religion"(4:48). In another verse the Quran states **"God says do not take two deities for there is only one God, and to Him they should reverence in devotion"** (16:51). Polytheism when external such as in idol worship is easily defeated and stopped by the physical destroying of the statues used as divine idols, and when it is *reya* it is likewise simply eliminated by performing solitary worship away from the masses, however the internal polytheism is difficult to overcome. It is for this reason that God devised a whole branch of the religion under the instruction of the prayer of Ibrahim the 'father of prophets' and the great prophet of God to include a section in the religion devoted to the extermination of internal polytheism, and this section is Ihsan. The internal polytheism of the ego, is difficult to destroy, however this did not stop Muslims of the past, who formed organised schools, formulated systems of struggling against the ego, and recorded biographies of pious men and women whose devotion improved with overcoming the ego, to the point that God accepted them as saints and honoured them with saintly miracles.

Allah says **"consider the one who takes their desires as a god worshiped, the Prophet cannot be for them a guardian. Don't consider that many of them listen or understand religion, for they are like cattle or even more misguided in way"** (25:43-44). The verse questions whether these egotistic people could be worthy of the Prophet's care, meaning to be included in the prayers he made for mercy, to get intercession on the day of judgment, and in this way this verse suggests those who do not practice Ihsan could not even be considered among the people of Muhammed. God describes those who follow the desires of their egos as being worse than animals, because animals are at least doing what they were created for, acting inside the system of their species, but they as people are not. God also describes these people who take their egos as gods like cattle, for by neglecting worship and following their desires they become like the animals in lifestyle. Those with a *nafs* main concern is to eat, drink, mate and sleep, but was it for this they were created? No. Allah says in the Quran **"God did not create the heavens and earth and what is between them without meaning and purpose" (38:27)**. And **"God only created the *jinn* and humans to worship God" (51:56)**. This clearly shows following the ego takes the person from the ideal of worship of God, what the Quran claims is the reason for their existence in the first place, to the derogatory world of animals, which are without the faculty of thought and the sense of shame. That by following one's own egotistical desires the person humiliates themselves into the likeness of animals. This is a dehumanisation that no self-respecting individual would welcome, and is used by God to encourage towards self-control and adhere to religious ritual. The Quran compares them to cattle, herded animals, such as cows and sheep, and this is to say without self-responsibility and guided towards excess consumption of food and recline. In acting like these animals they become legitimate to be compared to them, as they have become like them, they share description and attributes with them. Making it a true liking when a person is unemployed, reclined in leisure for hours, overindulging in food and drink, without increasing in religious knowledge nor attending of local mosque, and they become more in lifestyle to animals than other people. Behavioural and lifestyle similarities to animals is not only unacceptable when the person is human, but it is also considered very unproductive to spirituality, and God wishes they would spend their time instead in praising Him and devotion of worship.

The ego is the root of all human desires, it is the internal force of command present in the majority of people. The only exception of its absence is in some people who are lucky, and the Quran even calls them 'graced'. In the chapter of Joseph, the Quran says **"the minster's wife said she wishes not to claim innocence, for man's ego commands to evil, except those who God gives mercy, for God is forgiving merciful"** (12:53). Those whom God graced without an ego to command them to diverse desires, including evil ones of harm to the self and others are truly blessed. The commands of the ego, what are called desires, are typically self centred, excessive in amount, and unnecessary, and come to waste and destroy of the world to fulfil them to quieten the demanding ego. This is the reason God chose the commands of the ego to be illegitimate in Islam, in contrast to divine commands, kings and rulers' commands, or even the commands of parents, that in Islam there is religious obligation to fulfil them, because they are always towards balance, betterment of the person and improvement of the world.

The ego in terms of Islamic belief is an internal rival to God that sits in the heart diverting people from worship of God. God sent the branch of Ihsan and guidance to it in the Quran to overcome this beastly creature and free the heart to devotion. The ego is also the root of all sins and evils, as it does not conform to the divine commands of God towards deeds of charity and goodness, and the mention and glory of God. For this reason a quick route towards piety and devotion in Islam came to be the learning to disobey the ego and to remove it completely and destroy it in the heart of the believer. The Quran explains why God has interest in overcoming the ego, it says God sees the ego as a leader towards religious anarchy and play. The Quran says **"did they think they were created by God pointlessly and to God they were not going to return in the afterlife"** (23:115). This is a clear admonition that Muslims were not created without cause and aim, allowed to feel free to follow personal desires and an uncontrolled ego towards the external activities of animals.

The process of fighting the ego was referred to as being *'Aljihad Alakbar'* (The Great Struggle) by the Messenger (pbuh) compared to the *'Aljihad Alasgar'* (The Small Struggle) of the soldiers in battle, due to its difficulty and importance. The Prophet (pbuh) after he returned from battle said, **'We have come from the small struggle to the greater struggle' (Ibn Hajar)** it was said **'what is the greater struggle? And the Prophet replied "the battle of the believer against their ego"'** (Ibn

Hajar) and in another version the Prophet replied **"the internal struggle of the heart"** (Mala Ali Gari). And in the same way that those who do *Aljihad Alasgar* (the small struggle or war) could die physically in battle, those who do *Aljihad Alakbar* their egos die. The Messenger (pbuh) said '**Whomever wants to see a dead person walking should look at Abu Bakr (raa)**' and in another Hadith '**Whoever would like to see a man who is still walking on earth after he has met his death, he should see Talhah Ibn Ubaydillah (raa).**' (Ibn Asakir). That they lived in the world in a state of lack of desire and excess in using it as if were dead. They both achieved this by what the scholars of Ihsan call 'dying a death before death' by annihilating their egos. This is because while their bodies did not die in battle, their egos nevertheless died in *Jihadul-nafs* as they struggled against it for the sake of Allah. Both these companions were promised paradise by the Messenger (pbuh) and are considered among the greatest of Muhammed's companions. This death before death is said in the Quran **"people of belief should worship God in a truly perfect worship and not to die unless as believing Muslims"** (3:102) to die only after having already submitted, in a state of death ego. In one verse of chapter Rahman (The Compassionate), an alternative meaning is that God describes the people of Heaven as '**with destroyed egos**' (55:48). This is because absence of ego is a requisite to entering Heaven, so those who do not perform Ihsan in this world and battle their egos into submission to God will be forced to do it before settling to Heaven. The Quran says **"God removed from their hearts disappointment and became brothers on adjacent couches"** (15:47).

This is because Heaven is a pure land of balance and perfection, and the ego is excessive and destructive and unwelcomed there, and therefore no one is exempt to enter Heaven with an ego, that even Muhammed (pbuh), the greatest Prophet himself, during the night of his journey to Heaven the angel first did a quick split of his chest and removed the ego. Adam and Eve, when they chose to follow their ego during their stay in Heaven by eating from the forbidden tree, they likewise were quickly evacuated to Earth. The Quran says about those who did not do Ihsan in this world but had it done in heaven **"God removed from their hearts disappointment and became brothers on adjacent couches"** (15:47). This is to say the tension of desire, the bouts of aggressive greed that the ego is classically known for is removed from the hearts of the citizens of Heaven. Those who battle their egos in this world, need not such urgent spiritual treatment in heaven, and God praises them as already succeeded in purity, **"the people of precedence. These are the people close to God"** (56:10-11). This group of entrants of Heaven called The Foremost, are described to have different Heaven to the general people of Heaven, called The Righteous. The Quran says as a reward to entering Heaven with controlled egos, they are given choice and told to fulfil their desires as they please, **"and fruits of their choice, and meat of birds of what they desire"** (56:20-21). Most importantly they won't be told off for coming with an ego to Heaven, the Quran says **"they do not hear in Heaven pointless speech and no blaming"** (56:25). This is because the Angels in charge of removal of the ego from the hearts at the gates of Heaven, will not be offended by their prepared state nor need to explain to them the procedure of heart clearing which includes explaining the shortcoming of their heart's state. This means that they will be saved from speeches against the ego, and instead be taken directly to indulge in the rewards of their worship in their own Heavens.

The removal of the ego in this world is through a war against the ego, a battle to win the heart towards God and not worldly pleasures and excesses of the ego. Fortunately for the Muslims, some of the early Muslim companions of Muhammed (pbuh) were some of the greatest war generals in human history and were able to use their battle skills when they returned home against their egos, to gain discipline of worship of God. A soldier does not go into battle before knowing what they are fighting and what for, becoming armed with weapons and have a leader to guide and teach. Someone going into battle against their ego will need to know the same, in which case it is against the ego that lies between your two shoulders and for the sake of God, under the guidance of an expert following the way of the Messenger (pbuh).

The nature of the human *nafs* (ego) is animal-like, like that of cattle and other animals. It follows its whims and its desires such as food, sleep, doing nothing, or worse, attacking others, not different from the behaviour of animals. Purification (*tazzkiya*) is getting rid of the animal *nafs* for the sake of Allah, and this is why in the Quran the religious sacrifice of animals while uttering the name of God is also called '*tazzkiya*' (purification) (5:3); because the animal is being killed with the mention of God. Therefore, if the person is not purified of this animal *nafs*, the *nafs* will command them to sin except for those who Allah bestows His grace. In this state the *nafs* is called *Al nafs Al amara* 'The commanding ego'. It does this by commanding to and following its own animal desires, lusts and impulses and not the commands of God. The Quran mentions the commanding ego, saying **"man's ego commands to evil, except those whom God gives mercy"** (12:53).

The ego before it enters a state of commanding, is deeply troubling in the heart in a state of expounding with desire, keeping the mind unstable with explosive needs and wants. At this state the heart flares with desires, but not commands to them; merely deep feelings of wanting whatever it comes cross. It takes notes of what brands, what quality products and luxuries it may see advertised or owned by people they know. It is excited at anything beyond its means, but it is also irritant to their self and quick to defend their attacks, which is defensive arrogance. In this state the ego is called *Alnafs Alshuh* (the bursting ego). The word *shuh* means spreading or overflowing. The ego is called *shuh* as it is easily flared, and reflexes in the heart emotionally to objects or situations that excite it in providing pleasures to desires.

This is the worst form the ego can be in terms of personality, and most disruptive to society and destructive to its owner, as it's in a consistent state of anger and irritation, and aggressive and intimidating towards others, as well as quick to revenge to slight negatives towards itself. *Shuh* means radiating, such as a *shuh* pain is one that is spreading from point and throbbing pain for instance of burning is always described as *shuh* in Arabic. The *shuh* ego is pessimistic, argumentative, and disagreeing. God says **'and ignore those of angry natures"** (4:128), in the verse speaking about how wives should deal with husband's marital weakening, form marital desertion 'discourse' and 'avoiding her', God says here comes those who will disagree and object, and calls them *shuh,* and added that wives should even be generous to their husbands. The beginning of the verse advises to try to remain under his leadership and not to object to the change of course the relationship takes so as not to lose her wife status with him and lose her husband. God says he is aware there is '*shuh*' people who will be quick to object to this advice, due to their argumentative state of saying it's the men who should spend on the woman not women to give to husband to attract them back to the relationship. Having a *shuh* ego is not heroism, eloquence nor attains to justice. To want to argue and find fault in everything isn't praiseworthy, especially when out of context and has an amount beyond necessary.

The bursting ego is problematic to its owner as it invited them to disagreement, focuses their attention to objects and materials beyond their means, making them selfish and irritable. The Quran says **"whoever is protected from the anger of their ego, then they are the successful"** (64:16).

God says **"whoever is protected from the abhorrent of their egos then they are the successful"** (59:9). In this verse God says the description of those saved from this personality disorder, that they accept those who migrate to them, but those of *Shuh* are continuously repulsing people away with their bad manners and evil behaviour. This internal state of boiling from anger at finding so much objection and irritation in everything, leads to escape and the person escapes into following impulses and enters into the state of *Alnafs Alamara*, (the commanding ego).

At this state the person themselves may feel uncomfortable with frequency of desires, frustration at the distance of achieving them and is irritated that they became enslaved to desire. In some cases, greed of the ego may mean the person ends up bankrupt with large daunting loans, few friends due to being selfish and not developing relationships with others, as well as a life failure since time spent fulfilling desires takes a person away from their education and career. All this means that the person themselves may begin to agree to get rid of the ego and welcome religious rectification.

The person with the commanding ego (*Alnafs Alamara*) then becomes inspired of their rights and wrongs, and is then called the *Alnafs Almulhama* (The inspired ego). God says **"consider the ego as God forms it in balance. God inspires the ego of its blatant wrongs and good deeds of worship"** (91:7-8). This inspiration could be by the person becoming aware of their state or as a result of gaining religious knowledge that makes them acknowledge that their state is different from what is considered correct and required of them by God. The *nafs* in this state is still commanding, and may follow its false desires, but by being inspired of its wrongs it feels guilty about them, and this leads the *nafs* to become *Alnafs Allawamah* (The reproaching ego). God says **"God swears by the reproaching ego"** (75:2). This reproaching *nafs* is what motivates a person to spiritual purification. We are told by God that some purify it and others don't. God says **"they are successful those who purifies their egos, and losers are those who hide and ignores their ego."** (91:9-10).

Those who purify their ego do so in fear of God's punishment, leading them to restrain from following their ego's desires that are against God's commandments and that is the essence of the process of *Jihadul-nafs*. The Quran says **"as for those who out of fear of their Lord, deter the ego from desires. Then the Heaven is their abode"** (79:40-41). As the ego rebels against this restraining, it becomes a battle to achieve control of the ego and its desires and is thus called a 'struggle' (*Jihad*). Then when the *nafs* is fully purified in *Jihadul-nafs*, the animal *nafs* dies. Without the ego the person easily submits to the commands of God and gains discipline and control of their actions. In this state of death of the ego Allah bestows His peace on it and the person becomes peaceful, contented and relieved, and the *nafs* is then referred to as a 'peaceful ego' (*nafs mutmaina*). God says **"the peaceful soul should return to their Lord well-pleased and pleasing "**(89:27-28). This is also the state of the believers in the moments of physical death. This is because death is a permanent restraint from the world and all desires, and is thus a condensed state of *tazzkiya*.

God says **"the real security is for those who believe in God, and do not belittle their belief with acts of sins, and they are the rightly guided"**(6:82). This is to say the importance of controlling desire through restraint in struggle against the ego acts as a way of limiting wrongs in religions and sins that maintain religion. In a Hadith Qudsi God says **"I Swear by My Dignity, My Might, My Majesty and Highness, does a slave enforce My Desire on their desires, that I reduce their worries and remove degradation and need from their heart and replace it with continents and finding benefit, and I Swear by My Dignity, My Might, My Majesty and Highness, does a slave enforce their desire on My Desire that I increase their worries, remove contentment from their heart, make him be faced by poverty until they are reduced to a level that their destruction no longer offends Me. My slave gets closer to me through Nafila worship until I love them and and the best thing a slave can do to draw closer to me is to correct what is wrong and when he becomes like this, I become his eyes with which he sees and his hearing with which he hears, and his his heart that tells him what is right and wrong and if he prays to me I answer them and if he requests I give him. These are the slave which if I wanted to destroy the people of the earth, I look at them and for their sake I withdraw my wrath"** (Ibn Hiban). The desires of God are His commands and prohibitions, and the struggle of the ego is to enforce God's desires instead of one's own desire and in this way the believer's desires become in following to the commands and prohibitions of God.

The peace that comes with the death of the *nafs*, is due to the process of *tazzkiya* that includes the remembrance of God which makes the person feel peaceful, and signifies the end of the struggle against the ego which is a stressful process. Hence, those who practice the branch of Ihsan become peaceful, and God is pleased with them and blesses them with His bounties. God says **"those who purify are successful in religion"** (87:14) and **"those who were early to believe of the migrants and those who supported them to victory, and those who follow then in perfect worship of Ihsan, God is pleased with them and they are pleased with Him. God has prepared for them Heavens of running rivers and there they will abide forever, and that is the great win"** (9:100). This verse is also taken as evidence to giving these three groups of people; the two groups of companions; Muhajirin (migrants) and Ansar (hosts/victors), and those who practice Ihsan the title *Radia Allah Anhum* (God be pleased with them, shortened to (raa)) after their names. In Ihsan this title is exclusively said or written after the names of the scholars of Ihsan and does not include students, as scholars are considered to have reached a level of practice of the branch to merit the title. About those who practice the branch of Ihsan God says **"those who fight in the way of God, God will guide them to Him, and God is with those perfect in worship of Ihsan"** (29:69). It is with the perfection of the practice of Ihsan that a person is no longer just a *Mumin* (believer) but also gains the spiritual title of *Muhsin* (practicer of Ihsan).

The study of Ihsan teaches people to increase in *Iman*, therefore there is no need to wait until full belief enters their heart (complete the branch of Iman) before starting to practice Ihsan. However, those who are new to the religion should study it after studying the other two branches first. God says **"if they fear God and do good deeds, and then fear God and believe, and then fear God and perfect their worship in Ihsan, for God loves those who perfect their worship in Ihsan"** (5:93). This verse is the mirror of the Hadith of Gabriel as it speaks of three levels to the religion. It also advocates the study of Ihsan to follow the study of Iman and to follow Islam, which is referred to in the verse as 'do good works' to mean the physical worship of the branch of Islam. The Prophet (pbuh) said **'decrease your sins and death will be easy'** (Ibn Uday). This is because the person worries about his place in hell or Heaven, and knowing they have little sins, it then makes it easier to consider death. The Prophet Muhammed (pbuh) said that knowing Aisha his beloved wife will be in Heaven made death easy to him. The Quran says *'taqwa'* which is acting with God in mind, recognising God's existence and acting on that to make sure they do not sin so as not to merit God's punishment. That this state first motivates them to practice Islam and when it increases, they become firm in belief, and further until the person comes to the state of Ihsan in religion.

The ego (the *nafs*), is the innate internal state of the human being, what a person is born on. The existence of the ego is evidenced by the fact that God mentions it in the Quran, God says, **"Consider the ego and how it is formed by God"** (91:7). It is the overwhelming nature of the ego on the whole person, that God uses the word *nafs* in the Quran to mean 'the person'. The Prophet (pbuh) defined the ego as that **"which lies between your two shoulders"** (Ibn Rajab). The Prophet Muhammed (pbuh) said **"God's mercy I seek as not to leave me to my ego for a blink of an eye and to better my state"** (Dawood). In another Hadith the Prophet Muhammed (pbuh) said **"If God leaves me to my ego, God has then left me to weakness, shame, sins and wrongs and I have not trust except in God's mercy"** (Haithamy). The Quran says it is **"for those who wish to become straight in their religion"** (81:28), meaning sincere practice of it and to become straight in religion. The idea of straightness of the person is that the person's words and their actions are the same thus on a direct line, however those whose words say one thing and actions say another are bent, like a man being asked to return a loan and him later saying he isn't going to pay it.

The practicing of Ihsan is a spiritual journey in the company of a competent guide, expert in *Jihadul-nafs* and *tazzkiya*, to reach higher spiritual stations that gain God's acceptance (*rida*). The greatest incentive to practicing Ihsan, is the Prophet said **"God is Mohsin (practices Ihsan/perfects to His creation) and loved Ihsan"** (Ibn Uday) and the Mohsin is the one who performs Ihsan. In another Hadith, Prophet Muhammed (pbuh) said **"God is Mohsin and loves those who perform Ihsan"** (Haithamy). Therefore, the practice of Ihsan puts the person in the midst of the pious whom God loves, and it is usually people who appreciate this love and love God who endeavour to practice this branch in seeking the nearness of God. However, the practice of the branch is a command of God, and the Quran says **"God commands to justice and Ihsan"** (16:90) and Ihsan is to worship in the best way while practicing the branch of Ihsan. When a man asked the Prophet a deed to allow him to enter Heaven the Prophet (pbuh) replied '**practice Ihsan**' (Baihagi), when the man asked how does he know if he is of Ihsan, the Prophet said 'ask *jayranak*' commonly interpreted as neighbours, but it means those who will bail you, and traditionally in Islam this has been the scholars, for they used to give references to their students when they got into trouble. This means if you practice Ihsan to a level sufficient for your scholar to consider you Muhsin take that as a *bushra* (glad-tiding) you will enter Heaven. The Prophet said **"God is Mohsin, practice Ihsan"** (Ibn Uday). God says '**people who believe should enter into practice of the whole religion**' (2:208), and this means to complete all parts of your religion. This is to recommend and commend to the practice of Ihsan. Practicing the branch of Ihsan is to have all the necessary parts of one's religion complete when facing God for accounting on the Day of Judgment.

The Prophet Muhammed (pbuh) said '**my followers do not group upon a misguidance**' (Alzagany) and from Morocco up to Indonesia, and from Turkey up to Yemen the majority of Muslim countries have an Ihsan practicing tradition of Sufism. This in itself is a proof to its legitimacy even to people yet to be fully introduced to Islam. Knowledge of whirling dervishes, and famous Ihsan writers such as Rumi, and Ibn Arabi works in international Sufism literature show that there is a widespread acceptance, a product to the deep history this branch of Islam has and the rigorous authenticity to support its practice. God says **"God revealed to him the holy book, to clarify everything, and as a guide and mercy, and a foretelling of good to the Muslims"** (16:89). That the book of Quran explains everything on the religion and that includes what Ihsan is. God also says 'and by His words proves the truth to be true. Verily, He has full knowledge of what is in the hearts of men' (42:24). This is to say if Ihsan was true from Islam and from God, there will be verses on its subjects from God, that God supports what is true, by his speech, his words, that is the verses of the Quran. If Ihsan is doubted, then indeed all perfection and beauty is doubted, sometimes not out of malice, but beauty has such effect on people. It overwhelms, it bedazzles them, they can't believe their eyes, this is physical beauty, and spiritual perfection in religion has envy as well.

CHAPTER THREE

WITNESS OF GOD IN IHSAN

Witness is the pivotal idea of the branch of Ihsan. Witnessing is to be mentally present when you see, hear, touch, or smell a thing. It is not enough to say you heard if you weren't giving attention. To qualify to be considered witness the person must have been present in mind, in both cases it's hearing, but presence is different. In Islamic sharia witness based on this definition is essential in the cases of fornication and adultery. Witness in *shahada* is to say the phrase that a person witnesses that there is no god but Allah and Muhammed in His messenger, and this phrase is said to enter Islam when said as a statement you believe in. It is forced witness as it's submission, but then becomes a creed following increase of Iman and then a state of spirituality when witnessed as a practitioner of Ihsan. The branch of Ihsan, is to gain spirituality as to witness the miracles of God so as to believe in God firmly and witness out of experience, and this is the highest level of belief.

The Prophet (pbuh) said when the person dies their soul raises across the Heavens and towards the Throne of God (Al Baihaqi), and that this also happens in the small death, i.e., during sleep. Sleep is considered a form of death as the Prophet (pbuh) said **'sleep is the brother of** death, and the people of paradise will not sleep' (Ibn Hazm). This is because they will have no need for it, during the day they are free to do as they like, and will not require sleep because they will not get tired. Sleep is deprivation, and the people of paradise will not be deprived of anything and all their wishes will come true and so will not sleep. Nevertheless, in one verse, the Quran says they will have couches to lie on if they desired to recline. This is also, as sleep is a state of loss of consciousness and awareness. It is considered not befitting and as a reward we no longer have to experience it in *Jennah* (Heaven). God says **"God gives death to people while sleeping at night, and knows what they do during the day. Then God gives life to people as they wake up for a specified time. To God is the return of all people and then God will tell them their deeds" (6:60)**. Sleep is considered a type of death as when the person sleeps their ego dies, but as it is not a permanent death it is thus considered a small death. The Prophet's (pbuh) Morning Prayer was, '**Praise to God for giving us life after death and to Him is our return' (Bukhari).** The Prophet (pbuh) said that a true dream happens when the soul reached the throne, and an untrue dream is when the soul does not reach it (Al Haithami). The ascension of the soul towards the throne also happens in *Jihadul-nafs*, as the soul rises as the person increases in spirituality. In Islam since religion is organised spirituality, night time is great in spiritual reward as God descends during the last third of the night. Thus in spirituality the idea of night is quite common, and scholars and students endeavour to worship God during the night. In martyrdom there is a witnessing of God, in which they believe firmly in God that they are willing to die, therefore martyrdom is called *shahada* which literally means witness. In struggling against the ego of practicing Ihsan, there is also a witness, and the highest form is of course the vision of God.

This spiritual journey of the soul that is the result of *Jihadul-nafs* is mentioned in the following Quranic verse, God said **"if God wishes He would have raised them spiritually by the revelation but they chose to**

stick to the earth by following their desires" (7:176). They inclined to the earth means that they chose the *dunya* (world) and the physical world by following desires and sins rather than to nourish their soul which would have then elevated from God's mention and understanding of His signs. This misguided person mentioned in the verse is said to have failed spiritually and followed their vain desires instead of restraining their ego in *Jihadul-nafs*.

When the ego dies during purification, the body will be there, the mind will be there, and the soul will be there (but in a high state as it is raised towards the throne) but the ego becomes absent. The person then becomes a *shaheed* (martyr) whose ego died for the sake of God. Although the battle against the ego is very hard, thus making the *Jihad* of a more severity than the one in battle, and there is no pain associated with it as it does not involve the body. If with physical death the person leaves this world, in death of the ego, the person leaves the illusions of this world and can see the world in its truest form: as a finite world that is a place of test and a place to worship in order to gain reward for the next world. And this is the greatest preparation for the physical death.

As to the nature of the soul or it's rising, then that is something we have not been given knowledge of. God said **"they ask about the spirit, the Prophet should say the spirit is of God's issues and people are given of knowledge only little" (17:85)**. The word *shaheed* (martyr) in Arabic comes from the word *shahid*, which literally means a witness. Being a *shaheed* comes with it a witnessing, in the 'small' *Jihad* you witness paradise, as we are told the martyrs' souls are small birds in paradise (Muslim). In the 'great' *Jihad* you can witness the Face of your Lord full of Majesty and Bounty. The Messenger (pbuh) said '**you will not see your Lord until you die' (Muslim),** and considering that *Jihadul-nafs* is a greater *Jihad* than that of battle, the death of the ego in *Jihadul-nafs* can be seen as a greater death. This vision of God paves the way for being able to 'worship Allah as if you see Him', so that bearing witness that there is no God but Allah comes from truthfully witnessing Him and not trust alone. Thus their *shahada* (statement of belief) comes from *mushahada* (witnessing) and not belief alone, but as a direct witnessing of God's presence.

    Ali Ibn Abi Talib (raa) is reported to have said **'men are asleep when they die *antabahu* (became aware)' (Al Asuti).** He said *aware* as Allah is **"nearer to us than our jugular vein"** (Quran 50:16) yet are not aware of His presence except for few. When the person dies and enter the hereafter, they become aware of the truth. They realise the reality of the world, the reality of the existence of God and the truthfulness of the religion. While we are aware of the reality of this from believing in the message of the Prophet (pbuh) those who truly realise this in this world are those who achieved death of the ego in *Jihadul-nafs*. This makes them become aware without physically dying. People's attention to their ego's desires takes them away from and distracts them from being aware of God's presence and the truthfulness of the religion. This awareness in *Jihadul-nafs* happens as when the ego dies the person can then become 'aware' of the reality of the world and the existence of God. Just like a loud sound would wake someone who is asleep, regular *zikr* (remembrance and mention of God) and *Jihadul-nafs* can wake up a person and recapture their awareness of God's Presence. In a way *Jihadul-nafs* is about refocusing our attention, because concentrating on ourselves and our desires suppresses our awareness of God. Someone who deprives themselves from the words of God (the Quran) and His mentioning are deprived from the awareness of His presence. This is the wisdom behind God saying **'I am in the presence of those who mention me' (Muslim).** God could be said to be in the presence of all His creation, yet those who become aware and conscious of His presence are those who remember Him by making His praise. Thus, by His mention the slave enters His presence. Therefore, the process of practice of Ihsan is a spiritual awakening, and a stage of transformation guided by a knowledgable scholar. This is an awakening from the slumber that people gain from coming to the world, for in the Quran God says that God asked the spirits, **"made them witness is God**

not their Lord. They answered they witness God is their Lord"(7:172). That we have before known God and affirmed His divinity and lordship, but in entering this world we slept, and the revelation is meant to be an alarm clock to wake us up to the reality of the existence of God.

The Quran says **"on the day of judgement their tongues, hands and legs will give witness against them for what they did in the world"**(24:24). That after people wake up from death to Judgment Day they will come to know that God's existence is the Truth and reality beyond the evidence of this world. The truth will be so great on the Day of Judgment that even their body parts will speak the truth. The dead will start to come with truth; God says **"then when comes the drowsiness of death with truth, that is what they used to try to escape"** (50:19). That death brings a state of truth meaning realisation of the existence of God. It is not new knowledge revealed, but they are forced to believe the truth they denied in the world. The Quran says even the Christians will realise the truth about Jesus, that he was not a son of God, was not crucified, and was not a god to be worshiped. This is because the pain of the experience acts as a tortured interrogation to make them admit any truths they denied and any falsehood they deluded themselves about in the past.

The death of the ego is required to perceive God's presence because our mind's attention is as limited as our eye's gaze; just like we need to turn from one thing to see another, we need to turn our attention from one thing to give it to another. The Quran described this by says **"Allah has not made for any man two hearts in his body."** (33:4). It is the case that if we give a great amount of attention to one thing, it is accompanied by greater heedlessness of other things, and this is what the Quranic verse describes; that a person cannot be completely conscious of two things at the same time. Therefore, the death of the ego frees the person's attention and energy to concentrate on God's worship and become aware of His Presence, as God is always there but it is us who are not looking. While the existence of creation including our egos can take our attention from the presence of God, the existence of creation does not crowd God nor veil Him in reality, but only veil us from seeing Him. It is a mental veil that prevents us from remembering and knowing God even though He is very close to His creation. The Prophet Muhammed (pbuh) said **'between us and seeing our Lord is the cloak of majesty covering His face'** (Bukhari) sometimes it is a veil not physical but emotional, and a lack of understanding of His majesty makes us miss Him and not see Him.

CHAPTER FOUR

THE EGO

The word ego is called "*nafs*" in Arabic. The word *nafs* in Arabic literally means breath, and seeing the important of this to life they called valuable things '*nafis*', and the word *nafs* is also the word for 'self' as they considered the breathing was the gateway to knowing the self, as with it they are alive and express themselves. In Islam the definition of '*nafs*' which is a word that appears in the Quran many times is given by the Prophet Muhammed (pbuh) is **'your self which is between your two shoulders'** (Ibn Rajab) and this is to be clear since people romantically called their spouses '*nafsi*' or even valuables they owned as their self, to show how valuable they are to them, as if they are their own selves.

The ego is the internal force of command present in the majority of people. The commands of the ego are called desires, regardless of what the ego commands. God says it has no authority, it didn't create the person and it's not its God, so to follow it is stealing people from God. The danger of the ego is that it can command to evil, and that some people follow it causing them to commit crimes and sins. The command of the ego is not usually auditory but can be as simple as an inclination, or even an impulse. The ego is also the tool of the devil, so that when a person has an ego the devil can inspire them to sin, but if the person practices Ihsan and annihilates the ego in *Jihadul-nafs* then the person becomes immune from the devil and his evil whisper. The devil is thus an enemy to the believer, and the Quran say that the person should consider him an enemy meaning fight and protect from him. The ego when it commands it is usually subtle and this can be in the form of commanding excessive behaviour, that the person sleeps a lot or eats a lot. The ego commands to sins and this is dangerous to the person since the performing of sin leads to the hellfire and the punishment of God even in this life. This makes the fighting of the ego as very important in religion that there is this whole branch of Ihsan, where its practitioners struggle against their egos.

God says **"if they do not obey the Prophet, then know they follow their desires, and who is more misguided than one who follows their desire without guidance from God, and God does not guide the unjust people"**(28:50)

The human is created from mud, which is a mixture of water and earth. The earth in Arabic is called *ard* which is literally contentment. This is because when pressed on it, it follows by depressing, and as it follows command, it therefore contents. As for water it is pure, it has nothing to see, nothing to smell, nothing to taste, nothing to hear and nothing to feel, so it has no creation and no sense, so it is pure. The overall meaning of creating the human from earth and water is that it should be like earth and follow command, and that is the command of purity, so to follow the commands of God of being pure in worship. This way to create the human is so that it can be ready for the worship of God, which the Quran says is the purpose of the creation of the human. Therefore, the idea of *hawa* (desire) in humans is problematic and contrary to our nature as being made from mud, while to the jinn, who are created from fire and its movement, and its wind helping the flames to turn larger and wider and quicker, they are naturally creatures of desire. The ego to the spirit is like fat is to the body, a burden. Just as fat keeps the body from movement, the ego prevents the person from spirituality.

Impulsive and forced behaviour of the ego is the source of our regrets, losses and grievances. The person with an ego quickly fulfils the ego requests, but doesn't quickly answer the call to prayer – this is not fair to God. The ego is also a great liar, a person when they get a desire, it feels like fulfilling it is the end, however the ego desires again, such as if a person desires to eat food, then after they eat they desire again. This repetitive nature of the ego is another reason why a Muslim must practice Ihsan to destroy the ego in order to become free to the worship God. The ego is selfish, not only in regard to fellow humans, but also to God. It is stingy to consider other than itself even its creator. The Prophet (pbuh) asked God from being **"unable to reach satiety"** (Muslim).

The people of Ihsan always emphasise the evil of four, 'the ego, desire, the devil and the love of this world'. The ego is a disgrace; if society finds you a person who follows their ego and desire you lose face, you are not trusted, for you could follow your ego in important decisions. It also shows that you follow desire, easily bribed into actions of humiliations. The Prophet **"The worse slave is one who has desires that misguide them, and the worse slave is one who has desires that humiliate them to people"** (Al Albani). This is because the desires of the ego not only lead to the disapproval of God, but some desires could mean people become needy of other people, making them have to degrade to asking them or do things considered degrading in society so they become the laughter of others. The ego tricks the person to their own destruction as they follow the commands to sin and crimes, and become punished even in death. In the Hadith the Prophet Muhammed (pbuh) said **"when God gives permission to the spiritual destruction of a person He allows them to follow their desires"** (Ibn Uday). The human has been given free choice as a trust, and if a person has used their followed evil desires as their choice then they are dishonest with the trust. When Abu Bakr (raa) asked the Prophet (pbuh) to teach him a *dua* (prayer) to make the Prophet (pbuh) teach him to ask God's refuge from '**the evil of his ego**' (Tirmizi), this is the way the ego commands through its desires for things that could be harmful to the person – in this world or the next.

God says in the Quran "**his ego accepted for him to kill his brother**" (5:30). This is about the sons of Adam, who one killed the other, and this shows the severity of the ego command. It can even command the harm of loved ones and important family members. God is knowledgable of the most subtle things that the Quran says **"God knows what whispers in the heart of people"** (50:16) and therefore prayer is the most important tool in fighting the evil ego.

Those who not only belittle others but also expect them to follow and fulfil their commands could be said that their egos have overgrown not only to command them but also others, and these are the most in need of *Jihadul-nafs*. This commanding of others could be by intimidating them into doing what they wish, forcing them and not allowing them to have or express their own views, to acknowledge that they have an individual 'self' that is valuable and respected. Also disrespecting people's culture or taste or belittling their achievements and choices. These make people feel worthless, and are an oppression and injustice which Islam bans and forbids. The Prophet (pbuh) said '**it is a sign of belief to not concern or talk about that which does not concern you**' **(Al Nawawi)**.

Things in life come with a covering; peanuts even though have shells still have a thin covering, onions come with a covering as well etc. It is traditional cooking to remove coverings of fruits and vegetables. Even in the human body there is a part covered, which the cover that is removed in circumcision is the foreskin. They do this to make the fruit more edible, less distracted with the tasteless different textures of the coats. The human on the inside likewise has this cover, the Quran (2:7) says **there is a cover over the hearts and sight**. The ego is this cover in the heart that needs to be removed before a person can have vision of God and gain spirituality. The ego is like the incorrect time at a new clock, which the manufacturer expects the new owner to reset, and correct, but not to be followed. Likewise, the ego is the default system in the human before revelation which we are supposed to synchronise with the revelation. The clock manufacturers do not set it to one time as they expect it to be sold throughout the world and do not know where the clock is going to end up. However, God leaves the ego as a form of showing that it's a completely fee choice to worship him or not. Then those who choose to worship Him correct their ego to worship while disbelievers allow it to carry on in error.

The ego death in Ihsan, and not following desires, is temporary to this world. However, the Quran says in Heaven people will be fulfilled all wishes. God says **"in Heaven they get what they wish and God has more"** (50:35) and **"meat of birds of what they desire"** (56:21). The Prophet Muhammed (pbuh) also said men in Heaven will have the desire and sexual strength of a hundred men. This means that in Heaven desire will be expanded and fulfilled all in the command and acceptance of God. The disbelievers want to indulge in this world and therefore the Prophet said that this world is the paradise of the disbelievers and the prison of the believers (Muslim).

The Prophet Muhammed (pbuh) is considered in Islam to be infallible, and without ego and desire, God says **"and he does not speak out of his own desire"** (53:3), making him an example to follow by all Muslims. It is also a praise on his character that, he had no desires of his own, no biases and no needs or wants behind his religious teachings. His actions were divine commands to him which he practiced and thus doing what he did is practicing divine commands. The Quran praises the Green man who was a companion of prophet Moses (as), **"he has not done any of these things out of his own desire"**(18:82). The ego is the promoter and cause of most if not all evil, when the children of Israel started to worship a bull, the man who started it said, **"that is what his ego made him do"** (20:96), his self, inner self, his ego told him to do it, and he followed his whim.

CHAPTER FIVE

MONOTHEISM IN IHSAN

Monotheism in Islam is called *tawheed* and it is literally unification, or claiming oneness to a divine entity or being and this is an important belief Muslims hold about God. To say that God is one is called monotheism, to say god is more than one, or has different parts as is the Christian trinity division is called polytheism. In the branch of Islam, *tawheed* is a verbal utterance of 'there is no God but Allah', and in Iman is to gain a firm belief in His singularity as true, and in Ihsan it's allowing only God to be in a position of authority and command in our life. In Ihsan having an ego is considered to associating one's own will, as a partner with God over the person. In Ihsan there is a fighting against the ego and this frees the person from the burden of an ego that commands them to do evil and sin.

In Ihsan, a person with an ego that gives them desires is not considered to be monotheist as the Quran says **"consider one who takes his god to be their own desire"** (45:23). The presence of desire in the heart is another God with Allah, so to be monotheist is to eliminate the desire, and this is the practice of Ihsan. Complete belief in God is to place God only in command, in veneration, in place of love, and to have a place for God in your heart unshared with anything else, including the ego. The ego when present shares command with God, so it is like another god, and to eliminate the ego is thus the heart of true spirituality. God says in the Quran "**those who take god beside Allah will come to know of their mistake**" (15:96) meaning they shall come to see in punishment the error of their polytheism. This makes having an ego and desire to be a very serious state needing serious rectification by a scholar of Ihsan. Since the ego is concealed idol worship, it is thus called hidden polytheism. A worse state is not only to follow the ego as well as to worship God but to follow the ego and ignore the Lord's commands all together. God says "**so do not allow other things to be great as God while knowing**" (2:22). This is a command to not allow the ego's desires to command so that it is not great as God in the person's heart. The Quran says "**God alone we worship and from Him we seek help**" (1:5).

The best *tawheed* is not one of verbal utterance, but a physical reality gained through a programme of purification from desire of the ego that is the mini-god in the human. This brings into singularity the command over the person to be for God alone. This then fulfils the supremacy of God over all. The Prophet (pbuh) said '**let there be no obedience to the creation in disobedience to the Creator**' (Ahmed). The first manifestation of this should be disobeying the ego, which is a creation of God. God says "**that is because God is the truth, and what they worship instead of God is falsehood, and God is the high and great**" (22:62). God says when a slave choses to follow anything other than God that is a state of falsehood, of error and wrong and he commands what to do with this falsehood in another verse "**proclaim truth has came and invalid is falsehood, for falsehood is to be invalidated**" (17:81). God says we must perish and remove and destroy all falsehood beside him, and this is the command to remove the ego that disturbs the truth of following God.

CHAPTER SIX

THE GREAT STRUGGLE

Spiritual diseases make the person unpleasant to others as well as to themselves, especially when they come to be aware of them, and realise the goodness in being without them. Spiritual diseases are also sins or lead the person to sin, which are punishable by God. Also, spiritual diseases themselves can be uncomfortable or distressing, e.g., *hegd* (envy) is the experience of pain and anger at other's successes, and is very distressing to the person who envies. A person who has *hegd* not only has to endure its pain but the Prophet Muhammed (pbuh) said **"envy destroys the reward of good deeds like fire burns dry hay" (Abu Dawood).** This is because the envier wishes that the victim of their envy loses whatever good they envied, as well as not being content with the *gadar* (decree) of Allah. Thankfully there is a process of curing the person from their spiritual diseases, and as this process can be difficult – hence why it is called a 'struggle' (*Jihadul-nafs* lit. struggling against the ego or fighting the ego). This struggle is based on forcing oneself by going against one's ego and desires in doing what is right and refraining and avoiding what is not. *Jihadul-nafs* could be considered to be a form of *tazzkiya* as it purified the person from their ego which is the cause of the majority of spiritual diseases.

The term *Jihadul-nafs* is mentioned in the Hadith and is not a word made by the people of Ihsan. The Prophet said **'the best jihad is to struggle against your ego for the sake of God'** (Al Asyouti) and in another **'the best jihad is to fight your ego and your desires'** (Al Asyouti). God says **"whoever submits themselves to God and they practice Ihsan, to them will be a reward from God and neither will they become fearful or sad"** (2:112). To submit yourself, meaning by destroying your ego and for Him to be your only master. God says **"people should struggle and fight in the way of God to a true struggle"** (22:78). To struggle for the sake of God means **'wanting God's face'** (18:28). This means to do it not with the purpose of perfecting religion to enter Heaven at its highest level, but in seeking God' nearness, which is the most perfect and truest of jihads. The Prophet Muhammed (pbuh) said "**a weak believer is one who follows their ego's desire and then hopes God accepts them**" (Tirmizi).

The battling of the ego is best described by the metaphor of weaning of a child. The weaning is interpreted by the baby as a form of rejection and going hungry, while in reality it is an emancipation from feeding from another human and becoming independent of his mother. Likewise, our rejection of our ego, it takes us from being taken care of and suggested to by a created ego to living our life under the advice of the Wise true God. Sheikh Busairi says 'the ego is like a child if left to their own accord they grow up increasing in love of breastfeeding, but if weaned this link is broken'. This is a metaphor to mean the fighting of the ego is possible just like the weaning of a child.

The booty of *jihadul-nafs* is *fanaul-nafs* (the annihilation of the ego), and it is defined as when the person becomes exclusive to God, and securely attached to him, and linked to him after exiting the state of fulfilling desires of the ego. To become different so that no movement affects the person except they know it was from God, and no command he fulfils except if they knew it was from God, and they don't do any action except that God commanded or allows it, as permitted it in His revelation. When such is the person's state, they are called to have annihilated in God. It is an irrevocable state of the heart; when the spirit in this state it is said to have reached God, and is permitted to have presence with God and His vision. To reach a state of sole devotion to God, *tawheed* of slavery, that you serve none but God, not even yourself is allowed to command you to serve it, and this God then pats the spirit into a state of peace, and they are then termed by the angels as 'contented self'. Prophet Muhammed (pbuh) said God in a dream placed his Hand upon his back revealing to him knowledge, and this is absolute approval of him no different to the praise in the verses of the Quran.

There are Seven Golden Rules that a student must know in order to succeed in their struggle, one's ability to be cured is proportional to how much these rules are believed and followed. They teach the departure point (that illness is caused by the existence of the *nafs*), the journey (the hard work required and hurdles faces) and the destination (to be like Mohammed (pbuh)). Without them one is truly lost.

1. Admit to the Existence of Spiritual Health and Illness.

In this state the slave should read the stories of the *awlya* (saints) and their *karamat* (miracles) and also try and visit different sheikhs of different paths for blessings. Most importantly, let their stories inspire and motivate and not dishearten. For stories of their *karamat* can make a person feel like they took all existent blessing, on the contrary God is still Rich and His treasures are still full and what they were given is less than what a needle takes from the ocean. Their stories can be found in many books such as *Sifat alsafwa*, Orchids of Love, or *Tadhkirat al-Auliya'* (Memorial of the Saints) by Farid Adin Attar (raa). Otherwise, a person could just visit the websites of the different Sufi Paths for they usually contain a section about their Sheikhs.

It is worthy to warn from having a love of a specific Sufi that blinds one from appreciating other Sufis, and unless the person appreciates and loves them too, there is no moving from this state. There have been pious people who are stuck in this state for decades, for not appreciating the vast generosity of Allah to various people or appreciating the piety and knowledge of other Sufis. Do not be like those who believe in some prophets and reject others.

Reading the stories of the pious and prophets teach one about what spiritual 'health' is like, and stories of the cursed devil and of Pharaoh, etc teach what spiritual 'illness' is. There is a cure in looking at the pious, listening to the pious, and reading the works of the pious, because the pious are carbon copies of the Messenger (pbuh) and remind of health.

2. Admit to Spiritual Illness being Bad and Spiritual Health being Good.

We live in a time where it is considered praiseworthy and good to be bad. This is a disease too, and when one is spiritually healthy, they admit to illness being bad. Illness is of course is bad as it brings God's wrath, anger and punishment, and His punishment is great, His punishment is an eternal fire.

Noticing spiritual illnesses in others is a way of appreciating how ugly it is for the Prophet Muhammed (pbuh) said "**a believer is a mirror of the other believer**"(Zahabi). Health brings the benefit of the reward of Heaven. The person also lives a good life without unease that comes with sin, and will have a good death and hereafter. The Muslim needs to realise that spiritual disease is bad, they are a barrier from God, and can lead to sin which leads to the hellfire.

3. Admit to one own Inadequacy, Illness, and Imbalance

If one does not admit to illness when they have it, it is an illness in itself. When one becomes healthy from that they begin to notice their sins and their wrong action, as they are not similar to the pious and prophets.

Curing of spiritual disease comes in the order they manifest. Usually, people reflect their diseases on others, those who are hypocrites accuse others of hypocrisy, and those who are arrogant accuse others of arrogance. This is because the animal *nafs* is a selfish *nafs*, which not only commands bad actions but sees these actions as right. Another reason the *nafs* commands one to concentrate on the mistakes of others is to prevent attention from its own mistakes; also, by acknowledging another person's mistakes the arrogant *nafs* feels better about itself. It is the *nafs* biggest weapon: diverting, denial and avoidance. When one no longer denies they are ill, diverts their time and energy on others and does not avoid the medicine, one will be truly cured. The Prophet said "**a sign of belief is that the person doesn't concern themselves with that which is not their business**" (Tirmizi).

4. Admit to Spiritual Change can Happen

Stories of the righteous and those who were bad and became good, prove that change can happen. This removes the spiritual illness that is despair. Stories of prophets such as Moses (as) who God accepted as prophet even though he had killed a man, and likewise stories of the companions, such as Khalid ibn Alwaleed (raa) and Umar ibn Alkhatab (raa) who were great enemies of Islam but turned into its greatest supporters. There are also stories of the Sufis who some were thieves and drunks and Allah gave them guidance to the straight path. God is still God, and just like He gave them He will give to more. People need to just ask in prayer.

5. Admit to Help is Needed

The seeker of God must appreciate that there are scholars of Ihsan who have the knowledge of how to rectify them spiritually. They must choose the right help to cause change to their religious state. This means choosing a good scholar who is qualified and known for their piety. Then finding a scholar to actually listen and follow their command and not follow personal desires of the ego.

6. Know that Change is a Difficult Process that Requires Hard Work and takes Time

The practice of Ihsan is called the Great Struggle, due to its difficulty. It takes time to practice, months and years of hard work, and success from God.

Know that at times it would be hard, and may even seem impossible, just remember to do it to your utmost capabilities, for God does not ask people about that which they are incapable of. Know that purification is merely the method and not the goal.

We as humans have limited energy and time, so if we spend this time and energy in vein, then we have less time to spend in good things. Those who spend the night dancing will be physically too tired to pray, those who spend time watching TV have less time to contemplate the powers of creation of Allah in the universe.

7. No one is Perfect, and may not Succeed 100% in Maintaining the Spiritual Work

When performing worship and struggling against the ego, even those who are saints may find it difficult at times to maintain high level of worship let alone the beginners. Just to know that God forgives repetitive sinning, and rewards repentance and returning back to Him. God says **"those who committed sins should not despair of the mercy of God. God forgives all sins, for he is the most forgiving, most merciful"** (39:53).

CHAPTER SEVEN

THE ABSENT EGO

The term '*fana*' means 'annihilation' and it is used to describe the state of a person who has become oblivious to all, including their own self, except the object that he or she loves or contemplates. As a state, as a station it is the aim of Ihsan and is the result of *jihadul-nafs* after which the ego no longer exists. *Fana* expresses the person's love of, and the greatness of what caused *fana*. This absence of the ego brings with it a pleasure, as it allows the person to have undivided attention to what they love, and ignoring all else that would otherwise cause distraction. In the path of Ihsan, there are different types of *fana*, such as *fana* in *zikr* of Allah, an example the famous man who had his foot cut during prayer because he couldn't feel it at the time. There are also other *fana*, such as *fana* in your scholar (*faunal nafs fi al sheikh*), *fana* in the Messenger (*fanaul nafs fi alrasul*), and lastly, permanent *fana* (also called death) of the ego for God; *fanaul nafs fi Allah*. Annihilation of a physical thing is its destruction to a point that it no longer exists. The Quran says "**all things will be annihilated in the last hour, and only your lord will remain**" (55:26-27). The idea of annihilation of the *nafs*, the word is used as a metaphor to mean it no longer exists. This annihilation of the ego, is a destroying of a god worshiped beside Allah and is thus an equivalent to the destroying of physical idols worshiped by pagan disbelievers.

The state God wants all people to be in is an absent ego, it is a form of spiritual purity, of being then completely devoted to God without a distracting inner desire or wants, but to be completely present to God. Before annihilation of the ego, it is a guardian, but with an absent ego God is the only guardian. The Quran says **"who is better in religion than one who submits their self to God and practices Ihsan"** (4:125), so the annihilation of the ego and submitting to God is the best religion and makes one a Mohsin, i.e., a successful practitioner of Ihsan. God also says **"as for those who fear God and deter the ego from desire. Then the Heaven is their abode"** (79:40-41). The annihilation of the ego is deterring it permanently from desire, and so it is a high spiritual station rewarded with paradise. To those who love God and want His nearness, the ego is a veil, a distraction from God and with the absent ego the person can then see God and achieve the vision of God. The Green Man (Khadir), who is a pious man likewise was without an ego; he said to Prophet Moses at the end, before their separation **"and I did it not from the command of my ego."** (18:82) and indeed God supported him saying about the Green Man (raa) **"there they found a pious man who has been given mercy and knowledge directly from God"** (18:65). He was merely following the command of God rather than seeking any personal gain, and this was because he was with an absent ego. The Quran says **"whoever expects to meet his Lord, let him do good deeds and not worship anything beside God"** (18:110). The ego when present is a partner to god, but with no ego there is no polytheism and the person then can meet God in this world and see God.

CHAPTER EIGHT

THE SPIRIT

The spirit in Arabic is *'Roh'*, from a word meaning leaves or moves, and this is to acknowledge that it's the part of the human that leaves their body in death. The spirit is usually considered the opposite of the body. It is the unseen part of the person. The idea that it exists but cannot be seen is considered to mean that it is subtle in substance, just as the body is solid and heavy and thus we can see it, the spirit is light in weight and gentle and thus is not seen. The spirit is the awareness of other than the self, and the best thing to be aware of that is not us, is God. If a goat falls into a well, the other goats don't care, however, if a man falls into a well, other people come and surround the well, they make effort to get him out and cry with him about his sad fate. The reason for this is that humans have spirit, and awareness of other than the self, awareness of other people, and consider how they feel and help them. This is the spirit in action. The goats and other animals lack this and so they lack spirit and spirituality. The spirit is the source of meaning, and considering other perspectives. This means considering more than one meaning to a phrase or word, so acknowledging different perspectives which comes from awareness of others, all this is spirit. This means that Islam as a religion that considers the spirit, and the Quran has a whole chapter called "The Poets". Sufism (Ihsan) practice which is worshiping God through the spirit, is also famous for their much poetry, such as those praising the messenger and expressing love of God such as the poetry of Rumi.

The spirit is also the description of the thing, for once a person becomes dead their description leaves, because there are some things you cannot know by just looking at the body. What was their name? Their favourite food? Were they born blind or had an injury? Etc. Thus the word spirit is also used to mean the description of a thing, or what they stand for. For example, the spirit of the law is used to mean what it acknowledges or intends and not necessarily what the literal law says. This is because our spirit is our description and when our description is gone, so goes with it our spirit. When the physical body has changed so much our description is no longer maintained and then the angels come to take our spirit to the intermediary world of *barzakh*.

The unit of the body is hardness. What unifies the whole body, the bone, blood and arms is that they are hard and with weight, the description of earth from where it was created. The creations capable of recognising word entities are three, the humans, the angels and *jinn* (spirits/fairies). The angels were created first, and then the jinn and lastly the human. God created the jinn, from the flame, the angels from light and the humans from earth.

The truth of God comes in realising the existence of God, and this comes from the ability to recognise other than the self by the use of the spirit. The spirit is a human sense like that of sight of the eyes which allows people to see and hear with the ears, which allows people to hear sound, and the tongue which allows for taste of food. The spirit allows to recognise other than the self, and since no one is God in Islam, this means the imperative need of the spirit is to know God. Those with a sense of spirit will recognise God and those without any sense of spirit may ignore His existence. This is why the problem may not be that God doesn't exist, but that people lack the tool or spirit of recognising that God exists. This is why religion while for instance is truth is not usually considered a science, while Islam in Arab history was counted as a science, religion is usually counted as a humanity subject with art, literature and poetry as they also depend on the sense of spirit and meaning and appreciation of other existence.

The Spirit is an article that is gained when parents of the child are cousins or somewhat related. This is why people throughout history all over the world married relatives. The idea of paternal cousin parents is to allow the person understand metaphor (*mathal*), relative comparison (*giyas*), that are the basics of the spirit. There cannot be spirit in humans without parents of same origin, and no spirituality without spirit, and no religion without spirituality. This is because *giyas* (relative comparison) that a person uses to acknowledge others requires a point of comparison, a stable star to compare the moon's light to, and a point from which other points is measured. In cousin marriage the parents are similar in blood and flesh, and this gives the person born from such marriage a oneness that allows them to compare things back to them, such as if they see another person crying they consider what if they also were harmed and so they cry too. In marriage of different or blood strangers, the child comes from two different entities, and thus they lack a oneness that should come a point of comparison, and so they fail to understand others by comparing them back to the self, so they either have less spirit or none at all. The fact that people no longer marry cousins in places like the west, there is an increase in people being irreligious and some even atheists who refuse to acknowledge the existence of God. When parents are cousins, this is the coming together of similar blood and flesh so it's a pure union, and since marriage is the way of creating, a pure creation gives proof of a pure creator, God. This means children of cousin marriage are born with knowledge of God while children of strangers are born not knowing the pure creator since their parents are different and union of different is impure, so are born on atheism.

The understanding of metaphor is also part of the spirit. This is because the spirit is gentle and light, and so it is not literal and heavy. For example, a man wanting to express they came to a land fast, they may say, "I came quick, quick, quick" and tire out repeating the word "quick" but can instead use a metaphor and say "I came like flying". Traditionally Muslims understood reference to God in the Quran, having a hand or sitting on the throne to be metaphorical and not literal, but the sect of Wahhabism they consider them literal and they are the enemies of Sufism and spirituality, since they give no consideration to the spirit and are known for their obsession with physical Islamic worship such as keeping a beard or males wearing short clothes.

The act of spirit, *ruh* is to be able to take the mind to think about something distant to the self, this is why they called it *ruh*, which literally means "that goes", which is like what spirits or squirts to travel further, or project away from source. The most important thing a person needs to consider that is outside the self is God. Since God is not physical in Islam, the spirit is the best tool to know God.

The spirit is also important in knowing the nature of God, if description of God is meant to be literal or metaphorical. This is especially relevant to know since Wahhabis, a sect of Islam, understand and take verses of the Quran to be literal when traditionally they were considered metaphorical such as that God has a hand. The spirit is gentle and light, and so it understands metaphors which are usually the condensation of information, such as a person wishing to say they arrived fast says they came flying instead of saying they came really really really fast, using really many times. This gentle understanding of metaphors is possible in the state of the existence of a full spirit. The popularity of Wahhabism (or Salafis as they like to be called) an extreme sect which most terrorists belong to comes in the modern changes in society where less people are marrying cousins. These stranger marriages produce children without spirit who do not naturally understand metaphors and so find inclination to Wahhabism. But children from cousin marriages find natural understanding of spirit and so are inclined to the spiritual teachings of Sufism. This is why God commands in the Quran to cousin marriage (33:50) and prohibits stranger marriages (33:52). The Prophet Muhammed (pbuh) said **"the best wife is the paternal cousin"** (Ibn Algaisarani) and that a man to marry a stranger and ignore his cousin and not even look at her is a sign of the Last Hour (Alhaithami).

The spirit is mentioned in the Quran, God says **"they ask about the spirit, the prophet should say the spirit is of God's issues and people are given of knowledge only little"** (17:85). The Prophet Muhammed (pbuh) said **"Spirits are like armed soldiers, whoever agree become friends and whoever disagree become enemies"** (Muslim). The Prophet said spirits are like armed soldiers meaning very powerful, and that they recognise those similar and those different to them. In one Hadith the Prophet said spirits meet from the distance of three days, meaning if a person was to meet someone, both their spirits meet three days before their physical meeting.

Jesus (as) is called "The Spirit of God" in Islam, as he is pure, born without sexual union, and therefore is to the spirit of God who is whole in purity and holy. In Islam we also believe in the Holy Spirit, and consider it to be the angel Gabriel. God in the Quran says He supported Jesus with the Holy Spirit, so that Jesus was able to cure the ill and give life to the dead.

CHAPTER NINE

PURIFICATION OF THE SPIRIT

The religion of Islam believes in a pure God and therefore all worship in Islam begins with purification, such as washing with water before prayer or before reading the Quran. Likewise, getting close to God to gain His presence and vision in this world, requires purification of the spirit. The purification is called *tazzkiya* in Arabic and it is mentioned several times in the Quran. God says that He sent Prophet Muhammed (pbuh) to do *tazzikya* on the believers. God says in the Quran "**He is the one who sent to the illiterate people a messenger from them who recites to them God's verses and purifies them and teaches them the holy book and religious wisdom and if were before were in obvious misguidance**" (62:2). It is verses like this which make certain that the prayer of Abraham to send a prophet who will perform *tazzkiya* has been accepted and this is in the sending of Prophet Muhammed (pbuh). The aim of Ihsan is to enter the presence of God and gain vision of God, and this is not possible in impurity, because God is pure and only a pure spirit can conceive God. The Prophet Muhammed (pbuh) used to pray "**Lord, I ask you by your name the** pure who purifies"(Ibn Uday). The mention of God purifies the spirit just as water purifies the body.

God says "**they are successful those who purify themselves**" (87:14) and in another verse "**they are successful who purify their selves, and in loss those who hide and ignore their ego**" (91:9-10). This is to say religious success, and to be spiritually successful is to purify the spirit and to gain Vision of God. God is very keen that Muslims gain purity and purify their spirit. God said to Prophet Muhammed (pbuh) "**perhaps the blind man will become purified**"(80:3) admonishing the Prophet for turning away and frowning at the blind man. God says in the Quran "**God only wants to remove the harm of impurity from the Prophet's household and make them properly pure**"(33:33), therefore it is the wish of God that Prophet Muhammed's (pbuh) family should be pure and the believers should follow them in example.

The main way to spiritual purification is the mention of God and His messenger, and since they are pure, their mention purifies the spirit. The Quran says an animal killed with the mention of God is purified "**what is lawful is animal slaughtered by a believer mentioning the name of God to purify it**" (5:3) The spirit is also purified with the body and so keeping a pure body such as by performing the before prayer water wash and spiritual bath of Friday. God says in the Quran "**It has men who love to purify and God love the pure**" (9:108) and as God loves purity, He admits that those slaves who purify their spirit to His holy presence by giving them vision of His face. God gives examples of how Muslims can be pure, for example God says "**it is cleaner and purer for a divorced wife to return to her previous husband, instead of marrying a new man, and God knows and people know not**" (2:232). God says "**They are people who God did not want for their hearts to be purified, they will find in the world disappointment and in the afterlife a great punishment**" (5:41) and this is to say that to remain without purity in Islam is greatly punished by God in this world and the next.

The Quran mentions that the homosexuals in the time of prophet Lot (as) said about the believers **"remove them from the village they are people of purity"** (7:82). This verse shows that being people of purity is not universally accepted and some people consider them as inferior, but to God and His messenger they are the superior since God and His messenger are pure. God says in the Quran **"A mosque built on the foundation of piety is suitable for the Prophet. It has men who love to purify and God loves the pure"** (9:108).

CHAPTER TEN

DISEASES OF THE HEART

Disease could be defined as that which prevents function, and function is to fulfil one's aim. Our aim in life is to worship God. God says in the Quran **'I created the *jinn* and humans only that they might worship Me.'** (51:56). Thus, spiritual disease could be said to be all that which prevents worship or leads to disobedience of God, and this is the definition used by the Quran. God says **"the hypocrites and those with disease in their heart say God and His messenger promise is a delusion"** (33:12) and in another verse **'In their hearts is a disease' (2:10).** This is to explain why they are different and being in an irreligious state. Spiritual diseases are mainly caused by the ego, which is a divergence from state of religious obedience to God.

This malfunction of disease is accompanied with other disadvantages and the greatest of them is the risk of God's punishment. As the worship of God is fulfilled by following *Sharia* (commands and prohibitions of God) and the aim of this is to bring benefit and avoid harm. The one who worships God is on a healthy interaction with the world so that no damage is done to the self or others and that one come to be both beneficial to their self, others and the world. To do damage to oneself or others, which is a result of disease is a sin that can lead to God punishing the person in this world, the hereafter or both. The branch of Ihsan deals with purifying the person from diseases, so that they come to fulfil their function and aim of worshiping God. A process of refinement of the heart and spirit.

Just as what constitutes health so we may gain it is defined by God. What is considered disease so we may cure it is also defined by God, and they are what make a person go against the commandments and worship of God. The Quran is called *Al-Furqan* by God in the Quran, which literally means "The Discriminator", as it differentiates between what is to be considered right and what is be taken as wrong. God says **"blessed is God who revealed the law to His worshiper to be for the world a warning"** (25:1). Spiritual diseases are thus defined by God and therefore are absolute to all times and places and not changing from one time to another. What is health is what God wants us to be like and that is the character of the Prophet Muhammed (pbuh). God says in the Quran, **"they have in the messenger of God a good example for those who look forward to the meeting with their Lord, and the Last Day, and remembers God much"** (33:21) and that is because the Prophet Muhammed (pbuh) was of complete character and manners, and was perfect in his worship of God.

To have good character is worship, and is a sign of belief. The Prophet (pbuh) said **"the Muslim is he whom people are safe from the evil of their tongues and hands" (Bukhari)** and **"he has no belief if are not trustable" (Al-Baqwi)**. Bad character is injustice and sin, for it leads to harming other people, but also could prevent the person from entering paradise. The Prophet (pbuh) said no arrogant person will enter paradise, even if their arrogance was the size of a mustard seed (Muslim). Diseases make a person difficult to stand by society, for those of good character are loved by people and by God. The Prophet (pbuh) said, **'God loves the best of character' (Al-Iraqi)** and as we are told in the *Hadiths* that those of the best character will be on the Day of Judgment and paradise closest to the Prophet (pbuh). Spiritual diseases make a person easily accumulate sins, leading to loss of their hereafter and risk of hell fire. The Prophet Muhammed (pbuh) called those whose bad character erases their good deeds as 'bankrupt', for their good deeds are transferred to their victims as compensation on the Day of Judgment, leaving them empty of deeds and destined to hell (Muslim). The highest character is not refraining from hurting others or even doing good to others. The highest character is risking harm or loss for others or doing well to enemies, which is called *futuwa or farasa*. Hamza Ibn Abdul-Mutalab (raa) was known for his *futuwa*, and he risked his life by defending the Prophet (pbuh) in Mecca. Hamza (raa) was told that an influential man had attacked the son of his brother; the Prophet Muhammed (pbuh), but he was patient. Hamza (raa) went to the man and hit him back and said 'you attack a man while I am of his religion?' Hamza (raa) was not a Muslim at the time but said that to show his allegiance to the Prophet (pbuh) and protect him from further attacks.

Spiritual diseases happen when there is an imbalance from what God measured for us to be like in character, belief and action. God says regarding generosity **"let not people hand be miserly and held to their necks, and neither out giving in excess to become blameworthy and regretful" (17:29).** God in this verse forbids both being very stingy or very generous that you become poor, saying neither this nor that, thus commanding to what is in the middle. Thus, when the person does what is in the middle this would be considered health, yet when they go to either extremes, it is a sin and an imbalance that must be corrected. Disease is thus caused by imbalance and that imbalance itself causes other imbalances. The Quran says **"In their hearts is a disease and Allah has increased their disease"** (2:10). When a slave starts a forbidden habit it disinhibits them spiritually and their next sin becomes even easier, so that their disease increase. Those who lie will steal, and those who steal will fornicate, and those who fornicate will also kill, and those who kill will find it easy to disbelieve. It is also the case when a person becomes religious; they build a spiritual stamina with time that makes them able to perform progressively more worship.

As God's religion is that of moderation it is a preserver of the natural balance that God created in us and the world, and by following it balance can also be restored. Spiritual diseases can be an imbalance of the cognition, emotion or behaviour, when what God commands and the Messenger's (pbuh) cognition, emotion and behaviour encompasses balance and thus is a definition of health. When curing diseases of the cognition, emotion and behaviour the scholar is taking the student's cognition, emotion and behaviour to become like that of the Messenger (pubh). Allah said regarding the character of the Messenger (pbuh) **"the Prophet Muhammed has a great character"(68:4)** and hence God chose him to be an example to follow and be like. It is also because the Prophet Muhammed (pbuh) did not only invite to and preached the utmost of behaviour and character that God commanded, but was also described as being the first to practice it. Aisha (raa) when asked about the Prophet's character said '**his character was the Quran' (Ibn Hajar),** meaning there is no command or prohibitions in the Quran that he (pbuh) did not perform. An example of the Prophet Muhammed (pbuh) great character included being kind and forgiving to his enemies, and an example of this is visiting a woman who tormented him in the streets and when he once inquired about her absence and was told it was due to her being ill, he visited her. This visit led the lady to embrace Islam, for indeed it was the character of a Prophet. The Prophet Muhammed (pbuh) was merciful, kind, generous, courageous, patience, forgiving, modest and just. As a miracle it is reported that as a baby he only breast fed from one breast, leaving the other to his adopted brother. Even before his Prophethood he was regarded as trustworthy, upright, and just, and as a respectful man who was trusted to the point of having people leave their valuables to him before they travelled, and was nicknamed before his Prophethood '*Alsadig Alamin*', (the trustworthy honest one). He was also considered just and his judgment was accepted by the leaders of Mecca when they chose him to judge on which tribe of the city was to have the honour of restoring the black stone that is part of the house of

God. Sheikh Al Samman (raa) said in his poem in praise of the Prophet (pbuh); 'Muhammed is not a human like the rest of humans, but a gem among stones'.

The idea that there is wrong and right is understood as a person can understand the existence of two differing things at the same time, and this comes when the person is able to differentiate and name their two hands. Therefore, this is seen in Islam as the sign of the beginning of maturity in children, and it is in this state that children are made to sleep in their separate beds from their parents. The two hand are also a physical metaphor in Islam as the right hand is considered clean and good and used for eating, and handshaking and signalling *tawheed* in prayer, while the left is used for cleaning impurities from the body.

As the Prophet Muhammed (pbuh) is the example of health, the worst disease a person can have is to lack love for him, for how could you be restored to health if you have no love of health, or do not know what health is. Sheikh Al-Busayri (raa) a scholar who showed great love for and was expert on the love of the Prophet (pbuh) said in his most famous work of poetry, the *Burdah* 'the tongue would fail to recognise the taste of a drink in illness, and the eye would deny the sun's rays in disease' to explain the state of those who do not appreciate the state of the Prophet (pbuh) as it being a malfunction in them rather than a reflection of the Prophet of God. This state of lack of love for the Messenger (pbuh) is also sometimes due to them not knowing him, because for the majority it is simply due to them not knowing much about the Prophet (pbuh) and in order to remedy this state the scholar's first step was to advice and encourage the learning of the Prophet's *Seerah* (biography). A biography that none read was turned away without awe by it, for after studying his biography many including non-Muslims have found his character to be worthy of praise.

Spiritual disease is a state of being content in performing wrong actions, what God prohibited and what is considered abhorrent and immoral. The Quran says **"God has made prohibited immoralities,**

both hidden and exposed, and sins and injustice, and worshiping beside God false deities and for people to say about God what they do not know" (7:33). And **"God commands to good and justice and giving family, and forbids sexual immorality and abhorrent acts and prostitution, and God advices to remind they are evil"** (16:90). The level of spiritual health of a person is known by comparing the person's character to that of the Prophet's (pbuh), and its level of health is relative to that of the Prophet's (pbuh), and those whose character most resembles the character of the Prophet being the most in health.

Spiritual diseases manifest from the presence of the ego and can belong to one of three types or levels: of the cognition (mind), of sentiment (emotion) and of conduct; (behaviour and physical actions). Diseases of the cognition are when a person is not thinking properly. This could be caused by ignorance; if the person lacks knowledge, is in a state of heedlessness of knowledge, or holds wrong knowledge to be true. Or if they are not thinking properly as their mind is overwhelmed by emotion, affected by alcohol, mind-altering substances, trauma, or are ignorant of what constitutes correct thinking; logic. The possessing of incorrect knowledge of God or belief as well as constituting sin, or disqualifying the person from the religion can lead to stress or sense of ignorance and other unpleasant emotions. This is especially true if the person lacks knowledge, and could be reassured or made careful if in possession of knowledge. To correct thinking the cause of the problem in corrected, lack of knowledge or holding wrong knowledge is treated with learning; heedlessness of knowledge is treated with re-learning and repetition. Due to the importance and truthfulness of statements such as 'there is no god but Allah' the Messenger (pbuh) commanded their regular repetition.

As well as curing the disease of ignorance by being a source of knowledge of God, of the reality of the world, and of how we should worship God, the Prophet (pbuh) also corrected cognitive diseases or incorrect thinking and an example of this is when a Bedouin challenged the Messenger's statement that there is no such thing as infectivity (*adwa*).

The Bedouin said this could not be correct as a herd with one diseased camel usually gains other diseased camels after a while. The Prophet Muhammed (pbuh) corrected his cognition by asking him, if disease comes from infection, how then did the first camel become diseased? This is to say that the later camels that became diseased could have done so in the same way as the first camel and that the disease of the second camels was not necessary from or related to the first camel. The Bedouin chose his first explanation to be a fact, while the Prophet (pbuh) taught him to consider other reasons. This is a very modern scientific way of thinking.

The importance of this example is that it has further ramifications, e.g. blame. A farmer could be blamed if he let loose a diseased animal that goes to another field and afterwards another farmer's animals become diseased. Nevertheless, the Prophet (pbuh) forbade people entering cities with plagues or leaving them, and it is a sin to do so; this can be understood that infection exists in some diseases. What the Prophet (pbuh) tried to teach the Bedouin is to be open-minded; to not accept the first explanation as fact, but to consider other explanations, and other reasons, and not make one reason as fact especially if there could be other reasons or explanations the person may be heedless of. This is a very correct way of thinking; otherwise the person's knowledge of truth is constricted and could be erroneous. This is not too different from when a companion prayed 'Lord, have mercy on me and on Muhammed and no one else'; the Prophet Muhammed (pbuh) told him **'do not constrict what is vast' (Bukhari)**. This constricted way of thinking has the danger of leading to despair and sadness, but thinking that is humble and not constricted begets hope and more likely to find the truth. As God is grand being constricted shows lack of understanding of God and the reality of the world.

As the existence of God is the reality, disbelief in seen in Islam as a form of dysfunction of the mind, almost a psychosis, where the person is no longer in touch with the reality of the world. If a person chooses to ignore the existence of things in the world they enter a pseudo-schizophrenic state. A mental disease of the person alternating between state of realising the world and acting to the best of their health and other states where they hallucinate and possess delusions. They do not possess knowledge of the truth and this is the stand of the Quran that sees the disbelievers as not thinking properly, '*la yaqiloon*', i.e. lack sense and understanding, God says **"for they do not use their reason" (2:171)**. The Quran says **"but those who disbelieve invent a lie against Allah. Most of them have no understanding."** (5:103). The disbelievers and the believers who do not take the religion and worship of God seriously are also said by God to not be thinking properly. God says **"when they are called to prayer they take it in mockery and play. That is because they are people who do not understand" (5:58)**. This is because the existence of God is clear and absolute to those who think correctly. It is based on the existence of His signs, and the basic logic that each made thing must have a maker, and the world as collection of formed made things, must have a maker and that is God. God says **"God created the night and day, and sun and moon and stars as signs for people who understand religion"** (16:12). God made the change between the day and the night for our benefit, so that it may be light during the day for us to be safe and easy to manoeuvre and live, and dark during the night so we may be able to sleep and rest. God says **"God made the night for rest, and the day bright, and in them are signs for people who fear God"(10:67)**. The knowledge that we require as humans a dark night to sleep and rest, and light and clear day to be aware of the dangers from other poisonous and dangerous animals, uneven surfaces or be able to pick fruit and carry act out tasks safely. The power and might it takes to create the earth and sun and their movement in a way that there could be a day and night, are indeed signs of God, for only a God can have the power and knowledge to make it exist.

After a person becomes familiar to Islam, and then rejects it and becomes a disbeliever or accepts it and becomes a Muslim, the believers are no longer tested on gaining belief (but for the disbelievers it remains so), but their test is then patience at God's other tests; trials and tribulation and their seriousness in performing worship and obeying God's commands. Some after gaining belief they can lose it or it can decrease and gain doubt, then to them again belief becomes their test. This is a very serious test and thus the Prophet (pbuh) taught the prayer **'Lord, let not our test be in our religion'**, (Tirmizi) meaning if we were to be tested let it be in our worldly affairs, i.e. rather a valuable be stolen and having to be patient with that than doubt in the truthfulness of the Messenger (pbuh) or the existence of God. Usually people lose belief or it decreases as a punishment for lack of worship or disobedience of God. God said **"God followed their sinful deeds with hypocrisy in their heart to the day they meet God, for breaking their promise with God and for their lies"** (9:77). The other way people lose their level of belief, is if they perform certain serious sins called *kabair*, like magic, astrology, and fornication, which can lead the person to temporarily lose their state of belief, their *iman*. The seriousness of this is that if the person dies whilst in the state of performance of these major sins and had not repented, they could die as a disbeliever. *Iman* (faith) can also be increased by gaining knowledge of the religion, and the understanding of the Quran and Hadith. God says **"when the revelation comes down from God, they ask who is strengthened in belief by the verses. The believers become strong in faith and hopeful of Heaven"** (9:124).

In correcting cognitive diseases, the Quran and Hadith mentions, reminds and teaches many principles of correct thinking. The main cognitive disease the Quran and Hadith correct is people's thinking so that they could recognize the truth of God's existence and the Message of the Prophet Muhammed (pbuh); this is due to the seriousness of the ramifications of error in them, i.e., an eternal hellfire. The Quran and Hadith also corrects other illogical incorrect thinking that impact religion and spirituality. The Quran says **'Will they exchange the better for the worse?' (2:61)** to those who chose the life of this world above that of the hereafter, by neglecting the worship of God that promises an eternal life in heaven, to follow their desire of this finite inferior world. And it is based on this that those who concentrate on success of the world and not of the hereafter are not thinking properly or choosing what is higher and thus truly better for them. God says **'and remember that whatever you are given now is but for the passing enjoyment of life in this world whereas that which is with God is far better and more enduring.'(42:36).** Another correction of thinking is in following God's commands and ignoring the ego's desires. The Quran says **'it is possible to dislike a thing which is good for you, and that you love a thing which is bad for you.' (2:216).** This means that just because we desire something it does not necessary follow that it will be good or beneficial, and this is true of all sins, in that they have harmful effects in this world and punishment of God in the hereafter. Therefore to think about our actions and not impulsively follow desire would be to be thinking correctly, while those who follow their ego's command have suspended their mind altogether.

The second category of disease is dysfunctions of sentiment: diseases of emotion. A person has emotional disease if there is lack of emotion, wrong emotion, or wrong magnitude so that there is too little an emotion or too great an emotion to a specific thing, person or situation. To understand what causes emotional diseases, first the person must understand what emotions are for, how they occur, and what they serve. Our minds serve to allow us think and reveal to us what is wrong so we can avoid it or what is right so we can benefit from it and on this it commands us to action. The faculty of emotion commands to action, sometimes in a more powerful and even impulsive way, but unlike the mind it has no capacity to differentiate between what is wrong and right or beneficial and harmful. The emotion gets its direction from the mind, and thus when an emotion is established it acts like a short cut to command behaviour without thinking, and when the person does not use their mind they are merely following their feelings and desires, regardless of harm or benefit. There is a mental criterion for every emotion, and once after thinking the person finds that they have gained enough information and knowledge to fulfil the criteria for an emotion, the emotion develops. If an emotion is formed (and it's correct and suitable) it saves the time and energy thinking about every minute situation, and allows the person to act without having to think and yet do correct and beneficial actions, or in the case of disease of emotions the opposite.

To explain this, the example of trust, to trust someone takes a process of thinking and gaining knowledge to fulfil the criteria of trust. This includes that the person must be someone who does not lie, someone who likes to benefit others so they are not known to harm others, someone who has a history of being someone who can be trusted and if a person comes to fulfil these criteria, then feelings of trust develop for this specific person. As soon as a person establishes the emotion that they can trust this person, then they do not have to think every time they tell them something or analyse it for being right, or doubt its truthfulness, but instead accept it. This saves all the energy and time of thinking and investigating with each individual item. A person who comes to trust the Prophet Muhammed (pbuh) as being the Prophet of God will accept everything they say or do as correct, while those who do not, have to analyse and find physical proof of every statement the Messenger (pbuh) says, even when they are Muslim. This is the difference between the two religious states of just being a Muslim or being a Mumin, with the second being the state of complete belief and trust, and is a higher religious state. When the disbelievers of Mecca mocked the Prophet (pbuh) and told Abu Bakr (raa) that his 'friend' has claimed to have been taken to Jerusalem to pray and returned back in one night (when it took months to travel to Jerusalem), he replied **'If he said that then it's true. I trust him in what is greater than that: that revelation from God descends to him'** (Al-Albani).

As emotions develop by the mind giving permission once a person or situation fulfils the criteria for that sentiment, defects in thinking, and lack of complete knowledge of a person or situation can result in defects in emotions. This state could be a lack of emotion, or too great an emotion or too little an emotion, or projecting the wrong emotion to a particular person or situation. Treating wrong states of emotions developing from wrong states of mind is by correcting the way of thinking of the mind or increasing in knowledge depending on the case. Sometimes it is not the emotion that is wrong, but the direction of the emotion and intention behind it. Not all hate is wrong, and not all love is good, the hatred of what is bad is good and can act as a preventer from it, but the love of what is bad is harmful, while the love of what is good is beneficial and advantageous. The same could be said of the emotion of pain, discomfort or displeasure. For many future beneficial acts start by being difficult or a chore to some, like the following of restraining from sins, yet their benefit later discounts this initial emotion. In Islam the fear of people and worry of their harm is considered a spiritual disease and is misguided as a person should be in fear and awe of God, 'Who there is no might or power greater than His', and who by His permission all that benefit or harm befalls us. This negates the feeling that people can make us feel like they can be above or control us by threatening or harming us, because they can only harm us if God allows it to happen as part of testing if we would believe in Him and ask His help and be patient to receive His reward.

The third type of spiritual disease is diseases of conduct or behaviour. They are usually due to wrong thoughts or emotions that are the seed of and lead to wrong behaviour. As the person is not thinking properly or overwhelmed by emotion, they can take part in actions that are wrong (sinful). Part of the cure is to know and always remember that our actions have effect and that we must always think about the consequences of our actions. The consequence of sinful acts is the punishment of God in the hereafter, but sins can also have negative social and personal ramification in this world. As well as correcting thought and emotions, behaviour can be controlled by restraint. The fasting of Ramadan is a great trainer in restraint, and while in Ramadan people usually find it easy to completely restrain, due to the holiness of the month and great worship done therein in other months it is usually less efficient. This ability to restrain requires training; as it usually happens the first restraint is broken and the person returns to their negative behaviour. This process of re-restraining after failure can carry on in a cycle until the person completely leaves the behaviour, and this cycle is known in Ihsan as '*Reyadatul-nafs*'; 'exercise of the ego'. The Prophet Muhammed (pbuh) said God does not go weary of accepting a slave who repents after a sin, regardless of how many times this happens (Muslim). This means that a person who breaks their restraint is reassured that they will be accepted by God again, and their sin will be forgiven and thus not disheartened nor discouraged from restraining again.

In curing diseases of conduct, as well as correcting thinking by gaining knowledge and remembering it by repetition, healing can also be done by intentional arousal of pleasant or unpleasant emotions to control or perform actions. As incorrect diseased emotions can be very powerful in leading to wrong behaviour, emotions can also be used to lead to correct behaviour. Arousing the emotion of fear of God by knowledge and remembrance of the hellfire is a great restrainer of sinful, wrong behaviour, and the hope of paradise has led many people to perform great goodness and much worship of God. The second level of using emotions to modify behaviour is by association; associating pleasant emotions with pleasant behaviour, and unpleasant emotions with wrong or bad behaviour in order for the person to restrain from wrong behaviour in fear of the unpleasant emotion and find it easy to perform good behaviour by being attracted to the pleasant associated emotion.

In religion some of these associations (rewards or punishments) are innate from God, e.g. the Quran says, **'Is it not in the mention of God that hearts finds peace?' (13:28).** To become calm, have clear thoughts and feel contented are pleasant emotions associated with the mention of God, and are a great motivator to it. Hence, the mention of God in times of distress, yet as Muslims we must make regular His mention even in times of peace. Nevertheless, some associations are done by Scholars in curing their students. An example of this is that in the time of the Messenger (pbuh) grapes were hung in the mosque to encourage children to visit the mosque and associated it with the sweet taste of grapes. Negative emotions to restrain from sinful behaviour can be from a physical or psychological source. The Quran prescribes physical punishment using a stick that is no more in thickness than an index finger, to punish a disobedient (not in matters of cooking or cleaning or other household needs as in Islam they are not an obligation on the wife) or mischievous wife (or husband by his wife in at least the *Maliki* school of thought), but this has many conditions including that the head or face is not hit as this is forbidden, as well as that it should be restrained and not lead to bodily damage. Parents are also commanded to gently hit children over the age of ten if they do not perform *salah,* but this is after three years of training them from the age of seven. Physically hurting another person or an animal or even your own self without reason or for an unjust motive is considered a sin and forbidden by the religion. Nevertheless, these exceptional cases are allowed due to the greater benefit they beget as the person realises, they performed what is wrong and not repeat it. Pain to communicate there is an error and a problem is a natural phenomenon, in that our own bodies cause us pain if there is eminent harm e.g. touching a hot object, or pain internally, if a disease has caused damage to an internal organ. God has chosen to allow us use this, to prevent us from spiritual danger of hell.

CHAPTER ELEVEN

CURE OF THE HEART

The cure of a spiritual disease depends on the nature of the disease. Some diseases are cured by gaining knowledge, while some are cured by correcting the way of thinking, and some are cured by the Quran, which is a mixture of the two, as it contains the Blessing and Holiness of God's Divine words. God says regarding the Quran **"the revelation comes as an advice from God, and a healing for the hearts, and guidance and mercy to the believers"** (10:57). Other treatments for spiritual diseases include restraining from sin, making *zikr* (mention and praise of God), as well as specific exercises. Doing good deeds, *nafila* (optional worship) and the company of the pious also have a healing element that increases the person in good character and purifies them from spiritual diseases. Some scholars prescribe reading a certain portion of the Quran on a daily basis as the main way to cure and also perform *nafila* worship. Lack of knowledge or holding wrong knowledge is treated with learning; heedlessness of knowledge is treated with remembering and repetition. With repetition the person first learns knowledge by heart and so could then say it in the important moment of death. The Prophet (pbuh) said whoever says *la ilah ila Allah* at the moment of death will go to Heaven (Al Dargtni). With repetition the person truly realises the meanings of God's praises, and there is an increase in understanding of the religion and *ajr* (reward). Every time a Muslim repeats a praise of God and realises there is no evidence to the contrary, their belief increases, and awareness of God's presence increases. The cure of the ego is *Jihadul-nafs* and the prevention of excess desires of the ego until it is annihilated is deprivation from luxury as it suppresses the ego. This could mean eating simple food, deprivation from excess leisure and limiting unnecessary socialising. This is based on the Prophet's (pbuh) command that those who are unable to marry to make much fast; as it decreases their desire (Bukhari)

The curing of the heart differs from *tazzkiya* spiritual purification in that spiritual purification is to remove the effect of previous sins, while curing the heart is about stopping future sins and both are parts of the practice of Ihsan and the general basics to spiritual development.

The performing of sins can be viewed as being exclusively a spiritual disease demanding spiritual cure or a crime demanding punishment. Islam sees them as both without contradiction. Islam recognises that sins are a result of spiritual diseases, but as they are curable it sees being content with disease and not making an effort to improve as a crime against the self and others if the disease involves sins causing hurt or damage to another.

The cure in Ihsan isn't a sip of Zamam water or a pinch of black seed nor a drink of honey, all of which the Prophet Muhammed (pbuh) said contain healing properties. It is not a problem in the body that requires tablets and injections. It's a spiritual disease and thus requires spiritual healing. The spiritual cue is the Quran, the mention and praise of God and His messenger, and other spiritual exercises. The scholars of Ihsan have observed the changes in the heart of a believer with increase worship. The Quran says "**their hearts are affected by what they gained in sins**"(83:14). The people of Ihsan believe that good deeds also create a positive change in the heart as do sins change it.

At this stage the student must read the stories of the *awliya* (saints) and their *karamat*. Stories of the *awliya*, like the people who were trapped in the cave, *khidir* (the Green Man-the companion of Moses (as)) and other pious mentioned in the Quran and Hadith. God said **'verily in their stories are lessons for people of understanding' (12:111).** Their stories are found in many books such as *Sifat alsafwa*, *Orchids of Love*, or *Tadhkirat al-Awliya'* (Memorial of the Saints) by Farid Al-Din Attar (raa). While it is important for the student to learn about the stories of the Prophets and companions, it is the stories of the pious that are much emphasised, as while the spiritual health of Prophets could be attributed to their state of Prophethood and that of the companions to their company of the Prophet (pbuh), stories of the pious highlight what the common believer is capable of achieving spiritually and thus are the most inspiring. Their stories whilst entertaining are not for entertainment basis, they are an example of and education of what is religiously right and spiritually healthy. Their stories give us information of how they acted in piety and worship when faced by difficult situations. The power of religious commandments and teachings being practiced in the physical world (as should be) bring into it mercy, blessings and goodness. Their determination to choose spirituality and worship above worldly benefit further reinforce the superiority of belief and worship of God as well as provide a good example to follow.

Reading stories of the pious and the Prophets teach us about what spiritual 'health' is and what a healthy person is like. The stories of the cursed devil (*Iblis*) and of the astray like pharaohs, teach us what is spiritually 'illness' and what we must avoid. Physical interaction with the pious, of meeting scholars and the people of religious knowledge is essential to realising that spirituality is not mere theory but a reality that exists and will always exists. The Prophet (pbuh) said **'there will be goodness in my followers until the Last Hour'** (Bukhari). If possible, visit different scholars of different paths, and come to interact with others who take their religion seriously. The Prophet Muhammed (pbuh) commanded the companionship of good and pious people. He (pbuh) said '**a good friend and a bad friend are like a perfume seller and a blacksmith: The perfume seller might give you some perfume as a gift, or you might buy some from him, or at least you might smell its fragrance. As for the blacksmith, he might burn your clothes, and at the very least you will breathe in the fumes of the furnace**' (Bukhari).

The cure of diseases and its method is derived from the Quran and the Messenger's (pbuh) example when curing his companions. As the Prophet (pbuh) did not give the cure to every single disease, the scholars of Ihsan over the years have made formulas for diseases employing the laws used by the Messenger (pbuh), similar to the process used by the scholars of *fiqh* in making *fatwas*, for example using *giyas* (use of similar examples from the Quran and *Sunnah*). The human *nafs* when it is not purified is an animal *nafs*, and it is the cause of all diseases. It is arrogant, self-centred, selfish, lazy, evil, desires pleasure in what is bad or wrong, likes excessiveness and is never content. Thus it takes away from worship of Allah by leading the person to follow its commands and neglect those of God. The scholar of Ihsan identifies the diseases a person has, and can then provide them with the cures; they also guide the person through *Jihadul-nafs* in order to annihilate the ego and draw closer to God. This makes the scholars of Ihsan the doctors of the hearts.

Scholars cure the diseases as they manifest, and thus the process requires the student to be in physical contact with the scholar. One of the greatest diseases the *nafs* manifests is its command to be centre of attention, when only God is worthy of and rightful of that. A person with a *nafs* sees themselves as the centre of the universe, and everything they do is in perspective to what pleases their *nafs* and fulfils their desire, even if it is against God's commands. This is the reason God in the Quran describes it as taking their **'desires as gods'** (25:43). Therefore, it is battled in *Jihadul-nafs*, and purified in *tazzkiya*, and when this is perfected the *nafs* dies (becomes absent), and it no longer distracts from God and worship is restored to be only for God.

Knowledge of what is spiritual health and spiritual disease is not enough, there should be a distinction between the two and a belief that one is better than the other. It is important that spiritual health is seen as something desirable and disease as abhorrent, and the stronger these feelings are the more the person is motivated to perform *tazzkiya*. This comes from the realisation of the benefits of spiritual health and the disadvantages and adverse consequences of disease; both in this world and the next. This could be a result of noticing disease in others and not liking them or reading about them in the stories of the Prophets and saints and then acknowledging how unpleasant spiritual disease is. Being healthy and purified of diseases reduces the person's stress as they will be doing fewer sins which bring the worry or prospect of hell and the other health benefits that they become a better person, bettering their life and spiritual state, and through which they can expect a good death and hereafter.

To acknowledge and accept that spiritual disease is inferior and a shortcoming sounds simple, but it is not so for those with a *nafs*. This is because it is difficult for a person with an ego to admit something is a shortcoming or inferior if they possess it, even if it means being untruthful and unjust. This is because arrogance is an attribute of the impure *nafs*, and admitting that something they possess is inferior suggests a shortcoming in them and demands them to admit they are wrong or have weaknesses. The other difficulty the person who possess an arrogant *nafs* is with admitting that a characteristic is right or good if another possesses it, especially if they do not also possess it as it suggests that another is better than them.

One of the *Jahili* Arabs refused to become a Muslim and follow the Prophet (pbuh) because he said he would rather follow the liar of another tribe than the truthful one of Quraish (Prophet Muhammed (pbuh) tribe). This was because his tribe was a rival to that of the Prophet's (pbuh) and he did not want to further make Quraish superior to his own by declaring his belief in the Prophet (pbuh) who was from Quraish.

While this is an extreme emotion that has led to disbelief in God and His religion, there are lesser versions of it that include that which motivates people to perform *geeba* (backbiting) to belittle others, slander or making *shehadatul zoor* (false witness), which are very serious sins, but performed sometimes nevertheless to belittle others and maintain a level above them.

The other reason for the importance of realising that diseases are abhorrent and spiritual health is good is because it is not always the common view. Whereas the views of religion come from God and are absolute and unchanged by time, the views of society are shaped by those with the largest egos to suit their desires, and to make their own activities acceptable. This is further emphasised when they are a large number and their powers in society are greater. In human history sometimes society's views concurred with the views of religion, this is the case when the believers were majority or they ruled, but when the rulers and those who have power's views are contrary to religion, then society's views do not concur with religious views and morals. It is also the case that even if a society and its rulers are believers, society's views depend on their level of belief and practice of the religion. As well as their own egos, some social views are inherited from the views of previous generation who may not have been Muslim or from pre-Islamic times. This is why when one companion insulted another by calling him a 'son of a slave woman', the Prophet (pbuh) told him he still had *jahiliya* in him, i.e. the false beliefs of the pre-Islamic society (Bukhari).

The Prophet (pbuh) when asked if after the goodness of his time (the prevalence of worship and correct morality) there would be evil again, and he replied that there will and after that goodness will follow and so forth (Bukhari). This evil the *Hadith* speaks about is the prevalence of the lack of worship of God and the reversal of moral values in society. God said **"the people of Lot replied that they should banish Lot and the believers from their town as they are people of purity"** (7:82). In this verse the immoral majority commanded to remove a prophet (pbuh) and his followers for being people who were good. It is a disease too to not acknowledge that spiritual health is good and disease is bad. When a person is healthy of this disease they admit to disease being bad, and what is virtuous and good as superior, even if they do not perform them. This disease happens on a social scale when immoralities, crimes and sins are made to seem popular, and good characteristics are ignored or worse belittled. This is expressed in the belittling of their harms or praising of disease, e.g., that conning is an expression of intelligence, fornication as an expression that the person is desired by others or alcohol as a sign of sophistication. Or the belittling of good morals, e.g., kindness is seen as a sign of weakness, covering up in *hijab* is seen as a sign of lack of beauty, or wearing of loose Islamic clothes as unfashionable. This is sometimes because those of low belief or lack of knowledge of the religion, unable to imagine that there could be people who truly believe or have a level of belief that makes them perform its commandments so think there must be other reasons. Or they could be hypocrites or disbelievers who wish to lower religion and discourage its practice or show enmity to believers.

The command to evil is not just in forcing or recommending evil to people, but in also being labelled with low views or being ridiculed for practicing the religion. Then the wish to practice commands of the religion is hindered by the prospect of becoming what the general social view is against, or has derogatory views about. The battle is then two folds, one against their own desire and the second is going against the common belief, and this was the state of the worship of the Muslims in Mecca. If by practicing religion the person is harmed by merely a wrong image or view of them, then the Muslim should be patient with this, but if it will lead to bodily harm or death then the Muslims are allowed to not practice that which brings their society's wrath, or when possible to migrate. One way to overcome this is by knowing what you are doing is correct and know reasons and poof for it. You can ignore, but ignorance can fall to their incorrect views.

All people have the God-given right to free will, and can act to as they wish, and be equally free to practice what is religious or not. However, this does not mean that goodness and bad are equal, and spiritual disease is inferior according to the people, according to the Prophet (pbuh) and according to God. While the laws of the world protect people from the immoral and/or criminal from causing damage to others, the overall laws of God that command goodness forbid people to cause harm or damage to themselves as well as others.

It is possible that the views of non-religious communities or societies to concur to the superiority of good character and justice; spiritual health. This is due to their innate goodness and obvious merit. The beauty of spiritual health, that is the goodness of manners and worship of God, and refraining from hurting others is praiseworthy and considered good not only to those of belief. This comes down to our human state, the simple fact that things that cause hurt or pain, which comes from the expression of spiritual disease are detestable to people, and wish for them to be stopped, while the goodness of spiritual health that mean lack of hurting of others, and even doing good to them and being generous to them, means that people receive that in which they innately find happiness or pleasure. It is the *fitra* (the innate nature of people). God says **"people should establish the face for the pure religion, it is the nature of God and God made the nature of people to be pure. There is no change in nature of God"** (30:30). The Quran says the religion is to maintain that nature of humanity, not to allow it be corrupted and of course to correct it if it is made corrupt. The nature of humanity is that they detest pain and like and seek pleasure and the commands of God follows this, while the commands of the spiritually diseased and the human ego go against this innate nature of humanity. This is true as indeed the majority of people are good, and the criminals and people who do evil are only a few in comparison. Nevertheless, when society's views support these few, then people are forced to act against their *fitra*.

The acknowledgment that good is good and what is wrong is wrong, is a blessing. Umar (raa) used to pray to God to show him what is good as good and to help him to practice it, and what is wrong as wrong and to help him to refrain from it. The Quran says **"are the obedient believers like the disobedient disbelievers, they are not equal with God"** (32:18). The proof that the person acknowledges this is their love for goodness, the love of the people of goodness and loving God the commander of goodness.

The Prophet Muhammed (pbuh) was determined to cure his companions of their diseases and in helping them in battling their egos even when he did not mention that it is what he was doing. He also encouraged them to recognise the evil of the ego, and introduced them to its battle and of being aware of it by teaching them to make prayers. In one instance he told a companion he would teach him a prayer that would be of great benefit, then the Prophet (pbuh) added **"Lord, inspire me to what is correct and protect me form the evil of my ego"** (Bukhari). Which is the start of the practicing of the branch of Ihsan. It is also written that the Prophet (pbuh) said during *salah* in prayer **"I seek God's refuge from the evil of our egos"** (Abu Dawud), this means that the knowledge of the ego and its evil is something Muslims come to remember with every *salah*. This is because the ego is one of the main reasons for sins, as through it desires it makes easy and necessary to the person to fall into sin. The fact that the companions went into battle and thus risked death, acts as a way of *tazzkiya* for their egos. The fact that as they were building the Islamic community and government, they were under the constant instruction of the Prophet Muhammed (pbuh) and thus it did not leave a space for their desires, and they therefore achieved the highest of states.

There are examples in the Hadith of how the Prophet (pbuh) cured his companions and made them grow in purity (*tazzkiya*). When a young man asked the Prophet (pbuh) permission to commit fornication, the Prophet Muhammed (pbuh) approach was so to remind and teach him of its evils that at the end the man revealed that he no longer had such desire (Al-Iraqi). The young man's heart was diseased, as he desired to sin, lacked in *haya* (modesty), but also was arrogant that God's command would be broken for his sake. The Messenger (pbuh) responded to him by asking him if he would be happy if that (fornication) were to happen to his female relatives. And the Prophet (pbuh) then asked him in turn if he would be happy for it to happen to one of his female relatives, counting his mother, daughter, sister and aunts. And each time he replied 'no' and the Prophet (pbuh) then each time said **"other people do not want if for their relatives" (Al-Iraqi)**. This reminded the young man of the inferiority of fornication, but also that by committing fornication he was hurting the relatives of his partner, and that it is not Islamic to hurt others. The young man then said since then fornication became a thing most detestable for him. The young man's pondering on the bad consequences of his actions, i.e. that it will be hurting relatives of the lady involved, led the man to not want to perform such action, and saw it as wrong. This was possible because the young man had a healthy belief that a person should love for others what they love for themselves, but more importantly that fornication shows less respect and appreciation to a woman in comparison to marriage. The companion was honest that he wished not for a female relative of his to be given what is less, and based on this he was taught to not wish it on others. This was in following the Prophet Muhammed (pbuh) command to **"love for others what you would love for yourself" (Ahmed)**. This is because it's important to recognise that the other is similar to the self and similar must be treated similar. This oneness, is part of *tawheed*, thus the Prophet in a Hadith said that a true belief in oneness of God treats similar things as one. Islam sees fornication to lack the benefits, rights and dignity that comes in marriage and as such it is inferior and not deserving of a believer, woman or man. Islam sees fornication as a degrading experience, and this is why Joseph (as) felt pain and humiliated that he preferred jail than to be in such a situation.

Understanding the negative consequences to sinful acts, and that all sins have negative consequences is a powerful way to understand why they were prohibited, and also to avoid them. Sometimes it is not enough to just say that something is wrong or a sin. Scholars in using the method of the Prophet (pbuh) should always describe the worldly repercussions of sins, and the punishment for them in the hereafter. When the Prophet Muhammed (pbuh) described to the young man the meaning and negative consequences of fornication, it made him decide to refrain from it. The Prophet (pbuh) could have simply reminded him that fornication is a great sin that can lead to the hellfire. This is because for someone to refrain from a sin based on only hearing this requires that they be of very strong and deep belief, and as not all Muslims possess this, the Prophet (pbuh) instead employed a way that all Muslims regardless of level of belief can understand, i.e. the negative social and worldly consequence to sins.

Another example of how the Prophet (pbuh) cured his companions of diseases and increased them in spiritual purity was related by Abu Hurayra (raa). Abu Hurayra (raa) a companion of the Prophet related an incident when he was very eager and impatient to drink milk that it became obvious to the Prophet (pbuh). On noticing this the Prophet (pbuh) commanded him to instead offer the milk to all present, leaving Abu Hurayra (raa) to be the last to drink; an exercise in patience and restraint. Then once he started drinking the milk the Prophet (pbuh) kept commanding him to drink more until he could drink no more (Bukhari). This was an exercise to curb a wrong behaviour, increasing the companion in purity by teaching him to control his desire for food.

Part of knowing the ego is to know what it produces, which is desire. Desire is the emotion of wanting something very desperately; it is an intense emotion to deal with and can cause sadness if not fulfilled. As thus it is very controlling as the person has to submit to it in order to prevent the emotions that follow if they are not fulfilled. Desires can be for something that is wrong and thus leading to sins if followed. This makes it important to be able to control desire and have the ability to restrain from following it. Restraining of desire can also be from excess of what is allowed as well as being from what is *haram* and sinful. While the desire for food or drink in a state of thirst or hunger, as was the state of Abu Huraira (raa) is normal and the opposite would be considered dangerous and *haram*, it was his attitude and desire for excessiveness which the Prophet (pbuh) noticed and wanted to rectify. The Prophet (pbuh) wanted to teach him patience, control and restraint and increase him in spirituality.

What the Prophet (pbuh) did was to teach the reality of desire to Abu Huraira (raa). The nature of desire for the majority of indulgences including food and drink is what the scholars of Ihsan call '*shahwa kazba*' (false desire). It is called this because after the person fulfils them and they disappear they return, only this time in higher intensity as if were never fulfilled. They are also not truthful in that they do not permanently disappear forever after fulfilment, even if the person feels it will be the case while fulfilling them and thus overeats or drinks.

The other way of curing desire to excess, is from realising that excess is not right, and this is by experiencing the unpleasantness of excess when it is performed. This was the reason why the Prophet (pbuh) encouraged Abu-Huraira (raa) to drink even after having reached satiety, demonstrating to him in a physical way the unpleasantness of excess so that the next time his desire is controlled. Nevertheless, this curing of desire by experiencing the unpleasantness of excess of fulfilling it by overindulgence is valid for only *halal* desires. As drinking milk is not sinful, it was possible to overindulge in it, even though the Quran prohibits excess. This is because in this case the excess is allowed as it is done with the intention to cure, not to indulge. The other way we could say Abu Huraira (raa) was cured was by the experience of associating unpleasant emotion with both lack of behaviour (having to drink last) and excessiveness of behaviour (over drinking the milk on the Prophet's command). There became a mental association with lack of behaviour to be unpleasant, and mental association between excessiveness of behaviour also as being unpleasant. While each can be taught at separate times, for them to be done together by following excessiveness being unpleasant after lack being experienced as unpleasant, teaches that they are both equally unpleasant and thus a person prefers the moderation in the middle and gaining control of their desires.

Another way of teaching to restrain from sin is by acknowledging the enormity of sin. There are sins that people fail to see how they bring harm and thus perform them without inhibition. Some of these sins include backbiting and usury. God said "**neither backbite one another, do they wish to eat the flesh of their dead brothers, so they detest it**" (49:12). The Prophet Muhammed (pbuh) said '**usury is as great as a man who fornicates with his mother' (Al-Munzri)**. As all people agree on the enormity and abhorrent nature of these two acts, by equalling backbiting and usury to them, their magnitude is realised, and people then refrain from their practice. The Prophet Muhammed (pbuh) also equated the life, possessions, and the dignity of a Muslim as equal in sanctity as the month of *zul hijjah* (month of Hajj), the land of Mecca and the day of Hajj (Bukhari). This is to give sanctity to those who believe in God and worship Him in following the truth as holy beyond those who don't.

To cure spiritual diseases, the first step is to identify them. As they are obvious in speech, action or behaviour, anyone can identify them. Nevertheless, what defines a disease requires knowledge. An example would be of arrogance; the Islamic description of arrogance is described not as vanity of luxury in clothes and food or believing they are better than others, but rather as the expression of it. The Prophet (pbuh) said '**Arrogance is to ignore truth and belittle people' (Muslim)**.

Sufis (people of Ihsan) are famous for wearing patched clothes, and this is because it is the uniform of the people seeking God. Clothes cover the genitalia and shame, as well as our purity and when patches are worn this shows insistence of purity or wholeness of purity which is the description of God in Islam. The prophet Muhammed (pbuh) and his companions used to patch their clothes. This also teaches humility and the Quran says **"God doesn't like the excessive"** (7:154). *Khalwa* is seclusion and the Prophet Muhammed (pbuh) was meditating in a cave when the angel Gabriel came to him with the Quran and the religion of Islam. *Khalwa* teaches lack of socialising and excessive pointless speech, and the Quran mentions prophets and saints of the past fasting from speech. Serving the scholar of Ihsan, trains to obey the commands of God and His messenger. Stories of the prophets, the prophet's family, the prophet's companions and the saints, as well as visiting their graves, for blessings and to remember the reality of life and death. The Quran in the chapter of the cave mentions building mosques near the graves of the saints since they remind of God and people usually want to pray after they remember God. *Zuhd* is to take what a person finds essential and leaves what is not needed. This is to show that they are sincere in their want of the afterlife and their acceptance of only Heaven. The Prophet Muhammed (pbuh) taught **"leave what people have and they will love you, and leave what is in this world and God will love you"** (Ibn Hajar Alasglani). *Zuhd* is not poverty, the Prophet Muhammed (pbuh) prayed **"Lord, I seek your refuge from poverty"** (Bukhari). God says **"don't forget your share of this world"** (28:77). A very beneficial thing in practicing Ihsan is to give and work in charity, since correcting the wrong in the world shows an insistence of correcting the self in Sufism. In Sufism there are also brotherhoods. The Prophet Muhammed (pbuh) commanded to keeping good companionship and avoiding bad people; he described them like being in the company of a perfume merchant – that a person will smell good from their company – while bad companionship is like a blacksmith, you could get burned from their fire or the least smell bad from the smoke (Bukhari). Travel is also prescribed in Ihsan, the angels ask the people of hellfire **"was God's earth not vast"** (4:97).

There are other different exercises used to cure believers from their spiritual diseases. Those who love the *dunya* (this world) are cured from it by having to live away from society, in *khalwa*. Traditionally this meant to live in mountains and caves. Far from civilisation the person comes to learn to trust in God and appreciate that one can exist without worldly luxuries. Those with arrogant egos are cured by having to serve or beg to learn humility. Those with fear or anxiety of future damage or harm, or feel needy of others are told to repeat God's praise including 'my trust is in God and He is the best to rely upon' (*hasbi Allah we neam alwakeel*). Arrogance is cured by *'Allahu Akbar'* (God is great). *Alhamduallah* (thanks and praise to God) teaches dependence on God and increases happiness by reminding of His many gifts. Sadness from loss of loved ones or damage or loss of possessions is removed by being reminded that we are not here permanently because all belongs to God; (*ina lellah wa ina ilyhi rajioon*). Lack of *salah* (prayer) is due to the fact that the person has not mentally established its importance either due to lack of knowledge or forgetfulness, but the Quran also says that those who find prayer easy are the '*khashieen*' (those who fear Allah). A person can be cured from their lack of observance of prayer, by reminding them of the Majesty and Might of God and His severe punishment to those who disobey His commands such as prayer. The Prophet Muhammed (pbuh) said **"to gain a gentle heart, feed the poor and pat an orphan's head"** (Sahih Aljami). This shows how the Prophet considered the spiritual disease of being harsh and hard hearted and prescribes a spiritual cure for them.

Khalwa gives an opportunity to revise one's beliefs, gives time to think and reflect, and most importantly to worship undisturbed which is the aim of it. While *Rahbana* (becoming a monk or nun) is prohibited in Islam, nevertheless, Islam encourages *khalwa* which during the nights of Ramadan is termed *aetikaf*. The difference between *Rahbana* and *khalwa* is that while *rahbana* is permanent, *khalwa* is temporary. *Khalwa* is usually prescribed for students who have sinned much and need to replace them with much worship, those who are distracted by society, or as part of the training for becoming a scholar of Ihsan. However, generally it is not something that is prescribed much.

Other exercises scholars may command of their student is to wear patched clothes, called '*margoa*'. It is a *Sunnah* (the Prophet (pbuh) performed it), to teach them humility and not to be affected by other people's views, or be too concerned by the superficiality of how they look. Repetition of *istigfar* (asking forgiveness of God) also teaches humility as it reminds the person of their sins and shortcomings in religion. Visits to graveyards remove the fear of death, and serves as its reminder so that the person lives a more productive and spiritual life. God says **"people are busy in increasing their riches, until they visit the graveyard"** (102:1-2). Growing plants from seeds teaches patience and appreciation of the nature of time, that it can be slow or fast and accepting it. The company of people who are knowledgeable of the religion, students of Ihsan and the pious encourage worship as well as reminding of it. It helps avoid environments and company that brings heedlessness of God and the hereafter which encourages sins to be made or repeated. There should also be strict self-censorship from sins and sinful acts as well as performing them which increases the sickness of the heart, and so must be avoided to achieve *tazzkiya*. The Prophet (pbuh) said **'when a believer commits a sin, a black spot appears on their heart. If they repent and seek God's forgiveness, their heart is cleansed, but if they do more sins then that spot increases until it covers their heart'** (Tirmizi). The Quran says of this **"on their hearts is the stain of the ill which they do"** (83:13-14). This cover of the heart can lead to more diseases of the heart, a decrease in *iman* (to doubt the Signs of God), and a state of carelessness where the person finds it more difficult to respond to the commands of God. To refrain from sins requires the knowledge of what is correct and what is sinful, and this comes from knowledge of the commandments of God from the Quran and Sunnah. This should not be left to randomly coming across a religious fact or knowledge, but the person should make effort to increase their amount of knowledge of the religion. One of the least ways of gaining religious knowledge is the Friday Prayer, which part of it is two sermons on the religion. The second is reading Islamic books to build knowledge, and the most important of books is the Quran. Yet the most correct way is to have scholars on the three branches to learn from authentic correct knowledge.

The scholar of Ihsan decides what combination of exercises suits their student, and the type of cure used is left to their discretion. Even though there are many exercises, scholars usually choose to increase their student's *iman*, and that is mainly by prescribing for them to do a certain *zikr* on a regular basis. This is because once *iman* is increased it acts to restrain from all types of sins, and becomes a great motivator to worship and perform good deeds and a cure from diseases. This is also the case as exercises reveal a student's spiritual disease, and Islam teaches discretion in sins and maintains people's dignity. Therefore when choosing to prescribe spiritual exercises scholars usually choose to prescribe them to groups of students and not certain individuals.

In Islam the hellfire is also seen as a purifier. It is used to purify Muslims from their sins, while for disbelievers it is a punishment and thus it is permanent. Therefore for the Muslims who enter hell, their time will depend on the amount of their sins. The Prophet (pbuh) taught us the prayer to ask God to purify us using **'water, coldness and snow' (Muslim)** as opposed to the purification using fire in hell. This is based on the fact that patience in suffering erases sins, and while water erases sins when used in purification for prayer, cold and snow erase sins by their pain and discomfort which nevertheless is very gentle compared to burning in the hell fire. The punishments of this world (*of sharia*) are so that the person associates painful feelings with sinful actions thus reducing these actions, preventing further sins. The punishment of the hereafter is for the person to understand the seriousness of their sins, and the Majesty of God, and how wrong it was to disobey Him in this world.

There are sinful acts which God did not set punishment for in this world but will be accounted in the next. Nevertheless, for those of knowledge of religion and fearing of God it is the self-inflicted punishment of regret, and fear that one is going to be punished for it in the next world. This feeling of remorse not only makes the person less encouraged to sin, but is also rewarded for by God, as it shows fear of and reverence of Allah. The Prophet Muhammed (pbuh) said those who cried in this world out of fear and awe of God, will have a special status on the day of Judgement (Tirmizi). The other reason for psychological punishment comes from the love of God. It is a feeling of disappointment that the person was not able to fulfil the commands of God or that the person did something that God hates and this comes from a higher spiritual state. While the punishment of God is great, those who believe in God and obey Him and do good deeds have nothing to fear. The fact that there is a life after this is a wonderful gift. The knowledge of the hereafter gives reassurance of a lasting eternal life, justice and punishment of those who do wrong, and the prospect of a superior life in paradise.

CHAPTER TWELVE

STAGES OF IHSAN

The Prophet Muhammed (pbuh) described Ihsan as to '**worship Allah as if you see Him, and if you see Him not, then to worship Him knowing He sees you**' **(Muslim).** The Prophet (pbuh) described two states that differ on the certainty of God's existence ('as if you see Him'). The first state or stage is to worship God as if you see Him, and the second is to worship God knowing that He sees you. This certainty 'as if you see Him' mentioned in first type of worship can be from the Vision of God and this would be the highest state, or it could be from the witnessing of the manifestation of God's Attributes in the world. The second state which is for those who 'do not see Him', is to worship knowing that 'He sees you' based on strong *iman*.

The state of worshiping Allah knowing that 'He sees you' is known in Ihsan as '*moragaba*' (vigilance), and this does not require the guidance of a scholar of Ihsan. This state is based on the fact that God is all seeing, all hearing and is knowledgeable of our actions. God says **"follow what is revealed to the Prophet Muhammed from his Lord, and God is aware of what people do"** (33:2) and **"God knows what is secret and what is yet more hidden."** (20:7). In this state the person worships with the vigilance of one who is being watched, i.e. perfecting all their worship. This state does not require *Jihadul-nafs*, merely being careful and complete in worship. Nevertheless, it does require knowledge of worship and of *Aqida*. It is the belief in the truthfulness of the message of the Prophet (pbuh) and the existence of God as well as His attributes of being knowledgeable and seeing of His creation and our deeds that motivates to this high spiritual state of perfect worship. It is also in awareness of God's Might and in fear of His punishment that the person restrains from His disobedience.

The two states described by the Prophet (pbuh) describe the highest spiritual states of each of the two stages of Ihsan. The second stage, its highest spiritual state is to worship God in a perfect way in knowledge that He sees them, while the highest state of the first stage is to worship in a direct way of 'as if you see Him' after having achieved spiritual states of witnessing and becoming close to God. The Ihsan stage that follows vision of God its highest state is defined as to worship God as if you see him even when you do not see him. To 'worship as if you see', means with the certitude of His presence even when there is no vision of His presence. This is because the vision of His presence is not a continuous spiritual state (we wouldn't be able to tolerate it anyway as too much pleasure like looking at the sun which gives too much pain). This means that in the absence of the state of witnessing of God the person's level and manner of worship should be maintained as if in a state of witnessing Him. In this state the worship is not based on *iman* of His existence, but is out of *yageen* (certainty) of His existence that comes from witnessing Him, and this is a high level indeed.

The Quran differentiates between two levels of *yageen*: *Ilm al-yageen* (Certainty of Knowledge) and *Ain al-yageen* (Certainty from Sight). God says in speaking of the hellfire **"indeed if they had certainty of knowledge, they will see the hellfire. Then they shall see it with certainty of sight"** (102:5-7). These verses explain the two certainties; the first of Knowledge that is a certainty based on knowledge and the second of sight, which comes from personal witnessing. Imagine that in a house there were only two people, and a cup that was on a table was moved. The fact that you are sure it was not you makes it certain that it was the other person who moved the cup. This certainty is based on knowledge (that there is only two of you) and logic (that if it's not you then it's the other who moved the cup) and as it is based on knowledge alone it is thus called *Ilm alyageen*. There is a higher and stronger certainty, and that is the certainty of sight, *ain Alyageen* which would be for you to witness the other person moving the cup. The weakness of *Ilm alyageen* in comparison to *ain alyageen* comes from the possibility of other explanations, e.g. a gust of wind blew through the window and moved the cup, and its strength will depend on having evidence to dismiss these other explanations. The Quran says if only people would become knowledgeable of the certainty of the hellfire from accepting the message given to the Prophets (pbuh). God then confirms that people will see the hellfire, and after this then their certainty would no longer be based on the knowledge of the reports of the Prophets but from actually witnessing it, and then they gain certainty of sight (*ain al yageen*). The third level of certainty the Quran mentions is *hag alyageen* (certainty of truth). God says in the Quran **"that is indeed the certain truth"** (56:95). This certainty would be the equivalent of the person themselves moving the up, and this would be like a personal experience of vision of God.

The same two levels of certainty are also true of the existence of God. When there is no Vision of God, it is *iman* based on *Ilm al yageen*. This is based on the knowledge (the existence of complex creation in the world, e.g. trees, animals, birds etc) and the logic (that every created thing must have a creator, and that the powerful creator of the world is God), thus the Quran names the phenomena of the world as Signs of God's existence. This absolute nature of this knowledge, meant that people can have belief (*iman* in God) before or without seeing or witnessing Him. The obviousness of this argument also meant that throughout human history people believed in God. It was merely the nature of God that people were different on, and hence why God sent Prophets to correct our understanding of Him. Before the message of Islam, the companion Jundub Bin Amru (raa) said 'to this creation is a Creator but I do not know who He is'. The Quran says **"if are asked who created the heavens and earth, and controls the sun and moon, they will say God"** (29:61) but yet these polytheists mentioned in the verse worshiped idols instead or in partnership with Him, an act that God disapproves of and prohibited.

The Prophet (pbuh) said Ihsan is to 'worship Allah as if you see him' i.e. with certainty that is in the same level of *Ain alyageen* and this is after having witnessed the presence of God. Whilst the second stage of Ihsan, of worshiping God 'knowing He sees you' could be said to be based on *Ilm alyageen*. Worshiping during an experience of vision of God is *Hag alyageen* (certainty of truth). Nevertheless, the message of the Prophet (pbuh) and the evidence for the existence of God is so strong that a person can have certainty of Knowledge that is similar to that based on Vision, certainty of Sight. One of the companions told the Prophet (pbuh) that his certainty of Heaven was so strong that if he was to see it, it would not increase his belief in its existence.

Witnessing God's presence is achieved as the person experiences the truth of God's attributes or even Vision of God which could be granted by God to those who succeed in *Jihadul-nafs* in seeking His nearness. God says **'Those who have striven for Our sake, We guide them to Our ways, For verily Allah is with those who perform Ihsan'** (29:69). The certainty that is on a level 'as if seeing God' is possible if the person comes to have very strong belief in God or if there was Vision of God; but to have Vision is a high spiritual state that is exclusive to those whom God chooses to grant to His favour.

The state of worshiping God in this state of certainty of 'as if you see Him' is called, by the scholars of Ihsan, *mushahada* (witnessing). The state of *mushahada* is higher than the state of *moragaba,* when a person worships in vigilance of God's knowledge of them. The Prophet (pbuh) said if the person is unable to worship God in a state of *mushahada,* they should at least worship God in a state of *moragaba.* The Prophet (pbuh) said '*fain lam takun tarah fainahu yarak*' (and if you see Him not then know He sees you). The other reason for *mushahada* being a higher state than *moragaba* is the fact that it requires and is the fruit of a higher level of *iman* and certainty of God's presence that comes from greater knowledge and higher spirituality, and in some cases witnessing of God. Those who worship God in a state of vigilance of His watching their actions (*moragaba*) and also cautious of disobeying Him, i.e. the second stage of Ihsan, are motivated by fear of death, fear of God's punishment and/or in seeking paradise. Those who worship God in a state of *mushahda* do so because they take part in *Jihad-ul-nafs* out of their love for God and in seeking His nearness and Vision. And also in wanting His acceptance of them (*ridaul Allah*) and their wish to worship and praise Him as He is worthy of and deserves such level of worship. The Prophet (pbuh) praised a companion called Salim (raa) saying **'Salim has such intense love of God that even if he wasn't in fear of God he would still not disobey Him' (Zarkashi).** This is the worship of those who are on the first stage of Ihsan; worship out of Love of God, and not in fear of Him or in wanting His reward.

The first and higher stage of Ihsan is achieved by gaining knowledge of God, performing *Jihadul-nafs* and *tazzkiya* from disease of the heart that reduce the quality of the worship. Thus the first stage of Ihsan requires the guidance of a scholar of Ihsan. Whilst the second stage of Ihsan, which requires not *Jihadul-nafs* or *tazzkiya,* could be practiced without the help of a scholar of Ihsan. It is also the part of Ihsan that Muslims should be practicing normally and is the minimum a Muslim should aim to perform of the branch of Ihsan. The first stage of Ihsan requires a scholar as it involves fighting the ego that distracts the person from realising the presence of God, and that is through *Jihadul-nafs*, which is impossible to perform without a scholar. Scholars also guide through the high spiritual states of becoming nearer to God that a person without expert knowledge may not know or thus be able to achieve. The practice of the high spiritual states of Ihsan and the high spirituality they beget such as spiritual ecstasy can lead the person to spiritual intoxication and other blameworthy spiritual states, which can be avoided in having a scholar to refer to and who can correct. People start by worshiping God in *gaib* (His presence is not witnessed), and the belief in His presence is believed and the certainty is of knowledge (*ilm al yageen*).

The difference between worship that is merely worship in following His command and worship that is for *tazzkiya* is described in the Quran. God said to the Prophet, **"perhaps the blind man will become purified or will remember religion and benefit from the counsel"** (80:3-4). The Quran says perhaps the man's conversing and getting knowledge from the Prophet (pbuh) could cause him to cure his spiritual diseases (*tazzkiya*) and if not then at least he would have profited in getting *ajr* (reward) for listening to the teachings of the Prophet (pbuh). This is also the difference between the performing of optional worship (*nafila*) done as commanded by a scholar of Ihsan to perform *Jihadul-nafs* and *tazzkiya,* and that which is done by the person simply to gain *ajr*, which is the difference between the worship of the two stages of Ihsan. That worship in the lower state is for reward while in the higher stage it is for *tazzkiya*. This mentioning of the teachings of the religion as do scholars is called *zikra* and it leads the person to remembrance of God and the commands of the religion. Thus, it is beneficial for the soul and has great reward with God. This *zikra* (remembrance) even though a lower state than *tazzkiya* is the least the person can come out with in the study of Ihsan books or in the presence of the scholars of Ihsan.

The practice of the second stage of Ihsan, of being vigilant of God's watching over our actions is passive spirituality, as the person is not required to do anything other than worship in a good manner. The first stage could be said to be active, as to achieve it the person requires to perform *Jihadul-nafs* and *tazzkiya* as well as being conscious of the presence of God. The second and lower stage of Ihsan is obligatory on all Muslims to practice, and it is fulfilled by perfecting of worship of God out of becoming aware that God is watchful of our deed. The second and lower stage of Ihsan is also achieved before the first, and is the stage the person performs until they achieve the first. The higher stage of Ihsan that includes *tazzkiya* is not *fard*, but nevertheless as all Muslims have to refrain from sins that are mainly the result of spiritual diseases, those who perform *tazzkiya* are riding where those without *tazzkiya* walk. This means while the goal of refraining from sins and having a pure heart is *fard*, the method of arriving to it by becoming a student and doing *Jihadul-nafs* and *tazzkiya* or personal effort alone is left for the individual's choice. The other opinion would be to say that both stages are *fard* since they are mentioned by the *Hadith* of Jibril that outlines the religion, and since the commands given for the other two branches are the minimum for the other branches, it could be considered that these two stages are also both obligatory of this branch. Nevertheless, the practice of the lower stage naturally prepares the person and makes them want to study the first.

The study of the lower stage of Ihsan is based on three things: knowledge of God and desire to worship Him, awareness of His knowledge of all which happens in the heavens and earth including our actions, and knowledge of His punishment for those who disobey His commands and reward for those who chose to obey His command and worship Him. This means the practice of this part of Ihsan relies on gaining knowledge. Those who then intend to practice the higher stage of Ihsan must then take *baya* (spiritual pact) from a scholar of the branch. The scholar then guides them through *tazzkiya* and *Jihadul-nafs*, and helps to elevate them spiritually in order for them then to be able to worship God **'as if they see him'** which comes after His vision.

CHAPTER THIRTEEN

THE LESSER IHSAN

In Islam, we believe people are of three motivations. Those who worship in seeking God, and the nearness of God. The Quran says **"be contented with those who call on their Lord in the morning and evening, seeking His face"** (18:28). And below these are others who seek the good of the hereafter, of Heaven, and below them those who seek the world, and these the Quran calls 'delusional'. God says **"there are those who chase after this world and some that desire the Hereafter."** (3:152). Those who seek this world even if believers are by definition people who have not practiced the branch of Ihsan, and it is a state which they share with those of disbelief. God says, **"The life of this world is beautiful to those who reject belief"** (2:212).

The Hadith of Umar (raa) tells us of two states or stages of Ihsan, different in that in one the person has no vision of God. The Prophet Muhammed (pbuh) said **"Ihsan is to worship Allah as if you see Him, and if you see Him not, then to worship Him knowing He sees you"** **(Muslim).** This second type of Ihsan, as is described in the Hadith comes before the vision, in that they 'see Him not'. Therefore, their worship is not motivated by God, and His vision, but rather what is the highest after that, the want of Heaven and the fear of hell. This is achieved by worshiping God '**knowing He sees you**', meaning with the vigilance of the one who is watched. This state comes from understanding *aqida* that teaches that God is aware of our deeds and our actions. God says **"God is well acquainted with the sins of His servants" (25:58)**. They also are firm on the life after death, the Day of Judgment and the existence of Heaven and hell. Thus the first step in practising Ihsan, which is to practice the first stage of it, is to start caring about the hereafter. This is such that the scholars of Ihsan preached the concept of '*zuhd*', which is to curb from the excess want of this world.

About the state of Ihsan in which the person works in fear of entering hell and wishes to enter Heaven, God says, **"Those who out of fear of their Lord deter the ego from desires, then the Heaven will be their abode"** (79:40-41). The verse says those who fear God and His punishment in hell, are motivated by this to hold back from the sins and that which God made forbidden. Likewise, those of the stage of vision are motivated by the love of God to give up on that which they used to value and love (whether from possessions or desires). God says **"people will not reach righteousness until they give in charity of what they love, and whatever much people give God is of it knowledgable"** (3:92). Therefore, the motivation to worship and the type of struggle differs between the two stages of Ihsan.

The beginning of the practice of the branch of Ihsan, which is to practice the second state described that its goal is to enter Heaven and avoid hell, comes in changing from being a person whose aim is worldly into one whose goal is the hereafter. This comes in understanding the nature of the world, and gaining the ability to be content in it without excess (*zuhd*), and of learning about the hereafter and desiring success in it. This at first is not easy, and is a process of struggle but it become easy with increase in belief. When the person's certainty of the hereafter increases, they are more able to give up from the desire of this world. The main argument for Heaven, is that God is perfect, powerful and rich, so this world doesn't reflect the truth of God and so there must be a better world created by God, which is Heaven. The proof for hell, is that impurity of touch such as the friction of two woods create fire, and since God is completely pure, there must be an eternal hellfire that is a symbol of His purity.

Once the person becomes aware of the descriptions of hell and Heaven by increasing in the knowledge of the hereafter, they naturally desire Heaven and abhor hell, as their faith in their existence increases. This level of faith determines how much they do for this desire, for the more they believe in the existence of Heaven, and the more they desire it (by being aware of its beautiful description) the more they do of the deeds that lead to it. The more the Muslim becomes aware of the horrible nature of hell and the belief in its existence, the stricter they become in making sure they do not performs sins that make them qualified to enter it. Yet this desire should not become blinded that the person does not remember of the mercy of God that exists in some of His laws, including exemptions and simplified worship, in a state of illness, travel or inconvenience, where God gives licence. The Prophet Muhammed (pbuh) said **"God loves His slaves to use His exemptions"** (Ibn Hiban) as this shows *tawakul* and trust in God not to take you as a sinner for doing it, and as accepting the gift of mercy from God.

In the lesser Ihsan, the main feeling is of fear of God, just as in the greater Ihsan, the prominent emotion is of love of God. Fear of God has two main causes: firstly the idea of God that He has a power over us and we are weak and He is one, so there is no other God to stop Him from punishing us. The second idea is that God is so perfect without shortcomings, so is intolerable to wrong as it is not His description and so not accustomed to wrong, so doesn't allow it and punishes it severely.

This world we live in the Quran refers to as the '*dunya*' a word meaning low, in order to denote its value in the sight of God. Yet God tells us of its nature and reality. God says **"the life of this world is like rain water from the sky, it mixes with the plants on earth of what people and animals eat, until it grows to become colourful and beautiful. Then** people think they will use it, but instead comes to it God's command during the day or night, to ruin it leaving it as if harvested. It then as if wasn't rich the day before. In this way God details the verse for people to consider religion"** (10:24). This verse tells us that this world is temporal, not lasting, and not to assume its beauty and goodness are forever. In this sense the world is like an illusion, for all the attributes of permanence we may assume it to have, God tells us they are not true. Thus the Quran says **"the life of this world is nothing but an enjoyment of the deluded." (3:185).**

The Quran also emphasises the trivial nature of the world, by calling it play. God says **"the life of this world is like play and entertainment but the world of the afterlife is the main if they were knowing"** (29:64). This is because **"the pleasure of this world is little and the afterlife is good to those righteous"** (4:77). And the Quran also questions our attachment to this world by saying **"have they become contented by the life of this world instead of the life of Heaven in the afterlife, but the pleasure of this world is merely little compared to the pleasure of life of Heaven." (9:38).** And **"This life of the present is nothing but temporary enjoyment, but it is the Hereafter that is the home that will last." (40:39).**

The first step in practicing Ihsan is to acknowledge this difference between this world and the next, and the superiority of the latter. To also acknowledge that the **"best is the home in the hereafter, for those who are righteous" (6:32).** And it is this feeling that arouses the need to want to work for it by taking worship of God serious, and being keen in gaining much good deeds. The Quran says **"Such as took their religion to be mere amusement and play, and were deceived by the life of the world. That day shall We forget them as they forgot the meeting of this day of theirs, and as they reject Our signs." (7:51).** God praises those who achieve this sense of motivation towards the hereafter, the Quran says **"a person devoted in prayer at night standing and prostrating to God in cautiousness of the afterlife, and waits and yearns the Lord's** mercy. The Prophet should say are one who knows equal to one who knows not? Remembers those of deep understanding" (39:9). This understanding of the hereafter should mean that every hardship faced in this world in doing worship and in seeking success of the hereafter should seem negligible and trivial considering its relativeness to the torment in the eternal hellfire. The Quran says, **"Do not go forth to war in this heat, the Prophet should say the fire of hell is hotter by far, if they understood religion" (9:81)**. The pleasures of this world which may distract from the worship and working towards the hereafter must also be seen as inferior to Heaven. God says **"in it they will have all their souls shall desire, and in it they will have what they requested"** (41:31). The Prophet Muhammed (pbuh) said in the Hadith that there will be no illness and no death in Heaven (Ahmed). A garden of beauty that is spacious and each person lives in a way beyond the luxury of the richest of this world where houses are made of gold and silver bricks, and instead of earth it is musk and the grass saffron. Many servants and unlimited fruit and nothing is forbidden. People will be made beautiful, and will neither age nor their clothes wear out. It is a world that its most basic items of building are what is considered most expensive in this world, i.e. gold and silver bricks and musk mortar. And instead of salty seas, there are rivers of milk, honey, wine and clear water (Tirmizi) and instead of pebbles, it will be pearls and gemstones. Thus it is based on the best of this world and extrapolated. It will have markets and other social structures, and nothing is forbidden or out of reach. Yet what each person will get in land and palaces will depend on their level of good deeds. The Prophet Muhammed (pbuh) informed us in the Hadith that the person with the least amount in Heaven will have what will be equivalent in area to twice of this world (Muslim). It will be a peaceful place where there will be no hatred, even if people who entered hell before and lack in good character come there. God says they will be friends, the Quran says **"God removed from their heart evil, and they become like brothers on adjacent couches"(15:47)**.

The understanding of the world and the hereafter, also requires a belief in God as being just, and will deliver what He warns to those who reject His worship and disobey the commands of His message. This should bring into the hearts a sense of seriousness in the commands and prohibitions of God, that they are not said in a tone of unsureness or probability, but a firm promise from a majestic God. That when God promises Heaven it's a sure promise and when He promises hell it is likewise definite. God says **"when God gathers them to a day of no doubt, and they are judged, and each person will be awarded for the deeds they gained in the world, and no one will be treated unjustly"** (3:25). The mercy of God should not mean perceiving His commands as unserious, but rather as a reassurance of His understanding if we fail to follow these commands after trying, and this effort should at the very least be an intention. The Prophet (pbuh) commanded to work to goodness, with our hands, and if that is not possible then with our tongues, and if not then with our hearts (Muslim). The Prophet (pbuh) added that those who are on the level of hearts are the weakest in belief. Thus, knowing at what level the majority of our deeds usually lie is a revealer of our level of belief.

The practice of Ihsan should mean that the person seeks the hereafter, but does so in a way that God commands, meaning without a life of suffering or extreme deprivation. God says **"seek in what God enriched him with in the afterlife but still not to forget a portion for the life of this world"** (28:77). This is because the generosity and mercy of God, that we should enjoy the bounties He created in this world. One sign of this the scholars say is that the number of what He has forbidden of this world are few in number, a few dozen compared to the thousands He has allowed. Thus to overstep from what He has allowed into what is forbidden is a great act of folly and ungratefulness. The Quran says **"ask who prohibits what God made beautiful for people, and good food. Say it is for the believers allowed without punishment for it on the Day of Judgement"** (7:32).

The Quran says **"people find beautiful the desire of women and having children, and piles of gold and silver, and horses of good progeny, and cattle and farm lands. This is the pleasure of this world, and in God's reward in the afterlife is the best of places"** (3:14). This verse counts what is considered to be rich, and is the aim of those who seek the world. This type of *dunya* seeking and maintaining takes time and energy that means less time for activities of the next that could compromise even *fard* worship. Thus, it is discouraged to want. God says **"these have bought the life of this world instead of valuing the eternal afterlife. There will be no pardoning to ease their punishment, and they will not be given victory once they enter the eternal hellfire"** (2:86). God also says **"those who do not worship God, and look forward to the meeting with God in the afterlife, and are contented by the life of this world, and are pleased by it, and those ignorant of God's signs and revelation. Those to them is the abode of the hellfire for their sins"** (10:7-8). This is because in their seeking of the world they accumulated sins, in disobeying God and neglecting commands such as usury or stealing to accumulate such wealth. Those who have come to make their life goal seeking this level of life have been tricked. The Quran says **"and were deceived by the life of the world" (7:51).** The verse mentions the luxuries of life, and it is these what is usually referred to as '*dunya*' as it is not for a specific need or necessity, but for merely boast or enjoyment. This is evident in that they not do with any horse for a need, but bred horses, which are usually for show or business, and not a few cows to suffice the need for milk or meat but herds, and thousands of acres of land. The verse also included having more than one wife for no necessary reason, as well as accumulating gold and silver beyond what is to be regularly used. This is the world which if sought in ignoring the commands of God or going against them it is a great sin, but if in halal way that includes paying *zakah* (obligatory charity), and does not involve neglecting of *fard* worship it is considered to mean the person is not practicing the branch of Ihsan, as they are not working towards the hereafter but the luxuries of this world. Nevertheless, the seeking of such level of richness with the intention to spend them in the sake of Allah, is considered a *nafila* (an optional act of worship) and the person to be in a state of Ihsan, and this was the state of the companions who accumulated great money to spend in the way of Allah.

The next level of *dunya*, is to have a choice in that which is necessary and essential in life, an example is to be able to eat your favourite food, to buy clothes that are the style the person wants and not necessary what is sufficient to cover them. This level of *dunya* is not haram and God says about it **"say it is for the believers in this life allowed without punishment for it on the Day of Judgement"** (7:32). The Quran says they are safe in the hereafter meaning they will not be accounted for them, and should be accepted as a gift of God. Nevertheless, this choice is removed in the state of *Jihadul-nafs* as part of the purification process. This is as it helps in constricting the ego and its desires, making easy its purification. Therefore, during *Jihadul-nafs* it becomes necessary to avoid it and become content with what is needed, meaning enough food, with no choice (what is available), so to battle the ego. When the person gains control over their ego they are then allowed to return to this level of *halal* living and this is in accepting the verse. In fact, this level is recommended to seek in a state of Ihsan, as then the persons are reminded of the bounty of God, and as Ali (raa) explained, in this state he felt his praise and thanking of God were at most truthful.

The level under this is to not have what is considered essential and required for survival, and those without this the Sharia permits them to beg, and to maintain their life even if they have to steal what is sufficient for survival and the law of theft is lifted from them (no hand is cut) in an Islamic court. However there is emphasis that a Muslim must not lazy from work and rely on begging and *zakah* (charity), and the Prophet mentioned that God loves his slaves who are '*gani*' meaning sufficient of others.

Secondly, the person practicing this stage of Ihsan must develop an understanding of God that gives them reassurance in their worship. This is the reassurance that no one will be deprived of the good deeds they do, which is not only explicitly mentioned by God in the Quran, but also as a rule that God made forbidden for Himself all injustice. The Prophet (pbuh) relates in a *Qudsi* Hadith, God says, **"I have made forbidden injustice on Myself, and on you, so do not act with injustice" (Muslim).** For God to punish people for no reason, to take their belief or lower it for no reason, or to misguide them for no reason is all an injustice which God forbids on Himself. Nevertheless, God tests His slaves' belief by tribulations (*fitn*) and those not already strong in faith or good deeds can suffer from them. God also misguides those who sin repetitively or do injustice to others by misguiding them, and making them die *kufar* (disbeliever).

Such beliefs are not only incorrect but can also discourage them from worship, for the person may not feel that they will be rewarded for the good deeds they perform, or may be made to enter hell for no sins committed. Thus God reassures us by saying **"when every soul will be paid in full what it has earned, and they will not be treated with injustice." (3:25).** This belief that God will reward our good deeds and not punish us without sins made by us is called '*husn al zan billah*' (assuming good of God). In a Hadith the Prophet Muhammed (pbuh) said **"having a good opinion of God is part of the good worship of God" (Tirmizi).** God says in a Qudsi Hadith **'I will be as my slave believes' (Muslim).** This means that if the slave believes well of God, they will see that in reward, and if not, they will be punished for holding wrong beliefs about God. This is because we have no reason to believe that God will act ungenerously or with injustice, especially since His message emphasises the opposite. This good belief about God should include that when we ask for forgiveness to believe it will be accepted, and when we do good deeds we will definitely be rewarded for them in the hereafter.

Those of this stage should also be aware of the system used by God to record, judge and reward or punish us for our actions. Every person has two angels, one on their right and the other to their left who record their words and actions. However, the one on the left writes all sins with a delay in case we ask God's forgiveness. The Quran says **"no word a person says except there is an angel recording in vigilance their good and bad deeds"** (50:18) and **"people should not follow what they don't know, for the hearing and sight and heart, all are responsible for in the judgement of God"** (17:36). While God has provided us with free will to choose our actions, He nevertheless, accounts us for disobeying Him. The slave should also know that as well as our own knowledge of our deeds, the recording angels, God by His Might and Knowledge also knows about our deeds, in fact even before we perform them. This is a proof of His knowledge to the high angels, who find it written in what is called '*Alloh Almahfoz*' (The Saved Scroll). The Quran says **"do they not know that God is knowledgeable of what is in the heavens and earth, it is in a book recorded and that is easy for God to do"**(22:70). In fact before the Prophethood of Muhammed (pbuh) the *jinn* used to raise to the heavens to hear the angels speak about what is in the *Alloh Almahfoz*, and return and share it with the soothsayers who communicated it to people. Then after the Prophethood the heavens were guarded and shooting stars are used to send away the *jinn*. The knowledge of what state we will die, if people of Heaven or hell, has likewise been written. In one Hadith the Prophet Muhammed (pbuh) said that a person who beforehand is known to be of the hellfire could work all their life doing the deeds of Heaven and yet before they die, they choose the acts of the people of hell and thus become of them, and the opposite can be said for a person who did the works of the people of hell all their life, yet before they die they do the works of the people of Heaven, and their state has been beforehand known by the angels (Bukhari).

It is also essential to know that the system of accounting is not vague, of a general judgment that the person is 'good' or 'bad'. Rather is a minute system of accounting based on our deeds and actions, or what the scholars of *aqida* call '*kasb*'. God says **"God does not ask of people, except what they are capable of doing of worship. To each person will be the reward or punishment for their deeds."** (2:286). This verse is to say that the commands of the religion are not beyond being practiced. It is what all people can bear, and this means that each sin is counted and each good deed a person does is also counted, and hell and Heaven will depend on the total of each. God says **"whoever does a grain of good will see it reward, and whoever does a grain size of bad will see it punishment"** (99:7-8). That is each sin is accounted as one, yet out of generosity each good deed is counted as ten (or more if God wishes), and that is the ratio of sins to good deeds (Bukhari). God says **"as for those whose scale is heavy of good deeds. They will be in a pleasing life of bliss. As for those whose scale is light of good deeds, their abode is seventh lowest level of hell."** (101:6-11). This means that deeds are weighted, meaning that the quality of the deeds is counted as well as their number. This means that sincerity, effort, and capability is considered and the harder the person worked the more merit is given for effort. To explain this the Prophet (pbuh) said **"One dirham can be better than 100,000 dirham"** (Ibn Hazm). This he explained as one man had only two dirhams and he gave one in charity while the other was very rich, and even though he had much money the hundred thousand dirham he gave in charity, while is good, is not up to the level of one who gives half of what he has, especially if what they had wasn't much to start with. Knowing this principle of accounting means a person of this stage should come to account themselves, checking into their deeds, being honest on the amount of disobedience they do as well as the amount of good.

Umar (raa) is reported to have said accounting yourself before God takes you into account on the Day of Judgment. It is also reassuring to know that as long as the person follows their sins with good deeds, their balance becomes better than one who is sinning in lack of good deeds. This is also true of those who do not ask God's forgiveness or the type of sins they perform are considered of those that are great in the sight of God. This is because the performing of greater sins, such as alcohol, fornication, and theft can mean the burning of the person in the hellfire even if Muslim. In fact, those Muslims who burn in the hellfire before being moved to Heaven is based on their performing of great sins without asking for forgiveness for them, or not doing good deeds to compensate for them in the balance. God says **"If people avoid the great sins, God will forgive their lesser sins and enters them a good entrance to paradise"** (4:31). The person practicing the first stage of Ihsan should make sure they withhold from great sins, as a priority in order to get the reward for not practicing them, which is to have minor sins erased. When accounting oneself the intention should be to get a general view of the level of forgiveness or good deeds the person needs to do, and those who find that level would be wise to panic and try and change this. As a practitioner of Ihsan this should be a serious activity that leads to a change in the person's life. This could mean less hobbies, or even less work in order to spend daily time in asking for forgiveness or doing good deeds. This is the case since by concentrating on this world have obviously meant less time for activities for the next, and likewise to when the person becomes conscious of the hereafter and success in it needs to be able to bring it into their life as a priority above this world.

Therefore, as to start the practice of Ihsan, the person should perform *tawba*, a general acknowledging of sin and want of a general forgiveness, and an intention to thereafter refrain from sin as well as making specific *istigfar* for specific sins. A prayer from the Quran is to say **"pray that God does not account people for what they forgotten to do of worship, or pity mistakes in religion. Lord do not hold grudges for people's past sins, as God was severe with previous nations. Lord not to command people to that beyond their capacity. Lord to forgive, pardon and be merciful to the believers. Lord to be the believers guardian, and to give believers victory against those of disbelief"** (2:286).

The practitioner of this part of Ihsan should become knowledgeable of the prayers and acts of worship that earn the most good deeds, such as fasting on special days or praising God in certain words and knowing them by heart and say them to increase their good deeds and erase their sins. This also should mean that the person comes to learn how to perfect their worship such as prayer and fasting in order to gain the most deeds, knowing the criteria for their acceptance and what invalidates them. The Prophet (pbuh) said **"a person may pray, but are rewarded for only one tenth, or one ninth, or one eighth, or one seventh or one sixth, or one fifth, or one fourth, or one third, or half" (Abu Dawud)**. The person should also start to remove themselves from environments that encourage sin. God says **"Leave those who take their religion to be mere play and amusement, and are deceived by the life of this world." (6:70)**. What is most important is to gain knowledge, on what God forbids and what He commands, what the great sins are and what sins forbid Heaven, and what deeds earn the person Heaven. Nevertheless, sinful deeds done in a state of ignorance of the teachings of the religion are not equal to those done after knowledge or worse intentionally, and with each level the intensity of sin increases and the more severe the punishment. In a Hadith the Prophet (pbuh) said **"seeking knowledge is a religious obligation (*fard*) on each Muslim" (Al Asuti)**. Thus, depriving the self of religious knowledge is a sin in itself and an injustice, and a form of rebelling against the practice of the religion. There is no worship without knowledge, as how do we expect to know what God commands us to do in worship if we do not seek to know it, and there is no real practice without instructions to it. The Quran says **"pray Lord increase me in knowledge." (20:114)**.

The hereafter in Islam, starts with death, which enters the person into a world that is intermediate (called *barzakh*) between the *dunya* (this world) and the world of the Day of Judgment and Heaven and hell. God says **"behind them will be a barrier preventing them from returning to the world, until resurrection day" (23:100)**. In this intermediate world, the person is in a state of awareness as they were in this world. When Umar (raa) asked if he would have the same strength he had in his worldly life, the Prophet (pbuh) said it would be the same (Al Munziri). The person's state in this world of *barzakh* will be of bliss to those of belief and good deeds, and of torture and anticipation of hell to those of disbelief and evil. People will remain in the *barzakh*, until the blowing of the horn for the last day, and then people will be raised from their graves (their bodies will 'grow from the earth' (Bukhari) and their souls return to them) for the meeting of their lord for the Day of Judgment. The Day of Judgment has many names in the Quran, and one of them is *yom algiyama*, meaning the Day of Standing. The Quran says **"A Day when mankind will stand before the Lord of the worlds"** (83:6). The Day of Judgment is a stressful day, where people will be in thirst, and the sun will be a handspan away, and people will be in fear and terror. God says **"do not think God is ignorant of the sins of the unjust in religion, but God delays their judgement to a day when eyes stare in horror"** (14:42). It is a day that will be long, the Quran says **"the angels and spirits ascend to God in a day of fifty thousand years in measure"** (70:4). The Quran says **"the day when runs a person away from their brother, and their mother and father, and wife and child. To each on that day issues keeping them busy"** (80:34-37). Describing their state God says **"other faces on that day are frowned, anxious it will be done to it a calamity that breaks their back"** (75:24-25). Then the hell fire will be brought and shown to the people pulled by strong angels. The Quran says **"And on that Day hell will be brought within sight" (89:23)**. Seeing that people will say **"people ask on that day, how and where to escape"** (75:10). The Prophet Muhammed (pbuh) will then intercede to God in deep prayer to start the accounting. Then the accounting starts with the angels giving people copies of their books containing their deeds, and those of good deeds will be given their books on their right hands and those of hell will be given their books from behind and to their left hands. About their books people will say **"then the books of records are placed, and see the sinners anticipating what is in them. They say it's a disaster as the book of record does not leave out a small or great deeds unaccounted. They find all their deeds present and God is not unjust to anyone" (18:49). People are then judged by God and sent to either Heaven or hell. The Quran says **"people should become pious to the Lord, and fear a day when no parent pays for their child or child pays for their father a bit. The promise of God is true, so be not deluded by the life of this world, and do not be deluded by the deluded"**(31:33).

> Tears drip drop
> Because fear of God never stop
> Tears drip drop
> Because love of God in the heart crop

The person of Ihsan should become knowledgeable of what is needed for forgiveness to be accepted. This includes following sins with good deeds and asking for forgiveness soon after a sin, and when forgiveness is not accepted like when the souls of the person raises to their throat as they die or the sun rises from the west as a sign of the nearing of the end of times.

One of the roles of the Prophet Muhammed (pbuh) was to warn mankind that there will be accounting of all the deeds we do whilst alive in this world, and that there is a punishment for those whose deeds go against the commands of God. That God has prepared a hellfire to those who disobey His religion. God says **"Allah has prepared for them a severe penalty, evil indeed are their deeds" (58:15)**. This punishment is described as being **"a fire whose fuel is men and stones" (66:6)**. An abode where their food will be from *dari* a thorny tree which the Quran says **"no food will there be for them but a bitter *dari*, which will neither nourish nor satisfy hunger." (88:6-7)** and as for drink the Quran says **"when the people of hellfire beg for water, they are given** water like oil that burns their faces, it is a severe drink and a harsh place" (18:29) and that when it reaches their stomaches God says **"and be given, to drink, boiling water, so that it cuts up their bowels to pieces" (47:15)**. Their clothes will be out of fire to burn them, God says **"for them will be cut out a garment of fire" (22:19)**. For punishment, they will be poured boiling water that burns them from the inside out, the Quran says **"and poured over their heads boiling water. The boiling water dissolves their bellies and skin to death in the hellfire"** (22:19-20) and when their skin is burnt it grows another skin to continue the punishment **"and every time their skins are burnt off, they are replaced with new skins, so that they may taste the suffering in full" (4:56)**. They will also be made to drink in humiliation like animals with their heads lowered into a container in the ground **"they will drink like animals" (56:55)** and this is part of a **"humiliating punishment" (33:57)**. They will be made to climb high fire mountains, **"God will tire them to climb mountains in punishment"** (74:17) about it is said in the Hadith **"it is a mountain which when they lay their feet on they melt from its heat and as they lift it to avoid the pain their feet will be restored, and this will continue for 70 years until they reach the top, from there they will be dropped back into fire, and they reach it in another 70 years. They are told to climb it again, and this is repeated" (Al Munzri)**. In this torture they will be left chained (76:4) and about this **"they have chains around their necks and with chains they are dragged"** (40:71). They will be restricted and forever abide in it, God says **"every time the disbelievers try to escape from the overwhelming worry of harm, they are returned back to the hellfire, and are told to taste the burning punishment"** (22:22) and **"they will be forever in hellfire, with no ease of punishment, and they will not be considered for pardoning by God"** (2:162).

The religion of Islam, is to submit to God. As human beings if we are made aware of a danger we take heed of it, even if it is not in our presence either later in time or further in space. This is in knowledge of pain, discomfort and the worst pain that can befall us. It is these principles that made people 'submit' to another in avoiding pain, and with God is it the idea of hell that has made them submit or become Muslim, in fear of it. This is especially since the risk is too great, and warding it off is very simple and painless in comparison, i.e. the verbal declaration of belief and performing of prayer, fast and Hajj. Thus the second chapter of the Quran starts with **"the Quran is a book that contains no errors to give doubt about it being from God. It is a guidance for the pious worshipers who are cautious of the hellfire"** (2:2). *Mutageen* means "those who ward off evil". This does not include children and the mentally ill, for they have no concept of pain and avoidance, yet for those who understand this, submission is a must to them – as it is almost forced by the reality of our humanity and thus is called a 'submission', since it is without choice. It is automatic, and without choice for those of understanding. It is too severe a punishment to take chances on. This is not about it being true or not; if it's going to rain people will take umbrellas, if it doesn't rain we are safe. This was the case of man in war who before being killed by a companion he declared his submission to God.

Love and fear are similar in that they cause vigilance and focusing of attention to their source. Islam teaches that only God is truly worthy of fear and love, for His attributes naturally create love and His punishment is great and should and do strike awe and fear in the strongest and most courageous of people. Umar (raa) who was feared and respected by the most courageous of people, and when the Muslims of Mecca kept their Islam secret and immigrated in the dark without drawing attention to themselves, Umar (raa) made sure his conversion to Islam was made known to all, to the extent that he personally knocked door to door to spread the news of his Islam and when he decided to migrate to be with the Prophet and companions in Medina he stood high and proclaimed his famous words 'whoever wants to sadden his mother, widow his wife and orphan his kids should follow me behind this mountain'. Nevertheless, he was so affected by the Quranic verses that spoke about God's might and punishment that he used to become bedridden on hearing them. But then again didn't God say **"if the Quran was revealed to a mountain, then it will be humble and anxious from the great reverence of God"**(59:21).

To love and fear God is the essence of slavehood to God. God says **'call on God in fear and hope'** (7:57) and the greatest hope and wish is gaining His pleasure and His vision. Those who should fear are not the doers of good, it is those of sin and evil who should be scared. God emphasises that His punishment is great and very painful. This should inspire people from not sinning in fear of God's punishment. Therefore, the perfection of the practice of the lesser Ihsan is to be saved from hellfire and be granted admittance to Heaven.

We must return back to God
Before the hereafter the Quran told
To stop sinning and repent before we get old
To give charity and be kind, and never be cold
In one hand the Quran and prayer beads we must hold
Concentrate on mention of God most High
To pray with gaze lowered not staring up to the sky
To always speak the truth and not once to lie
To be patient with trials and not question why
To be content with God and not the goods we buy
Not to get angry, swear and at parents sigh
To love God and His Messenger and on belief we die

CHAPTER FOURTEEN

THE GREATER IHSAN

The Prophet (pbuh) described Ihsan in what can be categorised as two stages: one where the person is aware of the presence of God, and the second where the person becomes aware of God watching them. The greater Ihsan is the state described first by the Prophet as to worship God as if you see him. However, God's seeing us isn't an intrusion of impoliteness but a part of watching over our deeds to later reward those who obey and punish those who disobeyed. Thus believing in this leads to a state of less sinning and more good deeds. The slave's awareness of the presence of God, is a state of pleasure but also to affirm their belief and gain certainty in their religion. However, achieving these two stages requires knowledge and skill, and most importantly an inner change, which is achieved in a state of struggle against the ego –a hinderance to the state of Ihsan. The greater Ihsan revolves around seeking the presence of God to gain His Vision. Every teaching in this stage is about preparing the person to the presence of God. Every act is to make the vision possible, and all studying is to learn manners in order to be suitable in the presence of God.

The Greater Ihsan is called this as it's a higher spiritual state of worshiping God, of more quality and therefore it is more noble. The Quran says **"the Prophet should be patient with those who pray in the morning and evening wanting God's face, and not to look away** from them wanting the beauty of the world. Do not follow those whose hearts are absent from the mention of God and follow desires and their issue is in loss**" (18:28). This means the Quran recognises that there are Muslims who worship seeking God's face, His presence and Vision. The greater Ihsan, requires a scholar, while the lesser Ihsan can be practiced without a scholar. This is because for the vision of God a person must annihilate their ego by struggling against their ego and doing spiritual purification and curing the diseases of their heart, and they require a scholar of Ihsan.

The spiritual Quest in Islam is seeking God, the Prophet said **"whoever loves the meeting with God, God will love to meet them" (Bukhari)**, meaning that some do wish to get closer to God, in state of love, and God welcomes them, so taking practitioners of Ihsan to God isn't disliked by God but the opposite –loved– and this gave scholars permission to traditionally loudly invite people to the practice of Ihsan. The divine presence is considered the highest attainment, higher than the entrance of paradise; in fact some want to enter paradise to see God as one of its bounties is to enter the presence of God, and have vision of God, a guaranteed part of paradise.

In the study of the branch of Ihsan, especially in some stations the students are made to overlook the fear aspect (after it's study in the lesser Ihsan) in order to develop the love aspect, and that comes from the overemphasis of the mercy of God and His attributes and their remembrance. This is not to trivialise fear of God, but when the person is doing what God commanded they do not need to be reminded of fear, God said **"those who say their Lord is God, and become straight in religion, there is no fear on them and will not be sad"** (46:13). And **"God said to Moses to not be afraid, for with God, the messengers of God should have nothing to fear"** (27:10). The other reason that fear of God is not emphasised in the study of the greater Ihsan is because while fear is due to remembering Hell and the hereafter, love of God comes from the knowledge of God Himself, which is higher, and that worship motivated by love of God is higher than worship out of fear of God.

CHAPTER FIFTEEN

THE TRUTH OF GOD

In essence the branch of Ihsan is about gaining direct personal awareness of the reality of God's existence. This is not possible if He didn't exist, and likewise it is not possible to truly worship God if our hearts contain doubt of His existence. Therefore the topic of God's existence is an essential teaching in learning and practicing Ihsan. However as this knowledge is advanced, the religion isn't called Iman (belief), but Islam (submission), for God knows that the majority of people worship him due to a submission from a torture in hell rather than a firm belief in Him. God says "**most people even if the Prophet are keen are not true believers**"(12:103). The beginning of faith comes from contemplating the signs of God, and the middle belief is from contemplating the miracles either by hearing of them or witnessing them, and the highest belief is from the vision of God.

As to worship him in a state of Ihsan requires certain belief, God says "**God will show them His signs in the world and in themselves until it is clear it is the truth**" (41:53). That God didn't reveal the book of the Quran and left it at that, but promised Prophet Muhammed (pbuh) that he and his followers will be shown enough proof of God's existence, found in the world and in their own bodies, to remove doubt that it is a religion made up by Prophet Muhammed (pbuh), but indeed the truth from God. An important thing is that people do not reject the truth after it is presented to them. God says **"who is more unjust than one who falsifies against God and calls truth a lie when it comes to them, is there no place in the hellfire for the disbelievers. Those who come with truth and believe in it, they are the pious. They have what they want from God, and that is the reward of those perfect in worship of Ihsan"** (39:32-34). For this reason the study of God's truth, investigating it, is part of this branch, to the point that Sufism has been nicknamed, *ilm-al-tahqiq* (the science of truth).

The Quran counts more than two hundred signs of God, and they are discussed in my book 'The Discovery of God'. One of the signs of God is the night. In the night it becomes dark and people become stationary in sleep so they don't take any of the world as they do during the day. At night there is no fishing and no fruit picking, and so it is a time of deprivation and this is to show that God has a sense of self, and can give and deprive of His ownership of the world as He deems fit. Therefore the night is a sign of God. The Quran counts as well as the night, even the boats at sea. This is because boats made out of wood being in the sea is a sign that there is generosity and goodness in the world, that the wood that was once a thirsty tree is now placed in the vast sea. This makes even boats a sign of God. God is not only the truth, but truth is one of His names in Islam.

The religion of Islam is considered a true religion; a religion with proof and the God of Islam is a true God and has proof to exist. One proof of God considered in the Quran is cousin marriages. The unions of similar and compatible people is a pure relation and brings about the pure creation of children that proves the existence of a pure creator and God who is Allah. God says in the Quran **"Among the signs of God is God allows to be from own people marriage partners"** (30:21) and in (33:50) God counts cousins from paternal and maternal sides to be obligatory to marry. In Hanif beliefs of purity the human is considered a sign of God, and in many places in the Quran God speaks of people needing to see themselves and know themselves as a guide to God **"do you not see yourselves"** (51:21). This is because the human is created with a pure plan and it is centred on the face containing the form of the male and female, the nose appearing male and the mouth a female without joining, and with separation in the place where the moustache usually grows. This separation of the male nose and the female mouth is a purity that prevents opposites from touching or uniting which is impure. God says **"maintain the face to be pure for benefit of religion" (10:105)**, so in Hanif sexual union which is a joining of the male and female in the genitalia, since it tells of a truth of the existence of male and female and they can join and separate is a reinforcement to the face and acts as a confirming of truth of the purity of the face and religion and God. The pure human face gives support to spiritual purity in people and that they have a natural acceptance to purity and a pure religion. God says **"God created humans to worship"**. The Prophet Muhammed (pbuh) said **"in sexual union there is charity, betterment and confirmation"** (Muslim). The Prophet Muhammed (pbuh) said **"looking at a beautiful face is worship"** (Mala Ali Gari)

God says **"that is because God is the truth, and what they worship instead of God is falsehood, and God is high and great"** (22:62). God says when a slave chooses to follow anything other than God it is a state of falsehood, of error and wrong and he commands what to do with this falsehood in another verse **"proclaim truth has come and invalid is falsehood, for falsehood is to be invalidated"** (17:81). God says all falsehood beside him must perish and be destroyed, and this is the command to remove the ego that disturbs the truth of following God.

CHAPTER SIXTEEN

KNOWLEDGE OF GOD

Knowledge of God has a special place in the branch of Ihsan as it is considered a perquisite preparation in nearing to God, coming to love God as well as understanding His vision if given access to His Presence. In Islamic terminology it is called '*marifa*', and the title '*Al Aarif Billah*' (knowledgable of God) is given to scholars especially of Ihsan as a social status of dignity. This is because traditionally in Islam, knowledge of God is considered to lead to dignity due to its importance and honour. God says **"none encompasses the protected knowledge of God, without God permitting it first"**(2:255). God also says **"ask about God an expert in religion"** (25:59), this is why a Muslim must have a scholar of Ihsan to guide them in their knowledge of God and in their spiritual journey to the presence and vision of God.

As Ihsan is about experiencing the truthfulness of the revelation (the Quran and the *Sunnah*) it is thus imperative that the person must have knowledge of revelation. The revelation is also our guide to come to correct knowledge and experience, and to save us from deviance. Those who abandon it will not gain the intended benefit from their spiritual experiences and could harm their belief in the process. Spiritual experiences with lack of correct knowledge of revelation can lead to deviance, for they are then deprived of the correct explanation provided by the revelation. Thus they may try and explain things by mental deduction when it is known that through mental deduction alone most people cannot come to knowledge that comes in revelation; otherwise there wouldn't be a need for revelation nor Messengers from God.

Those who do not have firm knowledge of *aqida* and then follow the path of *Jihadul-nafs*, or do not take explanations of their spiritual experiences from Quran and *Sunnah* will also be deprived of the correct understanding and find themselves making personal efforts to explain their experiences, and thus may end up with erroneous beliefs. Thereafter, instead of their experiences increasing their knowledge of God and gaining a higher state of worship it leads them away from correct belief. Knowledge of *aqida* should be taken from experts, i.e. scholars of Iman (scholars of *Aqida*). The study of *aqida* need not reach expert level, but should be at least enough to know the correct beliefs the Muslim should have and know about God.

The branch of Ihsan was defined by the Prophet Muhammed (pbuh) as '*worshiping Allah* as if you see Him'. Therefore, before a person can practice the branch they need to have knowledge of what *worship* means, is, how it is done, and who *Allah* is. This is by learning *worship* as it is taught by the scholars of *fiqh*, as well as understanding knowledge about *Allah* as is taught in *Aqida*. Otherwise, how will they know *Allah* and how will they correctly *worship* Him? The stronger the firm grasp a person has of *Aqida* the more they are unshaken by spiritual experience towards deviance and misguidance, and historically after many experiences of spiritual error due to spiritual experience being more intense than *Aqida*, for a period of time some Ihsan school of thoughts in Egypt wouldn't allow their students to study Ihsan without first confirming they learnt *Aqida*.

The most comprehensive description God gives of Himself in the Quran, is **"there is nothing like God"** (42:11), this means He is one and He is unique, but also that we should quit comparing Him to anything you come across, as it won't be like Him. There is nothing like him as it's impossible, He is a One God, and also as He is not created, even when he creates what has his attributes such as Adam being able to hear and see, but it is still not like Him. The most important knowledge of God is His ninety nine names, as they describe God. A Muslim who loves God should watch the world and see the manifestation of God's names in the world, as a truth to the existence of God. For example, seeing a mother feeding her child is a mercy, and so it is proof for the existence of God who is merciful.

In Islam God is perfect without shortcomings, God says **"to God is the most perfect example"** (16:60). The Prophet Muhammed (pbuh) said **"evil is not attributed to God"** (Tirmizi), and this supports that God exists, because a God who is evil deserves to be destroyed and so has no right to exist, but a good God such as Allah, the God of Islam, naturally can be expected to exist without hindrance. God is one and powerful and if there were many gods, they would share the power of divinity, and thus become individually weak and can't elevate the harm, pain and suffering of creation. This was Joseph's argument in the Quran, that solving of problems in the world is a sign God is one in number. God is Rahman (compassionate), who allows breaking of law for mercy, such as using earth in purification in absence of water.

CHAPTER SEVENTEEN

THE GREAT CHARACTER

The Quran says about the Prophet (pbuh) **"the Prophet Muhammed is of great character"** (68:4). This is generally understood to be his best character towards his fellow companions and other humans, however that was obvious. This description is a praise from God considering the Messenger's character towards God, such as his eyes did not wonder during vision of God, the Quran says **"the Prophet's sight did not look away from God"** (53:17) describing the prophet's manners in the presence of God when he was above the seventh heaven. The behaviour the companions witnessed of Muhammed was likewise striking. Umar (raa) saw how his blessed ankles swelled from long standing during voluntary night prayer, and when Umar (raa) reminded him that he needed not do that as God has already promised him forgiveness, the Prophet said '**should I not be a grateful slave to God**' (Bukhari). This excessive thanking of God is usually considered the epitome of human character and a manner to reveal the person's internal beauty. The Prophet Muhammed (pbuh) said **"I was sent by God to complete the teachings on the best of character"**(Haithami). He also said **"those best in faith are best in character and they are those best to their spouse"** (Tirmizi).

Learning good character is very important in Ihsan, that some people said it is a definition of Sufism (Ihsan). This is because Ihsan is about entering the presence of God, and a person must be of good character as to be guaranteed they will be of good manners in the presence of God. Just like a bride is beautified for her groom, a believer is beautified with good manners to be ready to the presence and Vision of God. The branch of Ihsan is called Ihsan, which means charity in Arabic as charity is the most important good character of a believer seeking the presence of God. The Prophet found good character to be so important that he prayed **"just as You beautified my looks beautify my character"** (Baihagi).

Some of the most important characters the Quran commands include: don't lie (22:30), don't spy (49:12), don't insult (49:11), don't waste (17:26), feed the poor (22:36), don't backbite (49:12), keep your oaths (5:89), don't take bribes (27:36), honour your treaties (9:4), restrain your anger (3:134), don't spread gossip (24:15), think good of others (24:12), be good to guests (51:24-27), don't harm believers (33:58), don't be rude to parents (17:23), turn away from ill speech (23:3), don't make fun of others (49:11), walk in a humble manner (25:63), respond to evil with good (41:34), don't say what you won't do (62:2), keep your trusts and promises (23:8), don't insult others' false gods (6:108), don't deceive people in trade (6:152), don't take items without right (3:162), don't ask unnecessary questions (5:101), don't be miserly nor extravagant (25:67), don't call others with bad names (49:11), don't claim yourselves to be pure (53:32), speak nicely, even to the ignorant (25:63), don't ask for repayment for favours (76:9), make room for others at gatherings (58:11), if enemy wants peace, then accept it (8:61), return a greeting in a better manner (4:86), don't remind others of the favours you done to them (2:264) and make peace between fighting groups (49:9).

The Prophet Muhammed (pbuh) said **"good character will be the heaviest deed on the scale of a believer on the day of judgment"** (Dawud). Sufis are famed for their character with their scholars to the point that they kiss their hands and sit below them in the ground. It is related that the companions kissed the hands and feet of the Prophet Muhammed (pbuh)(Bukhari).

The religion of Islam in its teachings about the perfection, purity and superiority of God, teaches to respect God and believe He has good description. In this way God considers associating sons to God, which assumes he dies and need to be replaced and associates the impure sexual union to God since it's the way of begetting children. Therefore the God of Islam communicated in the Quran that the Christians claiming a son to god is an insult to God and therefore is disrespecting Him. The Quran insists that God does not have a son and in one verse God warns against making such a claim. The Quran says it was sent to **"warn those who claim God has a son"** (18:4). The Quran also negates the idea that God rested after creating the world, which is believed metaphorically or literally in the religion of Judaism. Again needing to rest is seen as a shortcoming to God, that God is not strong enough and is weak, and therefore again is an insult against God. The religion of Islam in upholding to the oneness, purity and grandeur of God means it is a religion that respects God and holds a high moral and character code. An expression of showing manners to God in Islam, is having an intention before worship, meaning making a conscious declaration to worship. This is like asking permission of God to do worship as not to intrude into the presence of God, and thus it shows good character with God.

CHAPTER EIGHTEEN

THE LOVE OF THE PROPHET (PBUH)

Love of the Messenger (pbuh) is a perquisite for and a sign of the perfection of *iman* (belief in God). The Prophet Muhammed (pbuh) said that a person's belief is not complete unless they come to love him more than all else, including one's self (Bukhari). In Islam there is also the love of the other past prophets, love of the companions (e.g. at his request the Prophet (pbuh) made prayer that the believers would love the Prophet's companion Abu-Huraira (raa)) and love between believers. One of the groups of people saved on the Day of Judgment is two people who love each other purely for the sake of God. The Quran prohibits that a Muslim loves anyone more than God and the Messenger (pbuh). God said **"the Prophet should tell them, if their fathers and children, and brothers and wives, and relatives, and money they have gained, and trade they fear will not profit, and homes they are pleased with, are more beloved to them than God and His messenger, and fighting in the way of God, then they should await the verdict of God to punish them, and God does not guide the disobedient"** (9:24). Differentiating between different types of loves is important, love of God is different from love of a son, and this difference is based on the intensity of the love as well as its expression. Love of God is expressed by much *nafila* (optional worship) while love of a son could be expressed by hugging him, giving him gifts he likes and even sincere prayers for them. Whereas when a person loves God, they would want to see Him, as was the state of Prophet Muhammed (pbuh) who used to pray **'I ask you Lord to give me the pleasure of Your Vision' (Nissai)**.

The love of the Prophet (pbuh) is a sign of complete *Iman*, as it is not possible to claim to completely trust someone or follow them if we do not love them. Surely the person who is worthy of trust and following, are also worthy of love. And it is impossible to love someone and not trust to follow them, unless their criteria of who is worthy to be loved is not inclusive of all good characteristics. This is because the good characteristics that allow us to trust someone are the same to love them. When a person loves someone they find it easy to follow their commands, and to want to please them, and since by loving the Prophet (pbuh) the person will be following his command to worship God, pleasing him means only increasing in worship and spirituality. The love of the Prophet (pbuh) acts as a shortcut to the perfect worship of God. It is related that once while Umar (raa) was in the company of the Messenger (pbuh), Umar (raa) told the Prophet Muhammed (pbuh) that he loved him. When the Prophet (pbuh) asked if it was more than himself, Umar (raa) replied that he did not love the Messenger (pbuh) more than himself (Bukhari). After a period of thinking, Umar (raa) then told the Prophet (pbuh) that he loved the Messenger (pbuh) more than everything including his own self, to which the Prophet then told him that he's reached the completion of belief. When Umar (raa) was asked about it, he said that he thought about the matter and found that the 'Messenger (pbuh) is of more benefit to himself than his own self'. Umar (raa) found that the Messenger (pbuh) fitted the criteria to be loved more than himself, and on this he allowed himself to love the Messenger more. There was initially a defect in thinking that led Umar (raa) firstly to love himself more than the Messenger (pbuh). Umar (raa) was heedless of who the Messenger (pbuh) was compared to himself. As the Messenger of God, he (pbuh) was more perfect than himself, was more knowledgeable of God than himself, closer to God than himself, and more worshiping of God than himself. When this defect in him was corrected he was then able to develop a healthy emotion that leads to his benefit. The better love of the Messenger (pbuh) means the better following of him, the wanting to be more like him in his character and worship of God and thus gain the pleasure of God, increase in spiritual station and receive the reward of the hereafter.

The Quran tells us **"God has sent Muhammed as a messenger from the people, who grieves when people are stubborn, and is keen people should believe and not enter the hellfire, and is gentle and merciful to the believers"** (9:128). The Prophet Muhammed (pbuh) was keen that we were warned about hell and encouraged us to paradise, he spend his possession, time and effort, he emigrate from his home city and even risked his life in war to make sure that the message of God reached the people. In life he prayed much for his *ummah* (followers) and in death he makes *istigfar* (asked for forgiveness) for our sins on our behalf. On the Day of Judgment he will intercede to God to lift punishment from the believing sinners. How then can we not love him, or know that he is more important and more worthy of love than ourselves? While we follow our desires and ignore religion we are doing what is harmful for us, yet by trying to get us to become obedient and worshiping of God, he is being more beneficial to ourselves than our own selves, and it is with the recognition of this we find that he is more worthy of love than our own selves. The love of the Prophet (pbuh) is also a love of admiration, for his good character, his devotion in worship, and his love of God are admirable by any standard.

Once the person come to love and trust the Messenger (pbuh) they can then trust and listen to what he tells us about God and in turn that gets us to love God, so in away the love of the Prophet Muhammed (pbuh) is a step stone towards the love of God. This is true because if it wasn't for the Prophet (pbuh) we would not have known about Allah let alone worshiped or loved him. Lack of love for the Messenger (pbuh) thus shows weak belief and as he is what is spiritually healthy and good; one who lacks love of the Prophet (pbuh) is indeed very spiritually diseased. And once this disease is cured, all other diseases are then easily cured. As when a person loves someone they would want to be like them. When the person comes to love the Prophet (pbuh) they then find it easy to emulate him and take him as role model. This means that the process of gaining good character and performing worship is easily done. Love of the Prophet (pbuh) can be learned and increased, as was the case of Umar (raa). If a person asks how they can increase their love for the Messenger (pubh)? The answer and the treatment to lack of love for the Prophet (pbuh) is realising who the Messenger (pbuh) was, what his character was like, how he lived his life, and what his teachings were and this is why the scholars of Ihsan usually prescribed reading the *seerah* (Prophet's biography) to increase their love of him.

Part of the love of the Prophet is the love of his family. The Quran says **"the Prophet asks no salary from the believers but only that the believers love his family"** (42:23). The Prophet said **"give presents it creates love"** (Ibn Almlgn). This means giving presents to the family and descendants of Prophet Muhammed (pbuh) to show them love and to negate hypocrisy.

Lack of love for the Messenger (pbuh) can be due to many reasons, including lack of knowledge of the Messenger, holding wrong criterion of what or who is to be loved. Anyone who holds a correct criterion to who should be loved and gains knowledge of the Messenger (pbuh), will love him. In the case of Umar (raa) his shortcoming in love wasn't due to lack of knowledge, for he was very close to the Prophet (pbuh) and was an early companion, but it was his own ego standing on the way. This is cured by humbling our egos to the noble status of the Prophet (pbuh) as he is the best of mankind. The Prophet (pbuh) said **'I am the best of** the children of Adam (as) and I do not boast' (Tirmizi)** and this is because he was a Messenger of God and closest to Him in worship. This is based on the Islamic belief that the most superior of people are the most pious, God in the Quran says **"the most honoured of people in the sight of Allah are the pious"** (49:13). As the Prophet (pbuh) was the most worshiping of God, he is thus considered the best of mankind. The Prophet (pbuh) was the seal of Prophets, meaning that there will be no other Prophets after him, he is also the leader of Prophets (pbut) and he led them in *salah* (prayer) in the Aqsa Mosque on the day of *Isra* and *Miraj* (ascension into heaven). The Prophet's (pbuh) revealing of his status is an important statement as it allows all Muslims to know their spiritual station compared to him, so we may appreciate him. It also makes us feel spiritually inferior and thus to aim to be like him and learn from him. If the person feels superior to him then they will be looking down at what Allah said as being the one with 'great character' but also will not take him as example, for it is difficult to be like someone the person feel they are inferior to them. This acknowledgment of the Prophet's (pbuh) status is expressed in using the title *Sayaduna* (lit. leader or lord) before his name. The use of this expression is curing, expresses spiritual health and the best manners of the religion and is also rewarded by God.

The companions found loving the Prophet (pbuh) natural, for Umar (raa) did not lack in love it was merely its level that the Prophet (pbuh) commanded him to attenuate. This is because the Prophet (pbuh) message uplifted oppression from in front of their eyes. His message taught justice and equality, for the Prophet (pbuh) made slaves equals to masters, and made it a religious deed to free slaves, he banned the killing of infant girls by their fathers, and diverted worship from inanimate statues to the worship of the one true God. Thus their love for him naturally came as they saw their lives change to the better by following him, believing in him and practicing his religion and they attributed this goodness to him (pbuh), which further intensified their love. Many who are born into Islamic societies or families forget the beauty of Islam as they forget or are heedless of the alternative; worshipping many gods or none at all, holding false beliefs about God and no guidance except what some people formulate from ideas. And while there can be justice in a non-Islamic society, as was the society of Abyssinia in the time of the Prophet (pbuh), nevertheless, the Islamic religion guarantees that it should exist in society. Thus, when examining Islam, it is most understood and appreciated when compared to other beliefs or notions, or even lack of beliefs.

Lack of love or little love for the Prophet (pbuh) is one of the first diseases that are cured in the path of Ihsan, and by curing it then the curing of other diseases easily follows. Hearing praise of the Prophet (pbuh) as is common in Nasheeds (Islamic songs) also can teach his love, for in them his character is described and praised, so they act as a reminder and teach us to acknowledge his goodness and finding it praiseworthy. The other way is to love scholars, as when a person loves another they come to love what they love too. As scholars love the Prophet (pbuh), loving scholars and others who also love the Messenger (pbuh) leads us also to loving the Prophet of God. Likewise the love of the Messenger (pbuh) leads to love of God.

The love of God and love of the Prophet (pbuh) does not negate the love of oneself as we can deduce from the wording of the *Hadith* 'more than yourself Umar?' Loving the Prophet (pbuh) and loving God is about increasing your love to them, not of decreasing your love to yourself. And if a person truly loves themselves, they would love what is best and good for it and that is *Jannah* (paradise). This is achieved by loving God and the Messenger (pbuh).

> Holy child of Mecca, you brought mercy to the world
> With your birth from cousins in spring time, a blessing to be told
> You were born a Lord from the master from the time of old
> You worked in trade for Khadija, with products bought and sold

Then an angel came to you in a cave and left you scared
He asked you to read many times, but your voice was not heard
A message came from God, that there will be hell and Heaven
Then Muhammed was raised by angel above the heavens which were seven
Above the seventh heaven Muhammed saw his Lord
After a journey to the far universe and paradise he explored
Muhammed met all the prophets and together they prayed
Muhammed lead the praying prophets and his words to God were said
The Meccans were harsh to Muslims, so to Medina they all travelled
There Muhammed preached Islam and stopped all those gravelled

There are many reasons why Muslims love Prophet Muhammed (pbuh); firstly Prophet Muhammed (pbuh) told us about a perfect God, one who does not die and have a son like the Christians and does not tire like that of the Jews, secondly he was the greatest worshiper of God, he used to stand up in prayer until his feet swelled. Thirdly he was of great character, he once visited an ill woman who used to place thorns on his path, and fourthly he will intercede, begging God on the Day of Judgment to forgive the believers. Fifthly he came with the Quran, the speech of God, which before was exclusive to the prophets alone. Prophet Muhammed (pbuh) is admired by Muslims for telling us about Heaven and its beauty, of life after death, and about the vision of God. The Prophet Muhammed (pbuh) saw God in this world. Prophet Muhammed (pbuh) is loved by God, and so Muslims love him for that. They also love him as he was very handsome, and had miracles that saved people.

His skin was tanned, when his religion was banned
This is how the Prophet Muhammed looked
His hair was bent, to the shoulder it went
This is how the Prophet Muhammed looked
He traded sold and bought, his height neither tall nor short
This is how the Prophet Muhammed looked

His nose was straight, like a sword not faked
This is how the Prophet Muhammed looked
His face was round, his head lowered modest to the ground
This is how the Prophet Muhammed looked
His hair was black, a few grey hairs
His sweat was sweeter than the musk in airs
This is how the Prophet Muhammed looked
He was handsome like the moon
He died 63 too young too soon

CHAPTER NINETEEN

THE LOVE OF GOD

The branch of Islam demands from its practitioners the use of all their body; their tongues in *shahada* (praise of God), their limbs in *salah* (physical prayer), their stomach in fast, their hands in *zakah* (charity) and their whole bodies to travel to *Hajj* (pilgrimage). The branch of Iman requires our mind to understand, learn and accept the articles of the creed of Islam. However the main work of the branch of Ihsan is the heart and spirit, how we feel about the religion, about feeling fear of hell and hope of paradise, and gaining love for the Prophet Muhammed (pbuh) and God. This side of the branch meant that its people became famous for their religious romanticism, of whirling dervishes, the poetry of sufis such as Rumi, and devotion of Rabia al Adawia (raa) came to gain worldwide fame. However, it also meant it was the point of its fall, of where it became trivialised, for those of extreme physical devotion considered unimportant the subtleties of the heart.

The love of God is the fuel of the believer's heart in wanting to be near to God and being in His presence. Muslims love God for many reasons: firstly God is perfect and complete in goodness, God says **"To God is the most perfect example"** (16:60), secondly that God has beautiful description, as described in His ninety nine beautiful names.

Thirdly God created us, and we love Him for that, just as we love our parents who created us in the world, and fourthly we love God because He commands to good such as charity and forbids evils such as murder. We love God as He is pure, and is the God of modesty, chastity and cleanliness. Other reasons for love of God include, His provision of food to maintain life, easing the hardship of hunger and death. God also cures the ill, and He solves people's problems. He also gifted us with life in this world and promises to give life after death in the eternal Heaven. God gives us children who carry our names and mean that we don't totally die in the world but there remains of us something living, easing the idea of death. God gave us sight, hearing and minds to be safe in the world. God's greatness and majesty, that he is a great king means God is admired and loved as people love strong things in the world. God's kindness and compassion in allowing people for instance of not needing to fast when ill or travelling, touches people's hearts and begets love. Lastly God sending prophets and messengers to warn of the eternal hellfire is an act of mercy that brings relief to people and as such allows to them to admire and love God.

The love of God must be intense, and great in the heart of the believer, so God would love them back and accept their plea for the vision of God. God says in the Quran "**whoever loves God should follow Muhammed, and God will love them and forgive their sins, and God is forgiving and merciful**"(3:31). This is to say to worship like Prophet Muhammed (pbuh) worshiped. The Prophet said that God said "**whoever shows enmity to a saint God declares war on them. My slave does not near to me with something loved to me than obligatory worship. My slaves continues to do voluntary worship until I love them. Then when I love them I become their hearing, their sight, their hand which hits and their foot which he walks, and I accept their prayer. I do not hesitate at anything like I hesitate at giving a believer death, knowing they hate death.**" (Bukhari). This Hadith tells us that a person must do their obligatory worship as they are beloved to God, and do voluntary worship (*nafila*) for God to love them. Then when God loves them He becomes their senses, meaning they have super strength, such as seeing or walking great distances in a short period of time, all as miracles.

God says "**people who believe should know whoever among them leave Islam, God will bring instead a people who God loves and they love God**"(5:54). This shows the importance of love of God that God insists for there to be lovers, that in their absence He will create a new people who love Him. The Prophet Muhammed (pbuh) said "**love God for His much givings and grace. Love me for God's love and love my family due to loving me**" (Tirmizi). What is a heart good for if it doesn't behold the beauty of God and falls head over heels over God. Only in intense love of God has a person truly understood God, as He is worthy of all love.

The love of Allah and the Messenger are for the person's own benefit since both are exulted of the need for your love. In human love each has need of each other's love. One benefit of the love of God and His messenger, is to help to better love, worship and follow their command, and it should come naturally with belief, for if worthy of belief are as most worthy of love. What should be most beloved to a Muslim is God, and this is a state of Ihsan, while love of the Prophet (pbuh) is the state of Iman (complete faith). The Quran sees it as injustice for a person to love other than God with a love worthy only of God, in intensity and devotion. God says "**some people take other than God, to be on level with God, and they love them with the love of God, but those of belief are stronger in love to God. If only the unjust in religion, would consider the punishment of the hellfire, and see that to God is all strength, and that God is fierce in punishment**" (2:165). The Quran sees people loving other than God with a love that only God is worthy of as an act of injustice (*zulm*). This is because what He is rightful of is being given to another, and that constitute injustice. Who or what is worthy of more love than God? Especially since regardless of who or what it is, He created it. How can we give preference to what He created more than Him? How can we love what is less than God, more than God? It is considered an injustice, as justice would be giving each their right. Those people who worship or love other than God are giving their object of love and worship a state that is not theirs, and that is injustice. The Prophet (pbuh) taught us prayer **'Lord, I ask that I come to love you and to love those who love you and to do deeds that makes me worthy of your love'** (Bukhari).

There are types and levels of love; the Quran mentions those who love other people or objects like their love to God, because this gives the love of God a special category of its own. All types of love are not the same and they manifest differently. The love of God, God commanded to be manifest in following His Prophet. The Quran asks the Prophet (pbuh) to say **"If you do love Allah, follow me: Allah will love you and forgive you your sins"** (3:31). When you love God you should express it, and it should become natural to follow the Prophet Muhammed (pbuh), by obeying the commands of God. The Prophet (pbuh) was an example in the worship of God, and following him means the perfection and strict observance of the commandments of God. This brings the pleasure and grace of God on the person and becomes a reason for God to love them and to grant them paradise. God's love to the person is expressed by granting *karamat* (miracles) as is mentioned in the Qudsi Hadith, that when God loves a person he increases the powers of their limbs and senses, and thus strengthens their belief (Bukhari).

Love can be a result of the loved thing's innate qualities, or qualities they expressed to us. God's love comes from knowledge of Him, and of knowing His attributes. In Islam we have been given a lot of knowledge of God, including His ninety-nine names that describe His attributes. But other than what we are explicitly told of Him, there are facts we can infer and understand from His commandments and prohibitions. His commandments to what is good of good character and beneficial acts, and His prohibitions from what is evil and naturally abhorrent lead us to know and believe that God is Good. While some view the existence of evil in the world as a sign that God doesn't exist, this is not the Islamic belief, as in the Quran we are told that the painful and unpleasant things that happen in the world are to test who are strong in belief and accept the decree of God. God says **"God trials people by giving them good or bad, as a test, and to God they all return"** (21:35). The other reason for the existence of evil is that it is not created by God, not commanded nor encouraged, but is due to and from His creation, who He has given choice to test them but are choosing to do evil instead of the good that He commanded. In fact God shows us how we could avoid evil and that is in the message He gave to His Prophets. The Quran advices **"ask God for help as the Lord of the sunrise. God's help from the harm of His creation"** (113:1-2).

As well as being good, the Prophet (pbuh) said, **'God is Beautiful and loves beauty'** (Muslim). A look into the world does support that God indeed loves beauty; in fact many artists find it enough to just copy landscapes to create beautiful canvases. The colourful fruits and flowers, the nice patterns of some animal furs or some bird feathers or some fish, all testify to the existence of beauty in what God creates. The absence of beauty or little of it that God also allowed to exist in some things, merely further highlights the beauty of beauty, and in humans this is merely a temporary state and test, for the Quran and Hadiths tell us that in paradise all people will be made beautiful, in levels that correspond to their spiritual state in this world. However, beauty is not only in physical form, but also in concept or notions, and even in character. Kindness and good manners can arouse in us a pleasant feeling that is not less powerful or less sweet than that of a beautiful face or form; and this is further highlighted when the person compares it to the pain of harassment or unjust attack. Allah says to the Prophet (pbuh) **"if Muhammed was severe in anger and despise towards people they would have left his gathering, so the Prophet Muhammed should pardon them and ask forgiveness for them and consult with them"** (3:159).

To love what is beautiful is seen as a natural consequence, and an element that defines beauty, and being able to ignore it or detest it is both unnatural and strange. The Quran described the effect of beauty of Prophet Joseph (as); **"when the women saw Joseph, they cut their hands and said, God forbid this is not a human, but must be an angel due to his great beauty"** (12:31). This means that to know God and know of His Beauty is literally to love God, for none come to know Him truly without loving Him. The beauty of God is revealed in His Beautiful ninety-nine Names and Attributes told to us in the Quran and Hadith; that include that He is The Merciful, The Forgiving, The Generous, The Compassionate, The Just, The Great and The Loving. While to fall in love with a person or a thing for its qualities is one stage, how this object of love interacts with us is the second. This interaction if negative can lead to the review of the first stage, or if positive an increase in love or maybe it just remains at the first level. A lover who is kind and gives gifts is bound to increase the love of the beloved for them, while one who treats them with disrespect could lead it to decrease. God gifts to us are innumerable, and His greatest gift is the gift of life, of existing, of living, and this is well contrasted with our hatred of and dislike of death, simply because we love living, love being conscious, not only of ourselves but of the surrounding world. God says **"do people not remember they were created before from nothing"** (19:67). We take out existence for granted, we feel like we existed eternally, but this is not true. Before our conception and birth we were literally nothing. We exist only due to the gift of life that God bestowed upon us, and it is the first and greatest gift. But God did not only give us existence, but He also gave us a perfect existence and form. He gave us faculties through which we interact with the world and enjoy it. The details of our form, the senses of smell, taste, bodies and thought. God says, **"God created the human in a perfect form"** (95:4).

God's other gifts, and He was not obliged to have given them, just the basics that insured our survival would still have been sufficient, but out of His generosity He chose to make the earth flat for ease to walk on and live in, the palatable river waters, the variety of plants, foods, and even the existence of spices. The Quran say **"if people were to count the giving of God, they will find they are too many to count, and God is forgiving and merciful"** (16:18) and **"God is of favour to people but most people are not grateful"** (40:61).

After creating us He did not forget about us or ignore us but sent us guidance in the message of His Prophets and Messengers, of what is right and beneficial and what is wrong and harmful. God also banned injustice so that people could live safely, and encourages being good to each other in charity and good character, so that people could live in harmony with each other. The seriousness of this He emphasised by promising to greatly reward the good and severely punish the bad. As well as testing us for belief, God supports us to the truth of His existence and Message by miracles of the prophets that are related to us through chains of honest knowledgeable people as well as those mentioned in the Quran, by *karamat* (miracles) of the pious and true dreams, which eases the test of belief and further supports to us His existence, and thus the worship of Him.

The love of God has many signs, and among them are finding pleasure in worship, the love of the religion and knowing about God, as well as the love of the Quran; His speech and wanting to see Him, and looking forward to meeting Him in the Hereafter. The love of God should be expressed in the following of the Prophet (pbuh) as God commanded. The most important expression of the love of God is to follow His commandments and to refrain from His prohibitions. This should be done not only to please God, but also to become nearer to Him, which is a natural desire when the person loves Him. The following of God's commandments is mercy, for God only commands to what is good and beneficial and has only forbidden when it is wrong or abhorrent. Nevertheless the doing of good is not counted by God as worship nor is it rewarded unless the person's initial intention was that it's done as worship and to fulfil God's commandments. The Prophet (pbuh) said **"actions will be rewarded based on intentions"** (Bukhari).

A man asked **"when is the last hour?"** And the Prophet Muhammed (pbuh) said **"what have you prepared for it?"** and the man answered **"love of God and His messenger"**. The Prophet Muhammed (pbuh) said **"a person will be with those who they love"** (Tabarani). The Prophet Muhammed (pbuh) also said **"whoever wants to be loved by God and His messenger, should be truthful in tongue, trustworthy with people and be good to their neighbour"** (Ibn Hajar).

Hatred leads to anger at the thing hated and may lead to its destruction. Love on the other hand leads to admiration, and that leads to want for the thing loved to remain forever in our awareness. Love of God is expressed as wanting constant mention of God, enjoying prayer where we are near His presence, and wanting to greet God in prayer as a way of promising safety to the people of God and the exalting of His religion.

The person who loves God, their greatest desire is for God to love them back. Thankfully the Quran tells us what God loves, so we may perform them to gain love of God. The Quran says God loves **"those who are pure"**(2:222), **"those who fear God"**(3:76), **"those who trust God"**(3:159), **"those who fight for the sake of God"**(61:4), **"those who are just"** (5:42), **"those who repent"**(2:222), **"those who are patient"**(3:146), and "those who perfect their worship of God, by practicing Ihsan"(3:148).

> The beauty of God is the drive to His love
> He created everything, gold, flower and dove
> We love our parents who created us
> So why not the great creator above
> God has the beautiful names, the perfect description
> His love is the cure to our hearts, our spiritual prescription
> Love of God, reflects true faith, our solid conviction

CHAPTER TWENTY

THE SCHOLAR OF IHSAN

The Prophet Muhammed (pbuh) had a guide in his physical journey to God (journey to heavens): Angel Gabriel (as). This makes having a guide *Sunnah* (way of prophet Muhammed), and if the Prophet Muhammed (pbuh) had a guide, what hope do we have without one? As mentioned before, scholars can correct the student if they enter incorrect spiritual states e.g. spiritual intoxication. They are also a source of knowledge and are a good example of piety and a role model in spirituality and character. A pious scholar is a physical manifestation of the Islamic ideals; making it easier to understand and emulate Islamic knowledge. Scholars have studied and are knowledgeable of spiritual states, and have expertise to identify diseases and prescribe cures. They are a living example of what health is; as from their own study of Ihsan have come to increase in spiritual state and cured their disease, and became most like the Prophet (pbuh). Their *ijaz* (licence to teach) acknowledges that they not only reached a certain level of religious knowledge and spirituality, but also have qualities that make them suited to be able to guide and teach. The *ijaz,* which is given by one scholar to the next, usually goes back in an uninterrupted chain to the Prophet (pbuh), called *silsila* or *isnad* which further authenticates the scholar and their knowledge.

The Prophet (pbuh) said **'the believer is the mirror of the believer' (Abu Dawud)**, to say that another believer can help us see of ourselves that which we might not have known. This is important in identifying areas of improvement, and the scholar is someone who can do this with honesty and sensitivity. This is perfectly true of scholars, as they will see illnesses that others may not. This is because scholars can identify what others may miss due to their lack of complete knowledge of what diseases are and how they manifest, or even what some people may deny in themselves out of vanity or arrogance. This greater ability for others to notice mistakes is the basis for *'alamr bi almarouf wa alnahi an almunkar'* (the command to good and abhorring of vice), i.e. that when a person sees what is wrong they must try to correct it and be encouraging and reminding of what is good. God said "**the believing men and women are allies to each other, they command to good and deter from wrong, and establish prayer, and give in charity, and obey God and His messenger. They will have mercy of God, and God is dignified and wise**" (9:71). As scholars are the most knowledgeable of what is *'marouf'* (right) and what is *'munkar'* (wrong), it makes them the most eligible for this job in society. Scholars have been through all the spiritual stations that the student may have or not have been through. They have knowledge of spirituality and thus can guide through the short cuts and safe paths. The scholar's job is the refinement of the student, as they raise them up and give them a spiritual breeding.

To have a scholar is important; although books act as a useful tool in gaining knowledge, this does not negate the need of a scholar to clarify or explain. Knowledge is something that is actively sought and it is found with scholars, so finding a scholar is the first step to knowledge. Also, religious knowledge is not a trivial thing that it can be taken from all people; there are liars and truthful ones, there are accurate and there are careless ones and thus must be learned from a scholar. Learning from a scholar guarantees that the person is getting correct, authentic, and accurate knowledge. All branches of the religion are learned from scholars who understand the branch and are of a level of knowledge to be able to teach, and spirituality is no exception. Parents are expected to teach manners and good character to their children, yet scholars of Ihsan are experts of and knowledgeable of all the details of Islamic character, and how to gain them. While parents teach their children character as part of their role as parents and so they become respectable members of society, in Ihsan the study of character is a religious obligation, a deed to receive God's reward, gain His acceptance and avoid hellfire – thus its study is taken seriously as is the performing of worship. The learning of character formally from a scholar of Ihsan is part of the practicing of the branch.

Jihadul-nafs is like surgery in that it requires accuracy and precision, and self-operating is bound to result in harm. An example is to feel regret about past sins without ending up in despair or learning one's religious shortcomings and doing *Jihadul-nafs* without it leading to self-hate.

It is part of the scholar's role to remove the student from incorrect spiritual states. This includes forgetting God's mercy and worshiping in complete fear, *itikaal;* when a person doesn't refrain from sins or doesn't do good deeds, only relying to be saved on the Day of Judgment by the intercession of a scholar, saintly relative, the Prophet's intercession or God's mercy. God says **"they claimed the hellfire will only touch them a specified time, ask if they have God's promise, for if God promised, then God does not break His promises. However, they are probably saying about God what they do not know"** (2:80). Another reason for having a knowledgeable scholar is their being able to acknowledge and distinguish diseases that are not due to the ego, or when they are not against the religion, and thus not to be corrected. An example of this is arrogance that can develop to defend the self from belittlement or attack. Arrogance as a self defence was shown when a companion walked arrogantly in battle, and the Prophet (pbuh) commented that while walking with arrogance is detestable to God, in this instance it was acceptable. This is because it was done to give the enemy an image of strength. It is also possible that some people intentionally reveal their worship in order to gain respect or stop other's harm and to prove they are good people or not worthy of such treatment. This would not be considered *riya*; the forbidden ostentation of worship as it is done out of need. For these reasons the judgment of people and the diagnosing of spiritual diseases and curing them must be for those experts knowledgeable of this branch. God says **"people of belief should not invalidate their charity by reminders of their generosity or by doing wrongs, as if giving in charity to showoff to people, and do not believe in God and the afterlife"** (2:264).

Itikal is a spiritually incorrect state (blameworthy) of loss in goodness, or careless in sin. When the Prophet taught Muadh ibn Jabal (raa) that that **"There is none who testifies sincerely from is heart that there is no god but Allah and that Muhammed is His messenger, except that Allah will save them from the hellfire"** when Muadh asked the prophet's permission to tell others the Prophet said **"I fear they would *Itika*l"** and Muadh then only told of this Hadith in his deathbed (Bukhari). This means that while the Prophet did not command nor prohibit him from sharing this knowledge, he was instead told to be aware that some may rely on just saying it and not do more good deeds, i.e. instead of taking it as a sign of God's mercy and generosity, to use it as an excuse to not do more worship.

Another state is *Itikal* based on good deeds; while a person who does much good deeds should feel in a better state than not, we must know that even if we were to perform worship every second of our life we would not be enough for one or even of God's gifts on us, let alone entering Heaven. It is by God's mercy and generosity and forgiveness. Thus *Itikal* on deeds shows a misunderstanding of God.

Scholars can guide the person through the different spiritual experiences unlike learning from only books which can only describe them. Having a scholar also means that the person can find guidance in understanding what they read, thought the explanations of a scholar. Without a scholar making *zikr* or doing good deeds can lead to vanity, arrogance, and *riya* (ostentation), meaning that they become invalid and the person is not rewarded for them by God, leading to an increase in spiritual disease. Scholars are always reminding of intention and priorities, which better structure worship and direct it to the pleasure of God. Those who practice the branch without a scholar usually concentrate on the performance of good deeds that are of physical worship and forget or neglect those of the internal, such as love of the Prophet (pbuh) and good character. This means that their performance of good deeds is eroded by their sins that come from lack of character or spirituality. Those who perform *Jihadul-nafs* with the support and guidance of a scholar, learn to better control their desires and restrain from what is forbidden, decreasing their sins and being able to perform more worship. The study of Ihsan and to increase in spirituality requires performing a lot of worship, and while a scholar will organise their student's worship, those without scholars find problems in maintaining a steady worship. This is usually that they overwhelm themselves by excessively worshiping. This results in boredom with religion or even neglecting worship altogether to be able to get a sufficient break. This excess in worship to the extent that it affects other parts of life is also forbidden. The Prophet (pbuh) said **'Your Lord has a right on you, your body has a right on you, and your family have a right on you, so give each their right' (Bukhari)**, while God's right are fulfilled in His worship, part of the body's rights is having breaks and rests as well as leisure.

This excess in worship is also dangerous as it can lead to difficulty with continuous practice of the religion. The Prophet (pbuh) said **'the religion is easy. Whoever overburdens himself in his religion will not be able to continue in that way' (Bukhari)**. Those who do excess in their religion are overwhelmed spiritually and/or physically, making it difficult to practice while those who keep moderation find it easier to continue to practice it. By going into excess they are also acting with injustice to themselves and their families, which is a sin. God described those who disbelieve and those who disobey Him and the Prophet (pbuh) as being unjust to themselves and doing harm to themselves. God says **'those whose lives the angels take in a state of injustice to their own souls' (16:28)**. It is injustice to themselves as by sinning and disobeying God they are harming themselves on purpose as they know it will lead them to His punishment.

In preventing excess of worship, scholars make students understand that worship is not only in prayer or in fast, but is also in visiting family (*wasl alrhim*), earning a *halal* living, the spending of money on family and even in showing affection to one's partner. The Prophet (pbuh) was asked how the person received *ajr* by being intimate with a husband or wife, and he replied **"if he were to perform them with other than the person they are married to, they would be considered a sin" (Muslim)**. This gave the principle that a Muslim is rewarded for acts even if they were not commanded if in doing their opposite would be considered a sin. That is because they are being rewarded for avoiding the sin and as such it is worship to choose what is not *haram* over what is sin. The taking of breaks from worship is also worship, as it is a command, and fulfilling it shows obedience to God and His Messenger, as well as it allows the person to be able to perform steady worship. Most importantly, without the guidance and command of a scholar there is no way of really testing the ego, for there is no resistance, so by definition there can be no *Jihadul-nafs*. The command of a scholar to perform certain worship or exercises to cure the person's diseases is the definition of *Jihadul-nafs*. Without a scholar it is the person (and their ego) that decide on the worship and as thus it is not *Jihadul-nafs*. It is impossible to self-purify as that requires knowledge of purity which is not gained unless the person has been themselves purified and knows the way to it. Lastly, just like Gabriel (as) purified the Prophet's heart, scholars purify their students, and thus can't be a self-done process. The Prophet (pbuh) said, Prophet Dawood (as) once walked by a group of men who were doing remembrance of God, and when he became impressed by their worship he was told by the angel that if a woman was to offer them herself they would gladly follow her. This state of performing worship but yet not restraining from sins or having bad character is what necessitates *Jihadul-nafs* and is corrected by it. The Prophet (pbuh) said **'an *Aalim* (scholar) is as much superior to an *Aabid* (Worshiper) as the full moon is superior to all stars'** (Tirmizi). This is based on the importance and value of knowledge, God said **'are those who know equal with those who know not? Only men of understanding will remember"** (39:9). It is the reason for this difference, and the inferiority of ignorance that makes a person in need of a scholar.

Who is Qualified to Teach Ihsan?

To become a scholar of Ihsan, the person must be authorised by another scholar of Ihsan in the form of (*ijaz*) after having finished their learning. A process called '*tashayukh*' and can involve a ceremony of coronation.

The Quran says to the Prophet (pbuh), **"say this is my way of calling to God with vision, and likewise those who follow me. Glory to God, and Muhammed does not worship false gods with Allah"** (12:108). Thus it is important that those who invite to Allah and guide His slaves to Him should also fit this description; of inviting people from their own personal experience of the truthfulness of the religion and witnessing that there is no god but Allah. This means after their own study of Ihsan they gained certainty in religion and faith from personal experience of spirituality. As this description has always been true of scholars of Ihsan, they have always been people who agreed on their sainthood, and some have even became more famous as Saints than scholars, e.g. Ahmed Al Rifai (raa), Abu-Midyan (raa) and Abdal-Qadir Al-Jailani (raa). The Quran commands that inviting to God be based on *basira*, which means vision, but is used to mean vision of the heart (realisation) as well as vision of the eyes. In Ihsan this means that those who invite should do so from a spiritual state of witnessing and having realised the existence of God. This means that they must have reached the highest of spiritual stations. The vision of God is not necessary to become a scholar of Ihsan, nevertheless the spiritual state of the realisation of His existence from the witnessing of His Names and Attributes that manifest in the world is a must. This comes as a result of the complete practice of the branch of Ihsan and it is what the scholar is expected to be able to teach to their students.

Scholars are required to have knowledge of sound *Aqida* beyond what would be expected of a student and a firm following of a *mazhab* of *fiqh*, if they have not reached the level of making *fatwas* in *Fiqh*. They should have had an Ihsan teacher, from whom they learned correct knowledge, proper understanding and has given them permission to teach. They should be able to differentiate between struggling against the ego in Islam and that of other religions, the different experiences on the path, and can use Ihsan terminology correctly in describing it. They should also be able to differentiate between true spiritual experiences that come from following the straight path of Islam and those that come due to shortcomings in practicing of religion (*istidraj*), mental illness, magic and satanic or *Jinn* influences.

It must be realised that each branch and discipline of the religion is of vast knowledge, and to reach a level of scholarship in more than one, as much as it is noble is usually not possible as it requires a lot of time and dedication and thus the specialisation of scholars. It is based on this that an Ihsan scholar does not need to be a qualified scholar of *aqida*, nor an expert to the level of *fatwa* in *fiqh*, or required for them to know the Quran by heart nor be a *MuHadith* (expert in Hadith) but instead their students must seek knowledge of other disciplines from their experts to further their knowledge and deepen their learning of other branches. Nevertheless, knowledge of all these branches and their principles is a must and a requirement.

Part of the requirement to teach Ihsan includes having facilities, such as guesthouses to accommodate their students and those who come to stay temporary as well as permanently, as well as teaching areas. As Ihsan is not usually taught in classrooms but by the company of and presence of scholars, scholars usually accommodate for this by having close contact with their students and even opening their homes for them. As teaching was traditionally without a fee, the scholars usually had some other part time job (or jobs) or other means of living (such as fees from Quranic healing). The expenses of having guests and students were met with this as well as donations from more affluent students and from charitable Muslims who wish to support the religion and its teaching and sometimes from government grants. Scholars also have to be available and easily accessible to students. As teaching took a large amount of their time, they always made sure that their marriage partners were understanding, supportive and accepting of this. Allah commanded the Messenger (pbuh) to say **'I tell you not that with me are the treasures of Allah, nor do I know what is hidden, nor do I tell you I am an angel. I but follow what is revealed to me.'** (6:50). This is the same for Ihsan scholars; they do not have the treasures of Allah, nor know what is hidden, and are not infallible angles, but only follow that which was revealed to the Prophet (pbuh). This is not in the way of expressing humility, but in teaching the reality of spirituality. Nevertheless, they do hold what is most valuable and priceless, the understanding of the religion and the knowledge of the path to God. The Quran praises "**men who are not distracted from God by trade**" (24:37) as scholars of Ihsan usually become dedicated to the teachings of Ihsan and spreading the religion.

In the Quran God commands the Prophet (pbuh) and by extension scholars of Ihsan, to show special patience and attention to and acceptance of students of Ihsan and those who become dedicated to the religion. God says, "**Muhammed should not turn away those who worship God in the morning and evening, wanting the face of God. Muhammed has no reason to judge them or they to judge Muhammed. Muhammed should not turn them away and become of the unjust**" (6:52) and "**the Prophet Muhammed should be patient with those who pray in the morning and evening wanting God's face, and not to look away from them wanting the beauty of the world. Do not follow those** who's hearts are absent of the mention of God and follow desires, and their issues are in loss" (18:28). These verses were revealed on a group of companions who lived in the Prophet's (pbuh) mosque, and were dedicated to the learning of the religion and practice of Ihsan. They were called '*Ahlul Sufa*' (people of the *Sufa*), and it is based on their name that the branch later came to be called Sufism.

The Great Scholars of Ihsan

As the branch of Ihsan is a practical branch, its teachings are not via the pen and the understanding of its concepts are not gained via intellectual reasoning alone, but are learned from personal experience and taught by scholars demonstrating them via their own lives before their words. An example of this was Rabia Al-Adaweya (raa) state of intense love of God teaching the spiritual state of loving God or Al-Hallaj (raa) teachings on the state of spiritual ecstasy and intoxication; Hassan Al-Basri (raa) teaching the state of asking for God's forgiveness. Burai of Yemen (raa) or Busairi of Egypt (raa) teaching us the state of loving the Messenger (pbuh). Through their lives and worship, they demonstrated the manifestation of specific spiritual states, teaching how to gain them and inspiring people to them.

As well as reports on their lives and teachings some of them have left guidance to those who came after them in their written works. Scholars like Abu Hamid Al-Ghazali (raa), and Abd Alqadir Aljailani (raa) who is known as the Sultan of the Saints, their leader – how can he not be when no Muslim who lived after him can claim to have been raised spiritually without his works, he indeed is the Sultan of Saints; *Sultan Al-Awliya*. His books make the backbone of the knowledge of the branch of Ihsan, his school of thought in Ihsan (called Qadiri path) is one of the most practiced, and many of the other schools of thought are based on it or branched from it. Ihsan schools of thoughts are called *Tariq*, which means path and is short for 'path to God', which is the path the person takes to journey to God.

Learning from the piety and worship of non-Prophets is well established in the Hadith and the Quran. The Messenger (pbuh) commanded Muslims to learn from his life and worship as well as that of his companions. He (pbuh) also related many examples of pious people from previous nations such as the hairdresser of Pharaoh's daughter. This is also an important element in preserving our understanding of how Islamic teachings translate to the physical world, which better explains the religion and makes it easy to follow after being demonstrated by others. As different scholars of Ihsan each emphasised a certain spiritual station in their lives, and we find that their teachings and school of thoughts usually emphasise it too. This has led to the growth of different Ihsan Schools of thoughts (paths) and is the basis of the differences between different *paths*, in that they trace back to different scholars of Ihsan. God says **"if they are straight on the path to God, then God would provide them with abundant water"**(72:16).

The paths (not different from the *Mazhabs* of *Fiqh*) scholars began are usually named after them, e.g. Tijani path, named after Sheikh Ahmed Al-Tijani (raa), Naqshbandi named after Sheikh Naqshband (raa), Ahmadiya named after Sheikh Ahmed Al-Rifai (raa) and Sammaniya a school of thought that was started in Medina by Sheikh Al-Samman (raa). All the Ihsan paths like Fiqh Mazahib are valid, and usually branched from main schools of thoughts, like the Qadiri path, yet all if not most have *Isnad* and thus trace back via one scholar after another to the Prophet (pbuh). Magzoubia path of Magazeeb of Damar in Sudan, descendants of Alabass (raa) there are the Alawayites of Yemen, they are the famous habaib scholars who are descendants of the Prophet (pbuh), there is the Shazaliya, there are the Tijaniya, Burhaniya, as well as there are usually national tariqas local to their lands. The Sammniya path emphasises love of Prophet Muhammed (pbuh), Qadariya emphasises *jihadul-nafs* and character with God, and Magzoubia emphasises the practice of truth and love of God.

Practicing Ihsan isn't about reaching in success the levels of these great ones, and it is not to become another Rumi, another Jailany or Saman, but it would be wonderful if it happens. It is about fulfilling a branch of the religion. It is not about a flamboyant display of your worship of God and his grace in giving you miracles. These names famous practitioners of Ihsan were scholars, and the chains of *isnad* for the practice of Ihsan form the Prophet and his companions, and thus their fame. However, the practice of Ihsan isn't about fame. Measure of its success isn't fame in sainthood, however if that happens it is a gift from God.

The books of biographical Ihsan, list hundreds of thousands of practitioners of the branch, their miracles, their names, demographics and scholars. This branch popularity since the third century after the revelation have mounted to its spread throughout the world, but most remarkable are the scholars, whose knowledge about them acts as guidance in Ihsan and thus paramount to mention. In some Arab tribes who descend from the Prophet and his companion, Sufi scholars and saints, since they are best in religion represent their people as royals. The Prophet said to a man who knew the chapter of the cow of the Quran by heart that he is a prince among the believers. God says in the Quran to the Jews who rejected the kingship of a man among them because he was poor in money, God says "**We have instead expanded to him in his knowledge and body**"(2:247), so this verse supports the leadership of the scholars of Ihsan to be valid.

CHAPTER TWENTY ONE

THE STUDENT OF IHSAN

The student of Ihsan is traditionally called *Murid* (wanter of God) a name given to them by the holy Quran. The Quran says '*yaridon wajha*' ("**they want God's face**"(18:28)). When a student is in constant presence with their scholar they are called '*huwar*', the Quran says '*gal al huwaryon nhn ansar Allah*' and they were the companions of Jesus. The Prophet (pubh) called some companions the title of *huwar*, which is a spiritual honour to gain as a title. They are called *huwar*, and it is related to the word '*huwar*' meaning verbal exchange. The practitioners of Ihsan are rarely referred to as *Mohsineen* (a word from Ihsan) outside of the Quran, and this is because to use such a title is to mean finished Ihsan, just as Mumin is used once the person practiced fully that branch of Iman. The third term used for the practitioners of Ihsan, is Dervish, and it comes from the words *dar wash*, meaning "wants face", meaning the seeker of the face of God and wanter of His vision (18:28). Another word for a Sufi is *faqir* (poor), as the Quran says **"people are poor for God and God is the rich and praised"** (35:15).

The student of Ihsan is unlike other students of other branches. They are the seekers of God, and are thus honoured in their quest. In fact the Quran advices their respect. The Quran says "**the Prophet should be

patient with those who pray in the morning and evening wanting God's face and do not look away from them wanting the beauty of the world"(18:28). People of Sufism are also called *Rejaal Allah* (men of God) in the Quran. It is a term that is used for both males and females. Another term is Magzoub (literally attracted) and it is used to mean those attracted to God, and are considered to be the great saints attracted by God's beauty into loving and worshiping Him.

CHAPTER TWENTY TWO

THE SPIRITUAL CONTRACT

The start of the serious learning of Ihsan is recognised by making a pledge of learning called *baya*. This is to recognise the seriousness of the studying of the Greater stage of Ihsan, and the commitment to it. It is also a vow of piety and of becoming obedient to God. To make a vow in Allah's obedience and to worship Him more, is a recommended thing, and is a great spiritual success if achieved. The Prophet (pbuh) said **"whoever vows that he will be obedient to Allah, should remain obedient to Him; and whoever made a vow that he will disobey Allah should not disobey Him" (Abu Dawud)**. The Quran says **"people should fulfil their oaths with God and not break their promises after confirming them. Count God as a witness and God knows what people do" (16:91)**

The details of *baya* are made on following the command of the Quran and method of the Prophet (pbuh). God says **"the Prophet should accept the oaths and pact of the women. When the believers come to the Prophet to give pact, they should declare they will not worship partners with God, and will not steal, and will not fornicate or commit adultery, and not to kill their children, and not to come with a blatant lie or fraud, and not to disobey the Prophet in what is** acceptable. Then the Prophet should give them the pact and ask God to forgive them for God is forgiving, merciful." (60:12). In the *baya* the Prophet (pbuh) gave to the men he added "**and whoever indulges in any one of them except the ascription of partners to Allah and gets the punishment in this world, that punishment will be an expiation for that sin. And if one indulges in any of them, and Allah conceals his sin, it is up to Him to forgive or punish him in the Hereafter**". The Prophet added: '**Whoever among you fulfils his pledge will be rewarded by Allah**' **(Bukhari)**. However the *baya* the companions gave to the Prophet (pbuh) was also political, to give an oath of allegiance in support of his message and authority.

The *bay'a* is usually physically represented by a handshake or in the some cases, for females it depends on the *fiqh mazhab* of the student and the scholar, and what it allows. Scholars who do not shake hands with female students usually substitute this with holding a cloth between them or a stick, or putting hands at the same time into a vessel of water to symbolise the contract that was made. For female students it can also be done orally as is mentioned in some *Hadith* that the Prophet (pbuh) did. The *Sunnah* of giving and taking oaths of being obedient to God's laws have been kept alive in the oath between the students and scholars in the beginning of learning the branch of Ihsan. God says "**help each other to fulfil God's commands and to worship God, and not help each other to sins and aggression, and fear God, as God is severe in punishment**" (5:2). The *Baya* is the formal contract of learning between the scholar and the student, and it establishes the validity that the person became a student to that scholar. It also preserves the transmission of knowledge and gives it authenticity, and is a condition for qualifying as a scholar of Ihsan. *Baya* also acknowledges formal students who have rights on the scholar and differentiates them from informal students who are responsible for their own learning; i.e. those who are performing the first stage of Ihsan and those who are studying the second stage of the branch of Ihsan that does not include *tazzkiya*. God said in honouring these oaths **"those who make an oath with the Prophet, they in reality make an oath to God. God's hand is over their hand, and whoever breaks their oaths do so against their own benefit, and whoever is fulfilling of their oaths, will get a great reward."** (48:10). Please note that Allah's hand is a metaphorical statement to show His agreement of the allegiance that takes place.

The *baya* means that the student's knowledge and spiritual wellbeing has become the responsibility of the scholar. The Prophet (pbuh) said **'every shepherd is responsible for his particular flock'** (Bukhari). *Baya* also acts as consent for the scholar to evaluate the person, make judgment about them and look into their weaknesses, things that would be considered *haram* (forbidden) if it wasn't for their role as a scholar. The *baya* also means that the scholar's command must be followed by the student, for while all scholars can and do command to what is good, the carrying out of these commands is usually left for the individual person if they want to do them or not. This is in following the Quran that forbids compulsion in religion, and also as the commands are usually general and the individual may or may not require them. In Ihsan the commands are specific and individual and for the individual's benefit and spiritual growth, thus the person has no freedom in choosing not to do them. This is also part of the *baya* that the student becomes obedient to the scholar, as was the condition of the *baya* the Quran gave, and the student promises in their *baya*.

The Quran said '**will not disobey the Prophet in any just matter**' (60:12). The disobedience of the commands of the scholar after *baya* will constitute the breaking of the *baya*, and while this does not invalidate it, it means the person is breaking their promise to be obedient to God and the promise to Him to become more worshiping in making *baya*. The breaking of promises made to God are considered a great sin, and as thus scholars only give *baya* to the most serious of students and to others only when they reach maturity to appreciate the magnanimity of the pledge they make. The taking of *baya* is thus considered a higher level of piety and effort in worship, and it is considered serious to merit a great reward when performed and likewise a great punishment if broken. Scholars have been known to reject giving *baya* if they felt the student was not ready, and some asked students to return after a few years if the reason was the student's life circumstance that would make them unable to perform all necessary commands and higher level of worship e.g. a man who is newlywed or a woman who recently had a new child. This is not different from when the Prophet (pbuh) asked a companion to reduce the amount of his optional fasts, but the companion maintained his wish to fast more only to later regret not accepting the Prophet's suggestion and found it overwhelming, but at the same time had to maintain it as he had made a promise to perform it. Scholars evaluate if the person has the spirituality and ability to maintain the level of worship required in *Jihadul-nafs* and *nafila* of Ihsan.

As *baya* cannot be forced nor is it given easily, in fact it is common to find that some relatives of scholars may not be formal students of Ihsan. *Baya* does not change the person's character into the better or increase them spiritually instantly, and hence it is possible to meet people in gatherings of Ihsan scholars who may not show perfect character. *Baya* is also an unspoken apology to God and all those who the person may come to trouble, as it is an admittance of one's shortcoming, awareness of them and a wish to improve them. Most importantly taking *baya* shows an intention to want to worship God in the best possible way and making an effort to increase spiritually, something that will be to the person's benefit on the Day of Judgment.

It is not appropriate that once a student has taken *baya* from one scholar to request another *baya* from another scholar. This not only shows lack of commitment and seriousness, but also disrespects the first scholar and belittles the first *baya* for no valid reason. Nevertheless with the permission of their scholar or if they do not explicitly prohibit it, it is usually the case that scholars allow their student to learn from other scholars as informal students. A student must always remember that when they took *baya* they were not merely making it with the scholar but also with God, i.e. a promise to God to become a better Muslim and fulfil a branch of the religion. Whoever doesn't fulfil their *baya* and its rules is breaking a promise to God, and that is a great offence. Those who do not invalidate their *baya* by permanently leaving their scholar or not following their commands are among those who God praised as being **"among the believers are men who are truthful in fulfilling their oaths with God. Some of them already fulfilled their promise and some still await but have not changed and are still determined."** (33:23).

God said **'whoever obeys the Messenger obeys Allah.' (4:80)** and by extension those who obey their scholars, for the scholar only commands to that which God and His Messenger commanded. This makes the obeying of the scholars as obeying the Prophet (pbuh) and God. While those who lived in the time of the Prophet (pbuh) were commanded directly by the Prophet (pbuh), those who came after him do not have that benefit and are instead commanded by his 'heirs'; the scholars. The Prophet (pbuh) **said 'the scholars are the heirs of the prophets' (Abu Dawood).** God says **"those who obey God and His Messenger and reverence God and be pious they are the successful in religion" (24:52).** Those who disobey their scholars break their promise to God, and their punishment for this could be as severe as the reduction of their *iman* and for their belief to be replaced with hypocrisy, and that is a great punishment indeed. God says **"among them are those who promise God if he gives them from His generosity, they will give in charity and become among the righteous in religion. Then when God gave them from His generosity, they were miserly and refused to give from it in charity and turned away rejecting religion. God followed their sinful deeds with hypocrisy in their hearts, to the day they meet God, for breaking their promise with God and for their lies."** (9:75-77).

This serious consequence of breaking the *baya* needed to become a formal student of Ihsan, gives seriousness and value to the *baya* as well as making it a responsibility for the scholar to only give *bay'a* to those who they feel are serious enough not to break it. It is better to not make a promise to God than to make one and break it. This is not only in making the promise of piety of *baya* but any other promise to God, e.g. the giving in charity, fast or other worship as gratitude to God if a certain wish would come true- called in *fiqh*; *Nazr*, and that is the reason it is discouraged by the scholars if the person feels they may not fulfil it. The making of personal oaths by swearing on God's name to do a certain thing is also frowned upon, and for those who do not fulfil it they have to do expiation of it, which is called *kafarat Alyameen*. The Quran says "**God will not account harshly on swearing on His name, but will judge if a firm promise is broken. The fine for breaking a promise sworn on God's name, is to feel ten poor people and amount average to what they eat in their family, or giving them instead clothes, or freeing a slave, and whoever cannot do this to then fast for three days. This is the fine for a broken swear on God's name, in this way God clarifies His revelation so people would be grateful.**" (5:89). As the study of the second stage of Ihsan (*moragaba*) requires not *Jihadul-nafs*, and is based only on knowledge of God's presence and watchfulness over us, it is taught informally without *baya*. *Moragaba* is also taught by scholars of other branches, albeit it is basics. It is most normal to hear a *faqih* (scholar of *fiqh*) encouraging the perfection of worship and reminding of the watchfulness of God.

The branch of Ihsan is for all, the young and old, the men and women, as long as they are Muslim and *mukalaf* (those who are accounted by God, i.e. reached puberty and sane) and wish to fulfil all branches of their religion. The Messenger (pbuh) said **'God does not judge you according to your appearances and your wealth, but he looks at your heart and looks at your deeds' (Muslim)**. No paternal permission is required as is the case for physical *Jihad* but those who have not reached puberty are only given *baya* in exceptional circumstances where they have shown great maturity and spirituality.

The reason that children are not accounted by God for their deeds, even if they sin neither could they perform *Jihadul-nafs* is because they lack an ego. This manifests in that they are totally dependent on their parents, even to tell them to eat, bathe and sleep. Children usually are ignorant of the consequence of their actions, due to lack of general knowledge (e.g. that being in the sun too long is damaging or that touching broken glass or a hot object will hurt them), but more so because they lack an ego, i.e. ability to decide on what is best for the self, and are unaware of their own self. This is different from an adult, who may do what is wrong, e.g. go in the sun after being aware of the consequences and ignore them and instead follow their own want, their desire. This awareness that there is a self, that could be damaged or must be pleased in adults, shows the existence of the ego. A child's desires are also aimless and usually due to curiosity or familiarity, and not due to an innate desire that is from the ego. The ego normally develops around puberty and that is when the person becomes accountable for their deeds in Islam.

The *baya* that is made between the scholar and the student gives role and responsibilities to both the scholar and the students .The scholar's role is to make sure that the students have sound *aqida* and knowledge of basic *fiqh* before the student is given *baya*. They also choose their *nafila* worship and guide them through purification of the ego and its battle. The student's role is to learn at least basic *aqida* and matters of *fiqh*, *especially* correct *tahara* (purification) correct *salah*, fasting and other matters of worship deemed necessary. They should also listen to and be completely obedient to their scholar. As the scholar's authority on the student is in matters of *nafila,* in this the student must show complete obedience, and as the *Sufis* say 'be like a corpse in the hands of its washers'. The student must obey their scholars in what they prescribe of *nafila* worship and even if that means they ask to reduce or stop performing other *nafila* worship you set on yourself, or to modify one they previously approved. This must not be misunderstood as including *fard* (obligatory) worship, which no one has the right or power to moderate as no one has the right to stop what God commands, or to create new worship as *fard*.

This total obedience to the scholar is the weapon by which the person fights the *nafs*. The *nafs* is commanding by nature and wishes to have control over the person's action, and by transferring these powers to the scholar after taking *baya* and following what the scholar commands instead of the *nafs*, the *nafs* is defeated. The *nafs* is tricky and is considered by the scholars of Ihsan to be in 'partnership' with the devil (vulnerable to negative inspiration). The *nafs* can trick from purifying it by commanding that the person does not perform that which they are commanded by the scholar, and this is by commanding that you modify it, either by increasing it, decreasing or varying it. If after being given the *nafila* (usually a set of *zikr*) the person feels they want to change it, this is the *nafs* wanting to express its command or an evil inspiration and both of which must be ignored. The main way the *nafs* likes to trick is by commanding an increase in the *zikr* (or other *nafila*) as it sounds noble and appears a good thing, but in fact is disadvantageous as it means the needed *nafila* for purification is not being followed, as well as increasing the intensity of *zikr* which is usually followed by stopping it as each person at a certain spiritual state has a certain capacity for *zikr* and worship. And even if a *zikr* sounds little at first, it is not when considering the person will have to continue doing it on a regular basis. This is in following that the Prophet (pbuh) said **'God loves worship that is continuous even if little' (Bukhari).** The best way to avoid following the commands of the ego is to follow what the scholar commands in detail and not what your ego commands and to remember that by obeying the ego the person is defeating the whole purpose of purification that aims to make them no longer under the command of their ego and desires but the commands of Allah Most High.

Scholars become acquainted with their student's life in order to recognise their personality, spiritual needs, and even clues or evidence to diseases. They also try to solve their problems by giving both theoretical and practical help when this is possible, but this is not a right nor should it be expected when a scholar has not the means or many other students. In some areas scholars of Ihsan have been known to even act as matchmaker by suggesting marriage partners for their other students, or even providing jobs by requesting of their affluent students to help their fellow students in providing jobs. All this so students are not distracted by matters of the world and can concentrate on their worship. This was also the *Sunnah* of the Prophet (pbuh) who helped companions who were looking for jobs or wives. It is this element of helping people that has allowed the study of Ihsan to develop into brotherhoods; brotherhoods who are keen on helping others as much as each other.

There are students who decide to become dedicated to the worship of God and the service of the branch of Ihsan, in the manner of the companions of the *sufa* (platform), who included Abu Huraira (raa) as well as students who assist the scholar in the running of the school and catering for the needs of guests or new students. This dedication to worship does not go against the teachings of the religion that forbid becoming a monk or nun, for as was the state of the majority of the people of the *sufa*, these students do marry and have families. These students, like the companions of the *sufa* relied on the Prophet (pbuh) for their livelihood and scholars accommodated this by having guesthouses and student accommodation as well as enough provision. Nonetheless, it is not the role of scholars to provide for other students materially or guard them against harm by physically stopping them from what is a sin or harmful. Their main job and duty is to teach better understanding and practice of the religion, and if this is achieved then they have fulfilled their responsibility.

The teaching of Ihsan is based on two Islamic principles; on the scholars' side the principle of *'amr bi almaroof wa alnahi an almunkar';* **"command to what is virtue and discourage from what is sin" (9:71)**, and on the student's side the duty of seeking knowledge and guidance from the scholars and those of knowledge. The Quran says **"people**

should ask the people of the religious reminder is they do not know a thing in religion." (16:43). This means that when the scholar sees what is incorrect in the student from character, behaviour or worship, they correct them. The students must revert to scholars if they come across that which they do not understand or know, so that their scholar may provide them with what is correct. People of the remembrance, people of the knowledge of religion as through their study God is mentioned.

Scholars differ in their personalities and *paths* (different Ihsan schools of thoughts) differ on their *nafila* and this is out of God's mercy so that there will be people who cater to the needs of all sorts of people. Some people are very gentle and sensitive and require tender treatment by their scholars for them to become more confident in the path, while others are stubborn and require a scholar who has a strong character to humble them in the path. It is from the Prophet (pbuh) treatment to different companions scholars get the *Sunnah* of varying their style and tone with different students. The Prophet (pbuh) was light hearted with Zahir (raa) a Bedouin who was not very confident, while he was stern with Umar (raa) when he came to declare his conversion to Islam when his first intention was to come to kill the Prophet (pbuh). The Prophet (pbuh) grabbed Umar's (raa) shirt and shook him to the point that Umar (raa) fell to his knees. This was because Umar (raa) was tall and strong and known for his great bravery and confidence, as well as having a reputation for harassing the early Muslims. The Prophet (pbuh) wanted to give Umar (raa) the knowledge that God created those who were strong and courageous enough to face his might, i.e. the Prophet (pbuh). The Prophet (pbuh) was also more covering of himself in the presence of Othman (raa) a companion who was very modest.

It is possible and does happen that a scholar sends a student to study from another scholar even if in a different school if they felt that the student would benefit from this. This also happens if that new scholar or *tariqa* (path) are known for their deeper understanding of a certain spiritual state and thus can help to get the slave to rise to it. Schools of thought whilst all branched from common schools, developed in certain eras, when for political or historical reasons certain spiritual diseases became prevalent, and this required a change in method or the type of *nafila* given to students. In the early centuries after *hijra* when the Muslims became affluent the most prevalent spiritual disease was love of the *dunya*, and thus the early teachings emphasised *zuhd* (renunciation of the world). People of Ihsan must fulfil their oath with God. The Quran warns **"Those who break their oaths with God"**(2:27). God also says **"fulfil your oaths and God will fulfil His oath"** (2:40) meaning to perform worship and God will grant them Heaven. The Quran praises that some believers fulfil their oaths with God. God says **"from the believer are men who fulfilled their oaths with God. Some completely their oaths to the full, while others await to fulfil it but are still determined"**(33:33).

CHAPTER TWENTY THREE

THE OPTIONAL WORSHIP

In fighting and purifying the ego, we are commanded by God and the Prophet Muhammed (pbuh) to maintain moderation. As this then helps to maintain the body, soul, and mind in optimum state. This means that a balance should be maintained, for the way of Ihsan is not of deprivation nor excessiveness, because deprivation and excessiveness can be equally harmful to the body and the spirit. It is a fact that those who deprive themselves from eating sufficient food, drinking, and sleep as well as harming their bodies may also become delusional, hallucinate and may even become psychotic. This is not the way of the Messenger (pbuh) who fasted and ate, woke up in prayer and slept, and married. In fact it was in his wife's Aisha's (raa) company that revelation from God most often came. It is also the maintaining of balance that assures that spiritual experiences are truthful and are not mere hallucinations. The Prophet Muhammed (pbuh) said "**the best issues is in the middle**"(Iraqi).

> Revelation wasn't from hunger,
> So that it stopped when you ate
> Nor was it from lack of sleep,
> So that when you slept it was late

Nor was it stopped by having wives,
So that when with Aisha the Angel would need to wait
But (and thus) it was from God on high Who has the Power to create

Allah said in a *Qudsi* Hadith: **'My slave does not draw near to Me with anything more beloved to Me than what I have made obligatory on them. And my slave continues to draw near to Me with optional worship until I love them' (Bukhari).** Allah said that there is nothing more beloved to Him to gain His nearness than obligatory worship, i.e. worship which He commanded us to do and that it in the performing of optional worship – additional worship the person may choose to do that makes God love His slave. Thus we learn from this that *Jihadul-nafs* should be on a regime of *fard* (obligatory) and *nafila* (optional) worship. Both these types of worship should be derived from the Quran and Sunnah, and should be as are described by the scholars of *fiqh*.

The *fard* worship has been established in *Sharia* and is unchanging and the is same for all people, but the *nafila* (optional worship) is chosen by the scholar of Ihsan according to the individual's needs and circumstance as they see necessary. To derive benefit the worship is then coupled with a change in the person's character in taking the Prophet Muhammed (pbuh) as an example. The learning of good character is part of the branch of Ihsan, and the Quran describes those who have good characteristics, such as generosity, controlling anger and being forgiving as achievers of Ihsan, *Muhsinin*. God says **"those who spend while rich and while poor, and those who do not become angry, and those forgiving to people, and God loves those perfect in the worship of Ihsan."** (3:134). In improving the person's character the Prophet's (pbuh) character is taken as an example. This is because God described him as having **"great character"** (68:4) and that he is an example to take. God says in the Quran **"they have in the messenger of God a good example for those who look forward to the meeting with God and the last day, and mentions God much"** (33:21).

In the same way that we derive our *Aqida* and *Sharia* laws from the Quran and *Sunnah*, we derive our knowledge of states of the ego, struggling against the ego and its methods from the Quran and the Sunnah. In addition, we notice that *Jihadul-nafs* in other religions is taken to extremes of deprivation, even that of Christians who claim that their religion is of love and forgiveness and believe that Jesus died for their sins. We notice that the most religious and pious of them, the monks abstain from marriage, and take a regime of extreme deprivation from food, drink, speech and social life. This in Islam is called *Rahbana* and it is forbidden. In fact the Quran says it was not prescribed upon them. God says **"They did a monks worship they invented, that was not prescribed to them by God, but did it in seeking God's pleasure"** (57:27).

Rahbana is not a better worship nor does it please God more. What is true worship and most acceptable to God is what He prescribes upon us. In a *Qudsi* Hadith God says '**My slave does not draw near to Me with anything more beloved to Me than what I have made obligatory on him' (Bukhari).** It is our obedience to what He commands us that gets us His pleasure. To invent our own worship and command it on ourselves and others shows arrogance, as it means we are assuming a right that is only God's, for only He can dictate what worship is and how we should express our obedience to Him. *Rahbana* (becoming a monk or nun) shows extreme deprivation from what is normal and what we need, and as thus goes against human nature and needs. To do what is against human capability is suffering and is thus punishment and goes against the mercy of God. God says **"God does not ask of people, except what they are capable of doing of worship"** (2:286). Seeing as it causes suffering it goes against the teachings of the Islamic religion of not just causing injustice against the self and others, but most importantly, it is pointless suffering, as it was not commanded. Islam teaches us to ask God to relive us of what we find overwhelming to practice, not overburdening ourselves. The Quran says pray **"Lord, do not command people to beyond their capacity"** (2:286).

Prophet Muhammed (pbuh) was sent with mercy and his mercy comes in teaching us the correct knowledge of our Lord and His worship. This understanding of his Lord is reflected in his *Sunnah* (way) of *Jihadul-nafs* and in his worship of God. He (pbuh) fasted and ate, worshiped during the night and slept, and married. Allah is The Mighty, The Majestic and The powerful so he fasted, worshiped during the night, and was many times silent, but his Lord is also The Compassionate, The Beneficent and The Loving thus he ate, slept, talked and married. This moderation in worship is also because God commanded that we worship Him in a state of 'fear and hope'. God says, **"they desert their beds to pray to the Lord in fear and greed, and from what they are given they give in charity"** (32:16). This is referring to the fear of God's punishment and the hope of Him answering our prayers and providing us with His bounties in this world and reward of paradise in the hereafter. The Quran says **"people should not worship anything except God, and the Prophet was sent from God as a warner about the hellfire and to give hope of Heaven."** (11:2). This means that while the Prophet (pbuh) was sent to warn people of the punishment of God if they disobey His commandants, he was also sent to give hope of an everlasting life in paradise to those who believe and worship God.

When the Prophet Muhammed (pbuh) was told that a companion promised to fast daily, another promised to pray all night daily and a third made a vow of celibacy, he (pbuh) said that his *Sunnah* (way) is to be moderate in fasting, night prayer and other worship and to marry, and that those who abandon this have abandoned his way (Bukhari). It is the command of God for Muslims to follow what the Prophet (pbuh) teaches. God says **"what the Messenger gives, the believers should take and what he prohibits them should refrain from"** (59:7). Those who wish to worship God more must do so in the example and command of the Prophet (pbuh) by not going into extremes of deprivation or worship. This is based on the fact that deprivation and excessive worship leads to harm to the person and may also harm their religion if it leads the person to stop worship due to spiritual overwhelming. It is also in following the Prophet (pbuh) that the slave gains the love of God. The Quran says **"whoever loves God should follow Muhammed, and God will love them back, and forgives their sins and God is forgiving and merciful."** (3:31). This means that as people of Ihsan, who love God and want God to love them, they must follow the Prophet Muhammed (pbuh) in everything in worship and religion.

CHAPTER TWENTY FOUR

THE MENTION OF GOD

Zikr is the mention, or remembrance of God. *Tazakr* is remembers, *'zakira'* is memory in Arabic. In Islam, the word zikr means the mention of God, His glorification and praise. It is a formal type of worship in Islam, commanded by the Quran and was exampled by Prophet Muhammed (pbuh) himself.

For the *nafila* to be chosen by a person other than the person performing the *nafila* is *Sunnah*. The Prophet (pbuh) used to prescribe the *nafila* for companions e.g. Ibn Umar (raa) who the Prophet (pbuh) commanded to perform night prayer. The Prophet (pbuh) said **'what a great slave of God Ibn Umar is indeed if only he performed night prayer' (Bukhari)**. The *nafila* does not have to be direct worship of God; the Prophet (pbuh) commanded one of the companions to learn a foreign language. Although this command was to benefit the Muslim community that they would be able to communicate clearly with other communities in their own language, it nevertheless was still a *nafila* for worldly acts done for the cause of the religion or the benefit of people as an act of worship and rewarded by God. This example teaches us that *nafila* does not have to be a certain *zikr* or other direct worship. Some scholars may not subscribe worship to students who assist in the running of the school when they feel that their carrying out of tests under the scholar's command is sufficient for their spirituality and *Jihadul-nafs*. This principle of helping people as a form of *nafila* is much emphasised in many Ihsan schools. *Ajr* (reward) is based on the number of people it will help.

Scholars of Ihsan differ in their methods of teachings; some allow their students to study books of Ihsan independently and freely learn from other scholars, while others are stricter and expect their student to ask permission before reading books or studying with other scholars. This is because reading books and listening to scholars is a religious activity, and what they prescribe from *nafila* will depend on how much they feel the person requires of worship, and other extra worship unknown to the scholar could overwhelm that. When a student asks permission the scholar becomes aware of what the student is learning and their level of knowledge as it changes. It is usually acceptable reading biographies of the prophets (pbuh), the pious and books of character and spiritual diseases without having a scholar or their permission to do so, but the rest require that the person has guidance or at least permission.

The majority of schools of Ihsan if not all make *zikr,* as their *nafila. Zikr* literally means remembrance, but it is used to mean the remembrance and praise of God. This is praise and remembrance of God by reciting and repeating His name and attributes verbally and asking His forgiveness and mercy, as well as praying for peace and blessing upon the Prophet Muhammed (pbuh). This choice of *zikr* is because relatively it is easy to do, anyone can perform it, as opposed to fasts and night prayer which need physical fitness, charity which requires financial ability, or *umrah* (pilgrimage) which requires means of time, money and physical fitness. Nevertheless, the command to have a portion of the night in worship doing *zikr* or *salah* is considered the most difficult and highest *nafila* to do, and is ascribed to the most advanced students. As the student progress in their study of Ihsan it is normal for the scholar to increase the intensity of their *nafila,* increasing their *zikr* from a few dozens or hundreds, to thousands or hundreds of thousands a day.

The *zikr* achieves two purposes; firstly remembrance of God restrains from sins as a few sins are done whilst remembering God and His punishment. It also acts as a sufficient *nafila* to make God love the slave, providing knowledge of God and increasing the person's awareness of God's attributes and hence helping the person to develop Love for God. Lastly *zikr* has great *ajr* (reward) with God. When it comes to spiritual development, knowledge of the spiritual states is the map, while *zikr* is the power and fuel. God commands **"those who believe, should mention God much praising Him"** (33:41). The Prophet Muhammed (pbuh) said *zikr* is **'the best of deeds, the most beloved to God, the most elevating of the person's spiritual station, and better than giving gold and silver in charity, and fighting in battle for the sake of God' (Tirmizi).**

As well as there being *tazzkiya* from spiritual diseases, there is *tazzkiya* from disbelief and heedlessness of God. When a person enters a state of Islam, they become spiritually pure, and this purity increases with the mention and knowledge of God. Purity is a gain in goodness and cleanness, and the person whose lifestyle does not include the spiritual is said to be in a state of spiritual impurity. The accepting of God's commandments to good, the purity comes in encompassing God as it adds a spiritual dimension of goodness to one's life. It is not a physical thing, but that holding impure belief about God or lack of correct belief leaves the person spiritually impure, if to say also not correct in religion.

To make *zikr* be most effective, there are guidelines from the Quran and the *Sunnah*, as well as techniques developed by those who practiced this branch. These should be used by students who have taken *baya* as well as those who practice the second stage of Ihsan, for they can make the *zikr* more beneficial. While students who have taken *baya* will be given a certain amount to do, those without *baya* should choose an amount they can maintain even if little. The Prophet Muhammed (pbuh) *zikr* following *salah* was limited to certain numbers, some praises of God he limited to thirty three times (e.g. *Allahu akbar* - God is Great), others just once. The limiting of the number of *zikr* to a certain number means there will be steadiness, and by limiting to a certain number there is less risk of going to excess as the person will stop as soon as the number is done. Making *zikr* limited to a certain number also makes it more affective in *Jihadul-nafs* otherwise it will be left for the student to decide, increasing and decreasing it depending on their ego's desire. As the amount of *zikr* is chosen by the teacher to remedy the student's spiritual disease, less *zikr* could mean that it is less effective and more *zikr* is not necessary. The same *zikr* on a regular basis brings a sense of easiness and stability while a *zikr* that is not limited or counted can create a sense of unpredictability that can bring a state of uneasiness or agitation as the person becomes less organised, or it can create excess spirituality when it is much. Because there are other obligations on the person worldly or otherwise *zikr* cannot be left unmeasured, and by limiting it allows the person to then be able to do their other responsibilities.

The other reason the *nafila* should at least be partly consistent of *zikr* is because in *zikr* there is the most mention of God; fasting is based on the ability to restrain and *salah* is mainly physical movements but *zikr* is entirely the mention of God and His Messenger. To realise the existence of God and thus strengthen *iman*, requires that the person remembers God's existence and this is achieved by repetitively remembering Him in *zikr*. *Zikr* is a very pure worship, as it can be done without people knowing, unlike fasting, or praying which people can see and therefore there is less risk of *riya (*religious ostentation). In order to bring the mind attention to God alone, the *zikr* should be simple, not complex like reading a chapter of the Quran, which as it contains *zikr* also mentions other than God. A Quranic chapter can hold many different topics that vary from worldly conduct to description of the hereafter and thus would not keep the concentration on God alone, as does *zikr*. Hence as the person spiritually develops their *zikr* should be more cantered on the mention of God. This can be to the extent that scholars do their *zikr* by the mention of God's name alone saying '*Allah Allah…*'. The Prophet (pbuh) said the world will not end as long as there are people saying **'Allah Allah' (Muslim).** The *zikr* of just repeating God's name *Allah* is not advisable to beginners, as when an advanced student or scholar says 'Allah', they know what they mean, as are knowledgeable of God, and come to know deeply His names and Attributes and what they mean, but this is not the case for most beginners. The other reason is that it is very powerful spiritually, and thus beyond the capacity of those new to the branch. This is because when done properly it can lead to high spiritual states, which can lead to *hal* such as uncontrolled movement like the companions who hopped, or losing consciousness like Moses (as) in the mountain. The mention of God, and the knowledge of His Majesty and Greatness, act like a strike of information that causes an overwhelming of the mind and body and an instant tiredness and sleep that induces fainting, or causes the soul to raise so quickly that it mimics sleep or death.

On the first few times when the person starts to make *zikr*, it can be difficult to concentrate especially if the person has many worries or concerns. The person might feel they are saying the words while they are not, at the same time being aware of their meanings as their mind diverts from one topic to another. But this does not mean that the person should give up but instead to continue doing the *zikr* even if they are not concentrating, for after a while they do. It is advised by some Ihsan scholars that at the beginning when the student is starting to make *zikr* they visualise their scholar in front of them in order to focus their attention. But also as it is the case that in the presence of the scholar they are most disciplined, visualising the scholar adds this dimension to their session of *zikr*. In the beginning it is possible that the person's *iman* may not be strong enough to really mean the words they utter in *zikr*. In this case they could seek knowledge in finding out proof for the individual praises of God, so that their words are spoken out of belief. Learning more about the magnificence and complexity of the natural world, really helps so that every *Subhan Allah* (glory to God), is said with full meaning and belief. If the person feels their *iman* is very low, then they should not leave it to the last minute in which it would be too late, but instead study the religion, and ask those of knowledge to learn more and further strengthen their belief.

In non-beginners the making of *zikr* without meaning could be considered a spiritual state of hypocrisy. God says **"They say with their tongues what is not in their hearts"** (48:11). Thus when saying the words, the student should concentrate on their meanings, e.g. when saying *Subhan Allah* (Glory to God) they should remember the complexity of the universe and then say the words out of truthfulness. When saying *Alhamdulillah* (praise to God) remember God's gifts on us. When saying *Allahu Akbr* (God is great), recognise the enormity of the world, and recognise that it can only be made by a God who is greater. When sending greetings of peace and blessing to the Prophet (pbuh), say them while remembering who the Prophet (pbuh) was, what he did, and why he is worthy of greeting and this comes from knowledge of his *seerah* (biography) as well as our own benefit of the religion that came to us from him. The person should also send prayers to the Prophet (pbuh) knowing that he (pbuh) is of no need of our prayers even if billions, for God and His angels send their blessings into him. God says **"Allah and His angels send blessings on the Prophet Muhammed"** (33:56). This removes the incorrect feeling that the person is doing the Prophet (pbuh) a favour, and teaches the truth that it is us who benefit. The Prophet Muhammed (pbuh) said **'for every prayer of peace sent to me, God sends ten prayers of peace to the person who sends them'** (Muslim). Sending peace and blessing onto the Prophet (pbuh) is commanded by God in the Quran and by doing it we obey God's command. God says **'Allah and His angels send blessings on the Prophet Muhammed, so those who believe should likewise send prayers of peace and blessings upon him"** (33:56). This is to teach us to be grateful and show respect to the one who without we wouldn't have been Muslims or learned the way to know or worship God.

After initial difficulties the person then may find that they enjoy making *zikr* much that they wish to do much more, but the person must restrain and only perform what their scholar has prescribed without modification. Those practicing the second stage must also try and maintain their usual amount, because if they increase their *zikr* (or any other optional worship) they will find that it is difficult to do the next time they want to, while if they stick to their certain count that is not the case. The Prophet (pbuh) said **'God loves act of worship that are steady even if little' (Bukhari),** and as excessiveness can lead to the person becoming overwhelmed and neglected, by maintaining the amount the person is more likely to continue on the same worship and thus be doing what God loves. Recognise that the desire to want to increase the amount of *nafila* isn't a desire of the spirit or goes with the teachings of the religion or the command of God that obliges to maintain the amount of *nafila* prescribed by the scholar, but it is the command of the ego and must be ignored. By following the command of the ego the person goes backwards in the path of purification, because the exercise of keeping a certain amount of worship aims to purify the person from the commands of the ego. The Prophet (pbuh) said a person's family and body have a right over them, and controlled worship means that the person will not be denying them or their own body of their rights. This means that it is important to take breaks from *zikr*, maintain prescribed *nafila* worship and not go into excess in worship.

While the student may become enthusiastic for making much *zikr*, when choosing the amount of *zikr* the scholars do be aware that this will need to be continued for long periods of time. They also take into consideration that life circumstances change, and this could mean the person is less able to maintain their *nafila*. This was the case of a companion who while the Prophet (pbuh) suggested less worship for him, reminding him that for every good deed God gives the reward of ten, he insisted that he was spiritually capable and begged the Prophet (pbuh) to allow him to fast much, but when he grew in age he admitted that he wished he accepted the Prophet (pbuh) original prescription (Bukhari). Those who are practicing the second stage of Ihsan and have not taken *baya* are free to make their own choice of the type of *nafila*, *zikr* or their amount, nevertheless should also keep a balanced life in order to fulfil other duties. Asking the scholar to increase the amount of *zikr* is not typical as the scholar usually does that without prompt if they think the student needs to, but the student should feel no hesitation in asking their scholar for permission for taking up other types of *nafila* such as fast.

The *nafila*, as well as containing what the student needs for their *tazzkiya*, should be based on and in addition to an existing *Sunnah* of the Prophet (pbuh). In *zikr* this means the prescribed for *tazzkiya* should be on top of the *Albaqiyat Alsalihat,* which is to say *Subhan Allah* thirty three times, *Alhamdulillah* thirty three times and *Allahu Akbar* thirty three times, which the Prophet (pbuh) did after prayer (Muslim). If the *nafila* is prayer then that should also be in addition to the *Sunnah* prayer, and the same if it was fast and so forth. The Prophet (pbuh) worship incorporated all *nafila's*, for his worship was most frequent and intense, so we have his example and direction in all types of worship.

The intensity of the *zikr* depends on its amount and frequency and they are chosen to be such that the person regularly remembers God. The Quran recommends that the *zikr's* intensity to be on the intensity of the mentioning and remembering of people of their fathers. God says **"when the pilgrimage is finished, mention God in praise, as used to mention fathers in praise or even greater to that"** (2:200). This verse was revealed about the disbelievers of Qurish who after they finished their pilgrims loudly mentioned their forefathers. They mentioned their forefathers as they were proud of them. The Quran demands that Muslims be more proud of God and thus to mentioning Him more than their own forefathers or what else they are passionate about. This verse also means that the intensity of *zikr* should be proportional to the remembrance of the person's worldly dealings, for they are a main cause of heedlessness of God. All worldly dealings require people to reveal their father's (or family's) name and this means that with greater worldly dealings the more the mention of their fathers. This verse demands that the mention of God should be based on the level the people mention their father, making the intensity of *zikr* to be subjective, and based on the amount of worldly dealings. It is the case that as the person's worldly dealings increases it is easier to become heedless of God and religion as the person concentrates on their worldly tasks. This verse commands that the intensity of the mention of God to be in parallel to that of worldly remembrance, in order to prevent the slave from becoming heedless. This is exemplified in that in many *Hadith* the Prophet (pbuh) commands to make mention of God on entering markets, as a person can easily become distracted and become heedless. This verse also encourages to the making of *zikr,* as it notes that people make much mention and remembrance of their families when it is God who is more worthy of mention and remembrance.

During *zikr* it is normal for the person to enter a state of *fana* and become unconscious of their self as they come to concentrate on the mentioning of God. This is called *fanaul nafs fi zikr*. The temporary absence of the ego brings with it a sense of peace and contentment that give a taster to *Motul nafs*; death of the ego. God says **"those who believe and their hearts feel peace and find comfort in the mention of God, should not the hearts find comfort in the mention of God."** (13:28). The intensity and length of this increases as the person progress up the path. If this state happens too intensely or for too long it may be required to lower the amount of *zikr* the student is doing, as long states of *fana* is a sign of spiritual overwhelming. The frequency of the *zikr* should be that it is performed at least during the morning and the evenings. This is taken from the Quranic verse that describes the worship of those who seek nearness to Allah. Allah says to the Prophet, **"Send not away those who call on their Lord morning and evening, seeking His face"** (6:52) and **"the Prophet should be patient with those who pray in the** morning and evening wanting God's face and not to look away from them wanting the beauty of the world" (18:28). If the intensity is to be increased, this could be done by increasing its frequency to include making it during other times of the day. God says **"glorify God in praise before sunrise and before sunset, and parts of the night they should glorify God, and the ends of day to gain acceptance of God"** (20:130). The Prophet (pbuh) performed *zikr* after every *salah* and this spread *zikr* throughout the day as the verse recommends. This also fulfils another command to make *zikr* after prayer, God says **"when the prayer is finished, to mention God"** (4:103).

The student should have a special place for their worship, one where they are not distracted nor distract. The Quran mentions Mary, Jesus' mother (as) as having such a place, God says **"every time that he entered her prayer chamber to see her, He found her supplied with food from God"** (3:37). As to manners of making *zikr*, God says **"remember the Lord with humility and in reverence, without shouting the words, in the mornings and evenings; and be not of those who are unheedful"** (7:205). While *zikr* can be done in all positions, the three mentioned in the Quran are whilst sitting, standing or lying on their side. God says **"those who remember Allah, standing, sitting, and reclining"** (3:191). *Zikr* made after *salah* is usually made in the sitting position, while group *zikr,* made as weekly boosters in Ihsan schools are usually made while standing, but in a few schools whilst sitting. Sitting is a good position for *zikr* as it shows humility, and is closer to prostration which the Prophet (pbuh) said is the closest position to God. *Zikr* made lying is mainly for when the person is ill or it is late evening or early morning *zikr*.

The *zikr* should be varied with many different praises of God that are each few in number than few types of praises that are each many in number. *Zikr* can be done for two purposes: when it is for *tazzkiya* and increasing spirituality, it is done on a repetitive manner with each praise of God being repeated, but *zikr* done for *ajr* is different. *Zikr* done for the main purpose of *ajr* is done by description, e.g. Glory to

God as many times as there are stars, or many peace and blessings upon the Prophet as there are grains of sand in a desert. When the Prophet (pbuh) found his wife Juwairiya bint Alharith (raa) making *zikr* for a long time, he taught her to say instead **'Glory to God as many times as are His creation, Glory to God in a manner and number that pleases Him, Glory to God as is the beauty of His throne, and Glory to God unlimited as are His words' (Muslim).** This was because as a wife of the Prophet (pbuh) she had many duties, and repetitive *zikr* would take too much of her time, and in this way she was to gain as much *ajr* and even more in less time. Scholars of Ihsan have formulated many condensed *zikr* and the most famous and widely used is Sheikh Aljezuli's (raa) *Dalail al khairat* which is based on making much praise on the Prophet Muhammed (pbuh). There is also *Jarid* mention of God, which is to slowly pull the prayer beads instead of counting bead by bead, and this is done in accepting God as rewarding greater reward than deeds.

Zikr can be done in *jahr* (loud) or *sir* (silent), but combining the two is the best method as it allows the person to ponder on the meanings, while a fluent *zikr* that is all loud or all silent is easy to lose concentration doing. Some companions did *zikr* loud like Umar (raa) as he wanted others to hear God's praises too, while others like Abu Bakr (raa) were known to have worshiped quieter. The permission of loud or silent zikir comes in the following verse, God says **"people can speak in public or in secret, and still God is knowing of what is in people's hearts"** (67:13). The person gets the benefit of both, but more importantly the effort to change from loud to silent alternatively is one of the best ways to maintain concentration on the meanings and benefit from *zikr*. This is especially helpful for beginners or those who have trouble concentrating. In addition, silent *zikr* is less inclined to *riya*, and acts to take the person from the physical world and sounds of the lips to the spiritual inner world of the spirit. In Islam there is also symbolic *zikr*, which is the lifting of the index finger of the right hand during *salah* to mean 'one', i.e. *Tawheed* of Allah. Concentrating while making *zikr* shows reverence, but also allows the person to understand the meanings of the *zikr*, and this is particularly important as *zikr* isn't about exercising the lips (even though the person gets *ajr* for every letter they make with their lips) but mentioning of God and praising him, and this is not sincere if the words are said without the person believing in their meanings or worse, not even being aware of them. For *zikr* to be effective in increasing the person's Iman and *tazzkiya* it must be done with sincerity, with the person being aware of the meanings and accepting them. This can also be achieved by making sure the person understands the meaning of the words and saying the words at a rate that is not too fast so that they do not contemplate the meanings.

Spiritually the two main things *zikr* impacts are the physical deeds and level of *iman,* making it the greatest worship a person can do. The more *zikr* the person makes the more their belief in God (as they remember Him more) increases, and by being in remembrance of God and the religion, the more good deeds they do the less sins they make. Nevertheless the most important and beneficial effect of *zikr* is increasing the person's spiritual station and elevating their souls in the heavens. In Sufism there is public mass mention of God, because when all people agree on celebrating the name of God who is the epitome of goodness, it is an unsaid expression of peace and safety between people. In Sudan, Sufis use prayer beads from the Balanites fruit called Laloob in Arabic, and since Laloob means "no bends" to mean being straight, it is used symbolically to mean they are straight and sincere and truthful to God in the worship. In Sudan they beat drums in mass mention of God in circles as a way of celebrating the name of God. They at the same time loudly repeat the name of God (*Allah*), and they dance by moving up and down at the same time that they bring their fists to their waist. This dance is supposed to mean purity to God since the waist is the place of the dirty genitalia and they moving their body from it means to negate meaning of impurity. Other Sufis such as those in Egypt turn from side to side to do a half circle to symbolise purity. The dervishes also whirl and spin to mean need since the circle is a shape symbolising need due to its many bends compared to a straight line, and they mean their need to see the Face of God. Other sufis jump at the mention of the name of God, to mean not leaving until granted Vision, and it is a way of expressing instance by not changing position. The Quran commands celebrating the name of God, God says "**they should celebrate the grace and mercy of God it is better than celebrating harvest**" (10:58).

The mention of God (Zikr) has many benefits: not only does it bring us closer to God, and increase our love of God, the inner peace that results can be good for our spirit. It also creates an attachment between us and God, and thus purifies us from worldly desires. Zikr also protects us from the devil; it is an easy worship that can brighten the face and soften the heart. Zikr also makes other worship easy, strengthens our Iman, and can bring us more luck and grace.

CHAPTER TWENTY FIVE

THE RESPONDING SPIRIT

The religion expects there to be a response to its teachings, the Quran says **"those who believe in God should obey God and the messenger of God when they command to what gives life"** (8:24). Likewise the spirit can respond to the mention of God and spirituality in practicing Ihsan. The love of God and His Messenger can get to such levels that it can lead to states of spiritual ecstasy, called *hal* (lit. state). Spiritual ecstasy can impact our faculties temporarily and lead to one of five states depending on its magnitude. It can impact the mind leading to linguistic confusion, and an example of this is the man mentioned in the Hadith to have confused his prayer saying '**Lord, you are my servant and I am your lord' (Muslim)** in happiness after finding his lost camel in the middle of the desert. The Prophet (pbuh) then added **'the man made a mistake from the intensity of his emotion' (Muslim)**. This state of ecstasy can happen when a person has found a new meaning in the Quran and/or Hadith, or learned something new in the religion or greater still increasing in the knowledge of God or becoming aware of God's presence that it makes them very happy that they become spiritually ecstatic. Sometimes their words could be so muddled up that they do not make sense, in which case the terminological word for it is '*tarjam*' (lit. translation), used to mean the spiritual and emotional ecstasy is being translated into the physical world. There is a Hadith that this state happened to one of the wives of the Prophet (pbuh). In English it is referred to as 'speaking in tongues' or glossolalia.

Spiritual ecstasy can also impact the emotions causing emotional confusion, leading the person to cry when happy or laughing when they are sad. Aisha (raa) said her father Abu Bakr (raa) was so happy when he found out that he was going to be the Prophet (pbuh) partner in *hijra* (migration) that he cried out of happiness. The state of ecstasy can also affect the physical body leading to increase movement like the companions who did *hijla* (hopped) in happiness in a circle around the Prophet (pbuh) when he (pbuh) praised them and said they were similar to him in the way they looked and in their manners (Ahmed). Or when great it could impact consciousness leading to loss of consciousness as it happened to Moses (as) after seeing the mountains tremble from the majesty of God; out of awe of God he fainted. These happen, as real and sincere emotions increase in intensify to the point that they manifest in the actions of the person. While the overwhelming of spiritual emotions is praiseworthy as it shows intensity of belief and love of God and love of His Messenger, excess emotion due to materialistic or worldly reasons is blameworthy and is frowned upon by the religion. Islam forbids excess mourning at funerals by loud screaming and very loud crying, and the Prophet Muhammed (pbuh) was described as smiling in situations that made others laugh (Bukhari). This is because they are not seen as worthy of such emotion, for the greatest loss would be loss from not doing worship and the greatest happiness should come from God and His worship. The Prophet (pbuh) also said **'The person who is strong is not one who could control their epilepsy but one who could control their anger' (Muslim).** Thus is the command to control emotion and praising it in Islam. That the real strength isn't in controlling the physical body, but in not reacting to the emotions of the heart.

The increase in intensity of spiritual emotions to the point that they affect our mind, body and soul are expected due to the magnificence of spirituality and majesty of God. The Quran says **"God revealed the best speech as a holy book of similar phrases to emphasise. Their skin stand on end in reverence of the Lord, then their skins and hearts become soft to the mention of God. That is the guidance of God, He guides whom He wishes and those misguided by God, find none to guide them back to God."** (39:23). This is to say that the Quran mentioning in truth of the punishment that God has strikes fear in people that their skin shivers in fear, but then the knowledge of God's Mercy and the fact that He is forgiving relaxes them that their skin moistens from perspiration as they relax (like exercise) and their hearts become soft in peace. In essence it described the Quran as impacting people to the point that it manifests in them physically. The response of the spirit to the mention of God, in order to gain spiritual experiences, is because the grandeur of God overwhelms the senses, and can lead to trances.

God says about lack of response is because their hearts have hardened, and became stone which is the most stable and lacking in motion of objects, while response is to move and change to command. The Quran says **"their hearts became hard after this, as if stones or stronger in hardness like rocks. However, some rocks bring our rivers, and some rocks crack open and water exist from them, and other rocks fall in reverence of God, and God is not distracted from knowing what people do"** (2:74).

Difference between spiritual 'perplexity' and spiritual 'intoxication':

Intense spiritual experiences can lead to a state of perplexity of being spiritually overwhelmed and it is sometimes called "drowning". Spiritual overwhelming is called intoxication when it impacts the mind and causes confusion and wrong believes, utterances or acts. This is symbolised by wine offered to Prophet Muhammed (pbuh) on his night journey to

God. In poetry the Sufis are famous for using the concept of alcohol as a symbol to say Sufism is so perfect and will not change from it, to mean it is the end just as alcohol is produced by the end of fermentation. Witnessing the face of God after death of the ego leads to either a state of *hera* (perplexity) or a state of *sukr* (intoxication).

Perplexity or bewilderment happens to those who have, understand and maintain knowledge of *Aqida* throughout. Their perplexity is a sign of awe and of overwhelming by the Majesty of God that is beyond the comprehension of their minds. Becoming bewildered is praiseworthy state as the Prophet (pbuh) used to repeat "glory to God" (*Subhan Allah*) as a way of expressing the grandeur of God. Some after death of the ego get into a state of Sukr (intoxication) a state of losing one's mind (*aql*). In the absence of the intellect one can misunderstand things and become unable to differentiate (e.g. between creation and Creator) as those are faculties of the intellect. The lack of *aql* is not a lack of thinking, but lack of correct thinking. The mind functions to understand and contain *Aqida*, so as soon as the intellect becomes un-functioning due to the state of intoxication, the person's *Aqida* then becomes very vulnerable to change. Hence, in the Quran drunks are commanded not to pray as prayer is for those with a mind that understands that there is a God and there is His creation who are commanded to worship, which is difficult to grasp in a state of intoxication. Also mad people who lose their *Aql* are excused from worship duty due to their inability to differentiate or grasp the concept of difference between Creator and creation. The Prophet (pbuh) made *dua* (prayer) to Allah to aid him with **"*Sakarat al mot* (drunkenness of death)"** (Tirmidi) which Al Gadi Ayad (raa) said it's because the 'intensity of the experience of death leads the person to lose their mind' in his explaining of the *aya* (Quranic verse) that talks about *Sakarat al mot*. **"And the drowsiness of death will bring truth, this is what they tried to escape"** (50:19). Seraj Ahmed (raa) in his explanation of Tirmizi said, 'death brings a state of confusion and perplexity that brings a state of heedlessness'.

The state of intoxication leads the person to disregard and not contemplate knowledge of *Aqida* or not taking explanations of their spiritual experiences from Quran and Sunnah, leading them to saying or believing lies about themselves and God. These believers are brought back their *aql* by *Aqida*, reminding them of it, and of the Quran and what it teaches us about God. To prevent this from happening, people should always increase their knowledge and have firm *Aqida* before embarking on the path of the ego death.

To state the importance of guarding the intellect and maintaining a clearly functioning mind, Islam prohibits the intake of alcohol and drugs that influence the mind, by making them haram. One of the reasons Mohammed (pbuh) was sent was to take us from the type of spiritual intoxication that existed in previous religions, for it is the misunderstanding of God which defeats the whole point of religion. In the Quran we are commanded to remind the believers of God, for it brings benefit to them. We remind them of God by telling them what was said about the vision and its chapters in the Quran, for it brings knowledge to them of what they are experiencing. This intoxication that comes with death is what has led the the Imams of Islam to say be both a scholar and Sufi (*fagih wa sufi*) and warned that if you be a Sufi without knowledge of revelation you go astray.

On the night Allah's Apostle was taken on a night journey, two cups, one containing wine and the other milk, were presented to him at Jerusalem. He looked at it and took the cup of milk. Gabriel said, **"Praise be to Allah Who guided you to Al-Fitra (the right path); if you had taken the cup of wine, your nation would have gone astray."** (Bukhari). In another Hadith in the heavens after meeting the Prophets he was offered the two cups and **"Gabriel said, 'Drink whichever you like.' I took the milk and drank it. Gabriel said, 'You have accepted what is natural, (True Religion i.e. Islam) and if you had taken the wine, your followers would have gone astray"** (Bukhair) this scene was also repeated in Al-Bait-ul-Ma'mur (i.e. the Sacred House) and then at Sidrat-ul-Muntaha (i.e. the Lote Tree of the utmost boundary, both mentioned in Bukhari. The word for astray is "*Tagat umatak*" something the Quran describes about Pharaoh, interesting that those who become intoxicated claim divinity like pharaoh. Difference is those pharaoh *taga* because of his arrogance and ignorance, and intoxicated because they lack knowledge or were heedless of it or misunderstood it. This is like the Sufi Alhallaj who said "*Ana Alhag*", meaning 'I am the Truth' which could be interpreted as he is claiming divinity. It would be lack of knowledge to say Alhallaj was like pharaoh, in the same way that Khidir would be accused of being a criminal.

The wisdom of having a cup of milk and wine of knowledge and confusion, as things are known by their opposite. Also, there is always a choice, there is no compulsion in religion. These Hadith explains to us why the Prophet (pbuh) and his companions (raa) were not intoxicated by God's love and thus professing false phrases such as '*Ana Alhag*' (I am God). It is because they maintained a sober mind by drinking the milk of knowledge. These Hadith also teaches that spiritual intoxication isn't a praiseworthy station as it will lead one astray. As it is not sunnah to get intoxicated, increase the intake of knowledge before journeying to your lord and throughout the journey. Know that the perplexity as a result of the Majesty and Greatness of God puts the slave in a position to gaining greater understanding of the verses that talk to us about God, and thus making us more worshiping of Him.

> For You Lord the women do Jihad(*Jihadul-nafs*)
> And the men cried their eyes
> By seeing You the knowledgeable are speechless
> And the spiritually intoxicated yelled their lies

CHAPTER TWENTY SIX

SPIRITUAL OPENINGS

In Islam when a supernatural event that breaks the normal laws of nature occurs it is a spiritual opening. When this happens for a Prophet e.g. the splitting of the sea for Moses (as), Prophet Abraham (as) not being burned by the fire or the splitting of the moon for Prophet Mohammed (pbuh) it is called a *Mujiza* (miracle). This is also the case if it happens to the believers in the lifetime of a Prophet as it is also attributed to proving the Prophet's Prophethood. When a supernatural occurs to a believer, the pious or saints it is called a *Karama* (pl. *karamat*). When we are born into the world we do not know what is possible or impossible, but then as we grow we learn what is normal and possible, and what is not possible, impossible. The spiritual opening is the breaking of these absolute laws.

A miracle or *karama* is the happening of what would be considered impossible except by the power and might of God, and thus they are signs and proof of His existence. Nevertheless, even normal laws are signs of God, even when we do not notice their magnificence. The fact that birds can fly, that living things can heal or repair themselves, and that from small things such as seeds can grow large trees. With some pondering you will find that the things humans are able to create are nothing compared to those found in the world. We cannot create things that replicate or reproduce; no chair makes another chair, or one table another table. Nevertheless, even the things people create are due to the abilities God creates in us and the structure of the world and thus are also proof to Him. However, for those who can no longer notice these signs or for further proof, God allows *karamat*.

Many people believe in God after witnessing miracles or *karamat*, and this is their reason and aim; to give evidence of God, His power and to strengthen belief. In fact many people pray for signs and miracles to make up their mind about religion and the existence of God. It is for this reason every Prophet that God sent was given miracles to confirm his Prophethood and the existence of God whom he invited people to worship. As the Prophet Muhammed (pbuh) is the seal and the last of Prophets, those who come after him have the chance to see and examine his first and lasting miracle, the Quran: God's speech. The Quran is considered a miracle because Prophet Muhammed (pbuh) was illiterate, yet in a time and place where poetry was valued to the point that the best poetry were placed inside the Kabba (God's house in Mecca) to elevate it like a trophy to its orator and no one debated or challenged the beauty, the perfection and the sublime quality of the Quran that make it impossible to be from other than God. Meaning they had a level of Arabic language knowledge to criticise if they saw fit, however their argument was that their pagan forefathers couldn't have been wrong. 1400 years later it is no longer only the perfection of the language but also the subject matter, as investigations into nature and the world made in science confirm many of the statements of the Quran on these subjects. The other Prophet's miracles can also be considered lasting and evidence for him. This is because they were witnessed by groups of people, and were preserved in writing as well as passed down via chains of truthful, honest, righteous, knowledgeable people or were mentioned in the Quran which God promised to protect.

It is a reality and a truth that just because people report to have seen or witnessed something does not necessary mean that it really happened.

This is due to the reality that some people lie and that some people could be mentally ill or their minds could be influenced by mind-altering substances. An example to the first is the workings of magicians like those of Pharaoh who in the Quran are reported to have made ropes and sticks look like snakes. This is in contrast to the miracle God gave Moses (as) whose stick God turned to a real snake, which not only looked like a snake but had the properties of snakes and ate the magicians' sticks and ropes. God says **"God revealed to Moses to throw his stick, and God turned it into a great snake that ate all the small snakes from the tricks of the magicians"** (7:117).

This to God is not difficult, and just like He created Angels from light and Adam (as) from earth, He can create a snake from wood. As to the fact that people can and do lie then that is a fact no one will disagree to; that as people we have the ability to tell falsehood and that some people do. The other explanation is that the person could be mentally ill, but that could be the case if the miracle or *Karama* witnessing was limited to that one person, and could not be the case when more than one person witnesses the miracle or *karama*. Another explanation for people reporting unnatural occurrences could be due to alcohol or hallucination caused by drugs, and while this could be true of some spiritualists of other religions, such as Shamans, or Rastafarians who smoke cannabis or Christians who drink wine as part of their religious rituals, such as the catholics mass where red wine symbolises the blood of Christ, this is not true of the Muslims to who all mind altering substances are forbidden, even in small amounts. The Prophet Muhammed (pbuh) said '**what much of is intoxicating, little of it is forbidden**'(Nissai).

Nevertheless, the seeing of miracles does not mean people believe. The Quran says if some disbelievers were thrown down a ladder to the heavens they would still disbelieve and say their 'eyes are tricking them'. God says **"if God were to open a gate in the heavens and the disbelievers to ascent it to see all the angels. The disbelievers would say their eyes were tricked and they are a people bewitched"** (15:14-15).

Karamat and miracles support that what the person is following is legitimate and truthful. However, in Islam there is the concept of *Istidraj* (entrapment), which is supernatural events happening to those who lack in righteousness as a way of punishment. This happens to false Prophets and hypocrites who just like they wish to misguide people; God punishes them by misleading them as the supernatural event leads them to believe they are correct. God says in the Quran **"the hypocrites when they meet those of belief, they say they believe. Then when they meet their demons they say they are with them in disbelief and that they were only joking in their belief. God will likewise mock them and God permits them to continue in their misguided arrogance in religion."** (2:14-15). This is also true of the miracles of the polytheists and those who insist on wrong beliefs about God after the truth has been made clear to them. God says **"God is established to judge each soul on its own deeds. They give to God partners then they should name them or do they tell God something God does not know in the earth, or is it a speech not to be considered much, but the disbelievers find beautiful their mockery and turn people away from God's way, and whoever misguided by God, has none to guide them"** (13:33). The verse says God will 'beautify to them their deeds' by granting to them miracles that make them think their beliefs and deeds were correct. This is because they are clear in error, for they have no proof that there is other gods who they worship with God, and that they are merely words they made. The world gives evidence to the existence of a God, as to saying there is more than one, that requires further proof they do not possess, and thus are insisting on error. God says **"this is the creation of God, so they should show the creation of those worshiped beside God, but the unjust in religion are in clear misguidance"** (31:11).

Those who practice the branch of Ihsan report more *karamat* as they happen to them and their scholars and other pious they come to know. The happening of *Karamat* is a sign of God which strengthens belief, and a sign of God's love to the person whom the *karama* happened to. It is also a confirmation that they are on the right path, and inspire good deeds and worship in others.

Supernatural openings (*karamat*) naturally reinforce themselves along the path as the person progresses up the path of Ihsan. The Quran says **"and they say if only a great sign from God is given to the Prophet. The Prophet should say the signs come from God and he is a clear Warner"** (29:50). *Karama* comes from a word meaning gift and the greatest gift from God is to strengthen belief, and this is what *karamat* do. Believing that miracles and *karamat* are possible also shows faith: belief that there is a God and also His abilities. As the person's *Iman* increases their openness to believing in *karamat* increases, and if they come to witness *karamat* their belief is further increased. This is because if the person has not witnessed a *karama* to believe that there can be a break to the natural laws, it is hard to believe especially on the levels of seas or the moon and that is the reason that makes *karamat* a sign of God when they do happen, for truly only a God could have the power for the phenomena described in miracles and *karamat*.

As the person's *Iman* increases and their belief in the unseen (*gaib*); the existence of God, Angels, the human spirit, *jinn* and dreams increases, it can lead some to be open to believing in all things spiritual, including superstitions. Yet while dreams can be true, finding meaning in the presence of birds (*taira*), eclipses or position of the stars is *haram* and forbidden in Islam. When an eclipse happened on the day the Prophet's (pbuh) son died and some attributed this to it, the Prophet Muhammed (pbuh) negated this, and said the eclipse is a sign of God and not connected to the deaths or births of people (Bukhari).

Having knowledge of what is true and what is false is a mercy so that the person does not get spiritually confused or become less able to interact with other people due to having strange beliefs and actions or even appear or become mentally ill. It is part of the teachings of the branch of Ihsan to be able to differentiate what is a true miracle of God from *istidraj* and be able to understand and appreciate the existence of superstition, magic and coincidence. When an eclipse happened on the day Prophet Mohammed's (pbuh) son died the Prophet (pbuh) rejected this linking. This is a teaching in coincidence, a concept that many spiritually high (*dervishes*) can become heedless of as they come to know and understand the Power and Ability of God and quickly label anything out of the ordinary as a *karama*, when it could have happened by accident or other normal phenomena they are unaware of. Not all *karamat* are equal, some *karamat* are greater and more profound than others. The simplest *karama* is a true dream. The fact that a person could see something in their dream and for it to come true accurately is neither normal nor ordinary, and it cannot be explained as anything but a sign of God. The greatest *Karama* is Vision of God in this world.

Dreams can come true and this was the case with the Messenger (pbuh) dreams and those of his companions. Yet true dreams are not confined to believers as the Quran tells the story of the king of Egypt in the time of Prophet Joseph (as), who had the famous true dream about the famine to come. While both believers and those who disbelieve may experience true dreams, the reason for the dream of believers and non-believers are different. To the non-believers seeing them is no more different than when a non-believer witnesses a miracle or a *karama*, it is a sign and proof for them to believe in God and submit to Him in worship. The dream of the believer is mainly *bushra* (glad tidings) that Allah has accepted their worship and they are of the pious who shall not fear nor will they grieve. The Prophet (pbuh) saw many dreams revealing the high spiritual states of and to give glad tidings of Heaven to some of his companions. The Quran says **'For them are glad tidings, in the life of the present and in the Hereafter' (10:64).** The Prophet (pbuh) said that this 'glad tidings' are true dreams that a person sees or are seen on their behalf (Tirmizi).

The signs of *ruya saliha* (truthful dream) are that it comes true, that it is beneficial and that the person remembers it. This is derived from Aisha's (raa) prayer when she prayed for true dreams. Other signs of a truthful dream are that the person has a peaceful state on waking up. A true dream is a sign of good worship and that the person is on the right path in their religion, hence it is a great *nema* (bounty of God) that should be celebrated when it happens, and in the *Sunnah* of Aisha (raa) even asked for in prayer. Dreams of *zikr* circles or religious gatherings, Prophets (as), the companions or the scholars and the pious, or hearing the Quran are all considered *ru'ya saliha* (truthful dream) even though they do not communicate future events, but nevertheless are spiritually beneficial, a sign of righteousness and a sign of a good hereafter to come.

As *karamat* are by God's power, will and permission for the slave they are not voluntary but only happen when Allah wishes. No slave of God is beyond the generosity of God, whoever they are and whatever they may have done in the past, God will strengthen them in the path and this can include the witnessing of His signs in *Karamat* if they fulfil what He conditioned, to cause Him to love them and make them worthy of *karamat*. In hearing about *karamat* it is important to realise and remember that *ina Allah ala kuli shain gadeer* (God is most capable).

Allah says in a *Qudis Hadith* **'I have declared war on anyone who shows enmity to a friend of Mine (*waly* –pious worshiper/saint). My slave does not draw near to Me with anything I love more than what I have made obligatory on him. And my slave continues to draw near to Me with optional worship until I love him. When I love him, I become his hearing with which he hears, his seeing with which he sees, his hand with which he strikes, and his foot with which he walks. If he were to ask Me for something, I would give it to him. If he were to ask Me for refuge, I would give him refuge. I do not hesitate in anything I do as I hesitate to take the soul of the believer who dislikes death and I disliked to annoy him'** (Bukhari). Firstly it is not literal that God becomes the person, as God does not change. It does not also mean that the person's organs and faculties become used only in what God loves, for that would suggest infallibility. It is an expression of God's love for the slave in giving them *karamat* so they have powers that only God has, and they still happen by His power and permission. They are His signs that strengthen their belief or His aid that helps them in their time of need to express His love for them.

God said 'I become his hearing with which he hears'; This is a metaphor to mean that God strengthens the slave's hearing ability so that they can hear what is usually inaudible, such as other people's thoughts, or even conversations taking place in a far-off land like the companions who heard Umar (raa) in Medina giving them direction to use the mountain's cover while they were miles away. 'His seeing with which he sees'; means that Allah increases the power of their sight such that they see Him or others that is usually hidden (*gaib*) such as seeing Mecca from a far land or seeing Angels, *jinn* or even paradise while awake. Sheikh Abdul-Qadir Al Jailani (raa) as a youth was able to see the pilgrims of Mecca from his home in Jilan in Persia. The Messenger (pbuh) used to tell the companions behind him to straighten their lines in prayer for he saw them even while they stood behind him (Bukhari).

God adds, 'his hand with which he strikes'; this is the same concept spoken about in the following verse **"the Prophet did not kill them but God killed them, and when the Prophet threw in war, it is God who throws"** (8:17). This verse was revealed when the Prophet Muhammed (pbuh) threw a handful of dust at his enemies in war and by the power of God that handful covered the faces of the whole army (around a thousand) and they were defeated.

A handful of dust does not reach more than a dozen nor can kill, but a hand that has been strengthened by the power of God can. This means that Allah increases the power of their hands such that a slight power can cause great consequences. God says I become 'His foot with which he walks'; this is when the slave can use their feet in a way that people are normally unable to, such as by walking on water, walking on air or walking long distances in short time. There have been practitioners of Ihsan who were said to have travelled between places in very short periods of time. They are termed *'ahlul khatwa'* (the people of the step).

The slave does not usually experience all of them, but whichever God wills when He wills.

Other spiritual experiences in the path include becoming spiritually aware of *fanaul nafs fi al sheikh* or *fanaul nafs fi al rasul*, either by it coinciding with seeing them in a dream or becoming conscious of their spiritual presence while awake. Another common spiritual experience is starting to smell the fragrance of the *awliya* (the pious), as a *karama*. This is similar to the smelling of the fragrances from the grave of Pharaoh's daughter's hairdresser by the Prophet (pbuh) during his *Isra*. This is possible because the smell of paradise can be smelled from a distance. In one *Hadith* the Prophet (pbuh) said it could be smelled from forty years away (Bukhari) but in other *Hadiths* a longer time is given.

This difference in length is because people entering paradise will depend on their spiritual stations, and while there will be some who enter paradise without judgment due to their very high station and great deeds, others have a longer distance. This is because the Day of Judgment length will depend on the person's piety, as well as the fact that God forbid some enter hell. On those who are of high spiritual station it is possible that the sweet perfume of paradise be smelled on them in this world and emitting from their graves. One of the Prophet Muhammed (pbuh) miracles was that he was described to have emitted a fragrant smell that was said to be sweeter than musk (Bukhari), and that it lingered even in the streets where he walked. It was very strong that one female companion collected the Prophet's sweat from his forehead while he was asleep to further beautify and strengthen the smell of her own perfume.

CHAPTER TWENTY SEVEN

THE ASCENSION OF THE SPIRIT

Islam teaches that all the prophets (*Alihim Alsalam*, peace be upon them) were Muslims and submitted to the One true God; Allah. God says **"there is no messenger from the past sent by God except God reveals to them, there is no god but Allah and to worship Him"** (21:25). The prophets of Islam started with Adam (as) and finished with Muhammed (pbuh), who is the final and last Prophet from God. The Quran and the *Hadith* of the Prophet Muhammed (pbuh) contain a substantial amount about their lives, worship, spiritual states and teachings. This is as there are lessons and examples for us from their lives and worship to learn from. The Quran says in their stories are lessons for us; to learn about God. Learn about how to worship God and lessons on spirituality. God says **"in their stories are wisdoms to people of deep understanding, they are not fabricated stories, but are truthful as confirmed by the Quran. They are an explanation to all things and a guidance and mercy to people who believe."** (12:111). This is why God chose to tell us about them in the Quran and the Prophet Muhammed (pbuh) mentioned them in the Hadith. In *fiqh* we find that many of the commands of worship are an example of the worship of the prophets of the past, like the slaughter of animals as did Abraham (as), to move between the mountains of Safa and Marwa like Lady Hager (as), and in *nafila* the Prophet (pbuh) recommended as a maximum the fasting of prophet David (as), who fasted alternative days. In the branch of Ihsan their spirituality is an example and their spiritual states teach us about the different spiritual and worship states of the path of purification.

As the student practices *Jihadul-nafs* there is a spiritual development that manifests in a physical evolution and a spiritual evolution. The physical evolution is what the student puts in and the spiritual evolution is what the student increases spiritually as a result of the physical evolution. The Spiritual development is that the person progressively gains more beautiful character and a higher spiritual state, and this could be described as an evolution. The two evolutions are much intertwined, yet for simplicity they could be considered separately.

The physical evolution includes taking up the characteristics of the physical worship of prophets (peace be upon them) starting with Adam (as) until Mohammed (pbuh) in the order they appeared in the physical world. The physical evolution happens as the person faces similar problems like the ones the prophets (as) faced and being able to solve them in their manner, i.e. in a religious way that follows the commands of God and what pleases Him. The physical evolution develops by increased knowledge of the religion, and the curing of cognitive, emotional, and behavioural diseases in *tazzkiya* and *Jihadul-nafs*, which infers on the person the spiritual ability to act in the manner of the prophets when faced by trials and tribulations that are similar to theirs.

In the spiritual evolution, the person takes the spiritual states of the prophets according to their spiritual stations and this follows their place in the spiritual world, i.e. their presence in the different levels of heaven as we told of from the *miraj* (ascension to the heavens) of the Prophet Muhammed (pbuh). This happens as the student's soul journeys through the heavens. The presence of Prophets in different and certain heavens is symbolic to the corresponding spiritual development the person gains when their soul reaches that heaven. While for the Prophet Muhammed (pbuh) it was a physical meeting with the prophets in heavens, to us it is a spiritual journey and development. The spiritual evolution happens when there is success in the physical evolution and the increased spirituality from making much *zikr*, *Jihadul-nafs*, and the study of advanced spirituality such as works of Ibn Arabi (raa) that further increases the person in spirituality.

Generally, those who go through the physical evolution but not the spiritual evolution, mainly because they have no scholar and thus lack *Jihadul-nafs* or are not doing enough *zikr* or other *nafila* worship can end up feeling very discontented spiritually. This is because even though they are feeding their body their souls are malnourished. And even though they are practicing the religion on the physical dimension, which leave them physically tired, they are not practicing the spiritual dimension which gives a sense of safety and contentment- due to the mentioning of God and pleasure from the increase in *iman*. Those who perform *zikr* and slack in purifying themselves from diseases and do not do enough physical worship look like hypocrites, for while they are truthful and experiencing spiritual states, their physical actions do not express it. This can also leave them spiritually unsatisfied, as the lack of physical development could mean lack in physical deeds and following of God's command that saves the person from His punishment. The Spiritual and physical development are intertwined but are laid out separately to aid understanding.

The Physical Evolution -changes in physical worship like that of the prophets

During the physical evolution, the person progresses by incorporating the spiritual character of the different Prophets (as). Progress occurs as a result of physical changing as the person comes across similar tests to that which the prophets (as) faced and acts likes them. This leads to a gain of spirituality and strength in *iman* that paves the way to the next physical change. This development is one people are conscious of and can happen in any order but are counted in the order the Prophet (as) came in chronological order, starting with Adam (as). The reason is that they usually happen in this order, and in this way progresses from what is easy to that which is hard. People usually have difficulty practicing the difficult tests of the later Prophets unless they have passed those of the earlier Prophets.

The Physical Evolution of the Lesser stage of Ihsan:

- Adam (as) - learning to restrain from what is *Haram* and excess in food.

Adam (as) disobeyed God by eating from the tree he was commanded not to. The Quran says **"God told Adam to live with his wife in Heaven, and to eat from Heaven as they wish, but not to come near a certain tree, and if they did, it will be sinful in religion"** (2:35). This was the first command God gave to humans and is the first challenge the student faces. In this state the person must learn to restrain from what is forbidden, and to ask for forgiveness when they fail to. The ability to restrain from excess food acts as a good trainer in being able to have control and also restrain from other forbidden things. The month of Ramadan acts as a trainer to restrain *completely* from what is forbidden, but the act of restraining from excess requires a different skill, i.e. the ability to restrain in the midst of indulgence, which is more difficult. In this state the student must learn to carry out both types of restraining. To be able to restrain *completely* from what is forbidden and to restrain *partially* from what is *halal* by not going into excess. The second is harder and takes longer to learn.

- Noah (as) - Recognising the gravity of sins and becoming independent of the people.

Prophet Noah (as) was called Noh meaning loud crying, as he used to cry a lot from *khashia* (fear and reverence) of God. For the student it should also be from remorse about past sins and time lost not in worship. This spiritual state is the fruit of knowledge of the hereafter and realising the reality of the world, i.e. that it is finite and inferior to paradise. It also comes from the knowledge of God's punishment and their wish to avoid it, and fear they may have qualified for it in much sin. This is the state of the *nafs-al-lawama* (the reproaching ego) that replaces the commanding *nafs* in the beginning of purification. It is the *nafs* that asks the person of their actions, why they do wrong, and is responsible for the feeling of remorse that follows a sin.

The state begins once a person establishes spiritual health and what is good and ideal from the stories of the Messengers, companions and the pious. The feeling that the person is not like them means that they have spiritual shortcomings. This leads them to regret and becoming sad about their past sins and their previous lack of worship. With this knowledge they become aware of their wrongdoings and spiritual diseases and therefore become regretful, tearful and asking for God's forgiveness. The feelings of regret and sadness are not relived except by the performance of worship, and much *istigfar* (asking God's forgiveness). It is a regret and sadness that is healing and preventative of sin. The Prophet Muhammed (pbuh) said on the Day of Judgment that those who cried out of fear and reverence of God will have a special station with God (Bukhari).

The other part of this station is that the person establishes that they should save themselves even when they see that other people are not preparing. This was the state of Noah (as) who prepared for the flood and built the boat while others watched. The person realises that Judgment Day and hell are a flood that the person must prepare and protect themselves from. Hassan Al-Basri (raa) an earlier scholar of Ihsan was said to have always looked as if he had just been through a disaster. This was from immense remorse and crying he did and intense fear of the punishment of God.

- Job (as) - the ability to be patient in tests and trials.

Prophet Ayoub (Job) (as) was trialled greatly by God. He lost all his possessions, then all his children died, and last became very ill that his flesh started to fall off. Nevertheless, it was only when the disease reached his mouth and he feared it would stop him from the mention of God that he prayed to God to relieve him from his suffering. Prophet Job (as) in the Islamic teachings is seen as an example of patience with that which God allows his slaves to have from pain and tribulation. *Ibtilas* (hardships) in the world are usually not to deliver punishments or a sign of God's wrath. They are to test the person's *iman*, and if they are accepting of the *gadar* (fate) of Allah. When the person is of *iman* then they are patient, and tolerant, but if not of strong *iman* they despair, become angry, and/or of little patience. Thus hardships act to reveal the person's level of *iman* to themselves and to God.

It is easier to be patient with tribulation when the person understands their purpose and the spiritual benefits in being patient in them. *Ibtilas* increases the slave with knowledge of their Lord. This is because trials bring a state of remembrance of God, as the person is forced by the pain to remember God and to pray to Him for relief. They also act as a break from the world and as a reminder of the reality and unpleasantness of pain and thus lead to fear of the punishment of hell. It also brings knowledge of the greatness of God in comparison to all else, as the person realises that it is only God who has the ability to help and this directs the person to God and His praise. Trials are also to purify the slave from sins. The Prophet (pbuh) said any tribulation that befalls a believer erases their sins, even the prick of a thorn (Bukhari).

- Joseph (as) - struggling not to follow desires and what is forbidden even in choosing a difficult option.

Joseph in Arabic is Yusuf. Yusuf, means one with apology, since many problems happen to him. One of the signs of strong belief is to practice the religion even when this could lead to worldly loss or hardship. This is because while it requires belief to practice the religion under normal circumstances, it required extra belief to do so when it could mean loss and the greatest loss is the loss of life. The companion Bilal (raa) was tortured in the hot desert by placing large rocks on his chest to force him to denounce Islam but he remained patient and steadfast on the religion. This is a reflection of his great belief in God that allowed him to tolerate the pain of the hot Arabian sun and desert. The other companion's readiness to die for their religion was also a testament to their great belief in God and the religion.

In this state the student learns to accept what is less in worldly benefit to gain what is more beneficial for the next world. An example is refusing a job so not to sell *haram* (forbidden) products or losing money by refusing *riba* (usury). This was the manner of Prophet Joseph (as) who chose to refuse a life of freedom and instead accepted prison rather than to disobey God. Joseph (as) said **'Lord! Prison is more desirable to me than that to which they invite me of fornication' (12:33)**.

In this state the student should read the *Seerah* of the Messenger (pbuh) and listen to *nasheeds* (Islamic songs) such as the *Burdah* of Imam Al Busairi (raa). This is to prepare for and to enter the next state; the state of loving the Prophet (pbuh).

- Jacob(as) - love of the Prophet (pbuh), and want to see him.

Jacob in Arabic is Yagoub. Jacob (as) intense love for his son Joseph (as) was to the extent that he became blind from crying at his loss. The Quran says **"and his eyes became dim from the grief with which he was filled" (12:84)**. This is because he loved the piety and goodness of Joseph, and realised from his dream and behaviour that he would be among the pious prophets, thus his crying wasn't from the loss of a son but separation from a fellow worshiper. This is the intense love that a Muslim should have for Prophet Muhammed (pbuh). In this state the person's love for the Prophet (pbuh) manifests in their want to visit his Mosque in Medina, and intense desire to see him in a dream. The state of

Jacob (as) was also one of being patient with the loss of what is beloved which is more painful that mere loss and more intense than it.

In this state the student should study the discourses of the *Awliya* (saints) such as *Gawseya* of Abd Al-Qadir Al-Jailani (raa), works of Ibn Arabi (raa) and *Concerning the Affirmation of Divine Oneness* by Sheikh Wali Raslan Ad-Dimashqi (raa). Also the study of God's Names, such as *The best means in explaining Allah's Beautiful Names* by Sheikh Abu Hamid Al Ghazali (raa). This is again in preparation for the next state which is the state of wanting the nearness of God.

- Moses (as) – Knowledge of God's Greatness and utmost devotion in the worship of God.

The Prophet (pbuh) said **'none becomes a true believer until their desires is the same as God's commands' (Al Nawawi).** This is to mean the perfectness of belief and strong *iman* that manifests in the desire to worship. This is the state of strict observance and following of the commands of God that was the spiritual state of Moses (as).

Those who believe accept God's commands and fulfil them, while those who disbelieve or are of low *iman* or lack of knowledge of the religion may find strange the physical worship. Why the need to bow, or walk around the Kabba (house of God in Mecca), or touch earth to make *tayamum*, God says **"those who believe know that it is the truth from their Lord, but those who disbelieve say: What does Allah wish to teach by such a similitude?"** (2:26). God says regarding the command to sacrifice animals, **'Their flesh and their blood reach not Allah, but the devotion from you reaches Him.' (22:37).** Physical worship is almost symbolic; to communicate belief in God and His obedience. It is not about the physical movements even thought they still need to be perfected, but it is about the feeling behind them that motivated the actions and behaviour which is worship. God says **"to be righteous is not physical movements of turning their heads in prayer to the east and west, towards the house of God. Righteousness is to accept to** heart to believe in God, and afterlife, and the angels and the holy books, and prophets. Righteousness is to give money while loving it as gifts to relatives, and as charity to orphans, and the poor, and the traveller, and those who ask needly, and to free slaves. Righteousness is to establish prayer, and to give obligatory charity on excess riches, and to fulfil promises, and patient in hardship and burden, and in situations of trouble. Whoever does these, have shown true belief, and those are the pious" (2:177).

Physical worship acts as evidence for the person that they are of the people of *iman* and thus feel more secure about their fate after death, and it acts as a testimony of faith. Physical worship also acts as a contract with God so that the person is not punished on the Day of Judgment, for God does not punish those who followed His commands and made sincere His worship. It is also important to realise that God's commandants while are worship they are for our benefit, and the benefits of society and this in itself is an enough reward, but there is also the reward of the hereafter. The proof that they are intended for benefit is that when there is harm in practicing the commandments of God or unnecessary hardship they are allowed exceptions in the law to allow for this. This includes the shortening of *salah* during travel or not fasting when ill. The other is to even go against the law when there is benefit, and this was the wisdom behind the acts of *Khidr* (The Green Man)(as). These allowances and exceptions in the law manifest and show God's Generosity and Mercy.

- David (as) – Restoring of balance.

Prophet Dawood (David), considered the importance of fulfilling and restoring the heart into a balance. His name Dawud is from the word cure, and thus he was once always in balance correcting his internal self to a balance. He rectified his spirit, just as Jesus who came after him taught to purify it. This is the reason this word 'dawa' is the word for medication in Arabic, as rectifies to restore to a previously healthy state.

- Zechariah(as)- Obsessive mention of God.

Once the person managed to keep a regular mention of God, it is found to his spirit as the best thing under the sun. Zechariah is a prophet from the family of Imran (Joachim), that included, Yahya (John), Jesus, his noble mother, Mary, and Zachariah was the husband of Mary's Aunt. He was a prophet of mention of God, and thus in charge of the temple and Mary as a permanent worshiper in the temple was one of his trustees, and he was her guardian. Thus he was the scholar of Mary, who taught her how to worship God in the temple. He was the first human to do repetitive mention of God in lack of tribulation as a form of worship. He was the father of John the Baptist, the maternal cousin of Jesus son of Mary. In this state the person starts to love the mention of God.

- John (as)- Understanding the Spirit.

Yahya (John), his name is John the Baptist, was the prophet of recognising the spirit. He is thus called Yahya, for the spirit is the eternal living, and unlike the body not destroyed once created. This is because God breathed of his own spirit and so associated with God, for the spirit recognises God, but the body is mere animal, and thus lacks association of God.

- Jesus (as) - Intense Spirituality.

Jesus (as) in Islam is called *Roh Allah* (lit. The spirit of God) to mean 'Mercy of God', yet he is not believed to be a god as the Christians claim but a noble Prophet. In the Quran God uses the word spirit as a metaphor for God's Mercy. Prophet Jacob (as) says in the Quran **"go and search for Joseph and his brother, and not to despair from the spirit of God, for only despairs from the spirit of God are people of disbelief" (12:87).** Jesus (as) is called the spirit of God to denote the mercy of his message. He (as) did this by manifesting God's mercy in reliving the suffering that comes from disease and death and he did this in the miracles of healing and reviving the dead. The Quran describes Muhammed (pbuh) as 'mercy to the world', this is to say while other prophets and men could manifest God's mercy, that the Prophet had his own personal mercy as a person, such as in asking forgiveness for his *ummah* (followers) in his grave, his intercession, his keenness not to overload his followers in tiresome worship such as '*siwak*'(brushing teeth) before every prayer, thus God chose him when he decided to send mercy to the world. Thus the Prophet Muhammed (pbuh) overwhelmed all other prophets in his characteristic of mercy, meaning as Muslims the attribute of mercy we associate to the Prophet Muhammed (pbuh).

This station starts with the loss of fear of death and disease. These two are the two greatest causes of anxiety to us, and while the state of being not afraid and not minding of death and disease is advanced, it nevertheless starts with the reassurance that healing is possible and even being brought back from death into the world is possible, as was evidenced and taught by the miracles of Jesus (as). The Quran says **"the angel told Mary, Jesus will become a Prophet to the people of Israel, coming to them with a revelation from God, also miracles of creating birds from mud and he blows a breath into them to fly away real birds, with permission of God. Jesus will cure the dumb, and the leper and raise the dead, with the permission of God. Also, he can tell what people eat, and what they hide in their homes, and in these are a sign of God, if people believed in God."** (3:49). The thoughts of illness and death keep the person occupied to the body and the physical world, and when this is released by hope from knowing, healing and reviving the person is possible and they are then released from the physical world and can experience high spiritual states.

This state is of experiencing spirituality, of *fana* during *zikr*, and of intense and frequent state of spiritual ecstasy, and *hal* and even spiritual intoxication, which must be corrected so that it doesn't become permanent. It is a state of understanding spiritual wisdoms and of being able to understand and appreciate the advanced works of spirituality of Ibn Arabi (raa), and the high spiritual states like Al-Hallaj (raa) and the experience of love of God. They may also witness *karamat* as a fruit of their observance of the commands of God in the state before this. In this state the student should concentrate on the restudy of the Quran and *Sunnah*. This helps increase their knowledge of God and quality of worship. They also act to correct spiritual intoxication so that the person is preserved from it becoming permanent.

- Muhammed (pbuh) – Love of God

This is the state of realising that we belong to God. Showing extreme obedience and humility to God in Islam is called slavehood to God. This state of slavehood to God was exemplified and perfected by the Prophet Muhammed (pbuh). The Quran says **"Christ would not feel proud to be a servant of God, and neither do the angels close to God. Whoever is proud to not worship God, and is arrogant, God will gather them all to His judgement" (4:172)**. The slavehood to God is an honour and a source of pride for it negates slavehood to all other than Him. The slave of God is a free man and thus Muslims carry their title of being slaves of God with pride. In fact many Muslims have as a name 'slave to God' in Arabic, and all names that start with Abdul' are different versions of this.

Islam is against the slavehood of man to man, and it considers it a great injustice and the freeing of slaves is seen as one of the greatest deeds of worship. It nevertheless acts as a metaphor to teach the slavehood of man to God. This means that He owns us, and that is because He created us and sustains us, but it also means that He has the right to command us, and we are obliged to follow His commands. The Muslims commonly say that Islam is a religion that 'frees people from the slavehood of man to the slavehood of the Creator of man'. The state of the slave of God is one of humility and complete obedience, and love of God. This is because God is the Most Merciful Most Generous, and thus we do not become arrogant of worshiping Him. God says **"those with God of angels are not arrogant from worshiping God and they glorify and praise God, and to God they prostrate in prayer"** (7:206).

People do not scorn of being slaves to God, for He is a good master, and a Just God. Even though slavehood is a position of degradation and pain, when the master is kind and generous it can be no different than being a servant. Zayd Ibn Al Harith (raa) who came to be the Prophet's slave before his Prophethood was an aristocratic Arab who became slave after he was abducted, to his father's remorse. Nevertheless, when his father heard of him being in the Prophet's household and came to free him, he instead chose to remain a slave in the Prophet's household. This is a reflection of the kindness and love and good companionship he found in the Prophet's (pbuh) household. Thereafter the Prophet freed him and adopted him as a son. Anas Ibn Malik (raa) a companion of the Prophet (pbuh) said he served the Prophet (pbuh) ten years, and he (pbuh) was never harsh in his tone to him, never told him off for not doing something or asking him why he did not do a chore (Bukhari). It is these manners and character that made Zayd (raa) come to love being in the Prophet's household as a slave and not as a free aristocrat elsewhere.

The Prophet (pbuh) worshiped God with great humility, love and gratefulness to Him. When the Prophet's (pbuh) blessed ankles swole from standing too long in night prayer and a companion became concerned and reminded him of his high status with God as a Prophet of God and the seal of Messengers, he (pbuh) replied "**should I not be grateful to God**" **(Bukhari)**. This is because as the person develops spiritually and knows the generosity of God on us, they realise they are too many to be thanked by verbal praise but need to be thanked by physical worship.

The Prophet Muhammed (pbuh) is called the **'Beloved of God' (Tirmizi)**. This state is of the most intense love of God. When the person gains this state it should be expressed in the following of the commands of God and the Prophet (pbuh). God said to the Prophet **"whoever loves God should follow Muhammed, and God will love them back and forgive their sins, and God is forgiving and merciful."** (3:31). An expression of the Prophet Muhammed (pbuh) love of God was his devotion in worship, and spreading the religion of God, and when he was given the choice of life or death by Angel Gabriel (as) he chose God's company. In this state the strict observance and following of the commands of God becomes out of love of God and it is also the way God commanded us to express our love of Him, and it is the way to gain His love.

The Prophet Muhammed (pbuh) state is also of the perfection of character, and Islamic character goes beyond good character with people; it involves good character with God. The Prophet's (pbuh) humility to people was expressed when he chose to eat with his servants. He also explained that he ate while sat on the floor to show humility to God by eating like slaves. By following fully the commands of God and showing the best of character the person become *Khalifatul-Allah fi AlArd* (God's vicegerent and representative in the world). This means the taking care of the environment, the animals (Umar (raa) when was Caliph said he feared that if a goat would trip in Iraq that God on the Day of Judgment would question him why he did not even the road for it.) and justice between people and the acting with mercy and generosity as does God, and to follow his commands as His representatives and to rule using His laws. This fulfils the reason for the creation of Adam (as) and placement on earth. God says **"God said to the angels God will be creating a deputy on earth"** (2:30). And **"God made people to be His deputies on earth"** (6:165). The plurality in the second verse denotes that this position of vicegerent was not confined to Adam (as).

The journey of the soul through the Heavens and to the Throne of God for the Vision is symbolic like the calling of the Meccan Mosque the house of God. God does not live in it and likewise God does not sit literally on the Throne. God is not confined to nor limited to a certain space. God can be lacking in body yet have its attributes is because there is nothing like God. The Quran says **"there is nothing like God and He can see and hear"** (42:11). The Throne of God is a testimony and symbol of His Kingship, for He is King over all.

The ascension of the soul is to understand God's name *Alali* (The High). That God is high and needs the person to experience a sense of elevation that comes with the ascension of the soul to acknowledge it. This is no different from the *imam* being in a higher platform and the people needing to raise their heads to see him which gives a sense of his elevated status. Just like the body is commanded to journey to the House of God in *hajj*, the souls journey to the Throne.

The journey of the soul through the heavens to the Throne follows the journey of the Prophet Mohammed (pbuh) during *miraj*. The Prophet's (pbuh) journey was a physical journey in body and soul and hence the *burag* (horse like animal) to carry his blessed body. For the general Muslims it is a journey of the spirit. The Prophet (pbuh) said when a person sleeps they die, and those that still have *rizq* (allocated sustenance) their souls are returned. In death we are told that the souls of both believers and non-believers are journeyed to the heavens, but disbeliever's souls are rejected entrance into the heavens and fall unsupported to the earth as a form of punishment (Bukhari). The journeying of the soul to the Throne also occurs during sleep. The Prophet (pbuh) said true dreams occur when the soul of a sleeping person reaches the Throne, and untrue dreams if they do not (Al Haithami). This is to say that the souls of people in this world do *miraj* across the heavens. This also makes the Throne as a place of truth, and there is nothing more truthful than the existence of God and knowledge of Him and His vision. The journey of the soul to the Throne during *Jihadul-nafs* is a journey to truth, and The Truth is one of God's ninety-nine beautiful names.

The Quran explains that not all people are on the same spiritual states nor do people remain in one. With increase in worship and belief, they increase in spiritual stations or what the Quran calls *'darajat'* or levels. God says **"they are the true believers in God, and they have stations with God and are forgiven, and there is a generous giving to them from God."** (8:4). That there are degrees or levels of belief and spirituality, is the principle behind spiritual development and evolution, i.e. that when the person is increased in belief, spirituality and good deeds they increase in spiritual states and degrees. God says **"the true believers are those who when God's name is mentioned their hearts are shaken, and if God's verses are recited their belief in God is increased and they relay on God"** (8:2).

Those who do not do *Jihadul-nafs* and *tazzkiya* and instead follow their egos and their desires are not elevated in spirituality. God says **"if God wished He would have raised them spiritually by the revelation but they chose to stick to the earth by following their desires."** (7:176). God also reproaches them and says **"they believers when are told to go out in the way of God, should not become heavy to the ground"** (9:38).

In Ihsan scholars also differentiate between spiritual states and stations depending on their duration. This gives us the difference between spiritual state (*hal*) and station (*magam*). *Hal* is a temporary state that lasts minutes, at most a few hours, while station is something that lasts a few years or even the person's whole life. The instance of Moses' unconsciousness from realising God's grandeur was a *hal*, the fact that he was of the law and strict in following God's commandments was his *magam* (station).

The spiritual development is one of changing spiritual stations from one to another that is more superior. But spiritual states happen during intense states of spirituality regardless of station. If a spiritual state becomes permanent e.g. spiritual intoxication, it could then be called a station. However, the permanency of spiritual states is considered a spiritual shortcoming. In the journey to God the student should always be improving and seeking higher states and stations. It is important that the person experiences spiritual states as they experience spiritual stations, even spiritual intoxication as was the state of Umar (raa) on the announcement of the Prophet's passing away, which reflects strong belief and spirituality. What is blameworthy is if they are allowed to become permanent.

Spiritual evolution corresponds to an increase in spirituality. This happens as *zikr*, *Jihadul-nafs*, *tazzkiya* and good deeds act as spiritual keys to open new higher spiritual states and stations.

The spiritual evolution follows the journey Prophet Muhammed (pbuh) took to the Throne of God and its steps outline the spiritual developments during the study of Ihsan. The journey from Mecca to Jerusalem is known as *Isra* and the journey from Jerusalem to the Throne is called *Miraj*. The stations of *Isra* could be gained in the practice of the second stage of Ihsan without a scholar, but the stations of *Miraj* require the guidance of a scholar and the study of the first stage of Ihsan. It is out of God's wisdom that the journey to Him is made clear in the physical journey of the Prophet (pbuh), in that the stations of *Miraj* show the stations of the first stage of Ihsan, and the chronological order of the position of Prophets in different heavens correspond to the spiritual development.

In their journey to God the student must be steadfast in their goal of becoming near to God and not getting diverted, what in Islam is called *al sirat al mustageem* (The Straight Path). The Quran says **"God is on a straight path"** (11:56). This agreement and harmony of the religion, as well as being beautiful, is a proof that it came from God. God says **"do they not ponder on the Quran, if it was from other than God, they would have found it in many contradictions"** (4:82). Contradictions come from errors in logic or if one statement is false, and what comes from God would be expected to be perfect, thus the Quran says its perfection is a sign that it is from God.

The spirit is affected by a wake and sleep, and by level of awareness of God which is the true awareness, for our awareness of sounds, smells, touch and taste of created things is negligible in comparison. That it is a traveller, and thus the word '*roh*' i.e. thing that leaves and comes as the *roh* is that which leaves when the person dies. The soul is with whom he loves, the Prophet Muhammed (pbuh) said **"a person is with one who they love"** (Bukhari). When a person loves God their spirit travels towards the throne, it is the Mecca of the souls. The Prophet called Abubakr (raa) as a dead person, for his soul has left his body and is in the throne of God.

The Spiritual Evolution - As the soul elevates throughout the heavens

The stations of the Greater stage of Ihsan (Isra)

- The Prophet (pbuh) started *Isra* by being taken to Medina where he prayed

This symbolises the love of Medina and more importantly the love of the Prophet Muhammed (pbuh).

- The Prophet (pbuh) was then taken to the mountain of Tor where God talked to Moses (as)

This is the establishment of love for God's speech the Quran, and the following of God's commandments. Realising the revelation is an invitation to return to God.

- Then he (pbuh) was taken to Jesus's (as) birthplace

Jesus's (as) birth from the Virgin Mary (as) was a miracle and a proof of God and His power. In this state the student's *Iman* increases and then becomes more believing of miracles and *Karamat* and expecting them.

- The Prophet Muhammed (pbuh) saw the *dunya* (this world) as an old woman

This is the state when the person realises the truth of the world; that it is transient, finite, and that what it provides is negligible compared to the pleasure of the permanent Paradise. God says **"the life of this world is like play and entertainment, but the world of the afterlife is the major world, if they were knowing of religion"** (29:64). That is to say that this world is not serious but rather play compared to the *Akhira;* the Hereafter. The Prophet (pbuh) said what is left of this world is the same as what was left of the life of an old woman, i.e. that the world will end and that this is not far. This makes the person realise that concentrating their effort on it is not wise as the person will leave it, and that a person should be more concerned with building for the permanent *Akhira*. The Prophet (pbuh) said the world is like a traveller sitting under a tree to rest and then leaving it to continue their journey (Ibn Hajr). In this state the student gains a state of heedlessness of the *dunya* and all their concern becomes of God and working for the next world.

In the Hadith of Gabriel Muhammed (pbuh) said this is your religion, and the fourth question asked by Gabriel was when was the hour, and scholars of the religion consider this to be the fourth and last branch of the religion, the knowledge of the End of Time, as it contains great signs of the power of God, but the most important belief is that the world is finite, and not divine. It seems this station in spiritual development inducts the Muslim to the fourth branch of the religion.

- The Prophet Muhammed (pbuh) then smelled a good fragrance emitting from the grave of the hairdresser of the daughter of Pharaoh. In this state the person reaches a spiritual state that they are prepared to die for the sake of God. This was the state of the hairdresser of the daughter of Pharaoh, who died when she was immersed in boiling oil for refusing to worship Pharaoh, and choosing to worship The One True God. It is the state of admiration and appreciation of the saints, for the person can only truly appreciate them when they come to experience their spiritual states. That is when they realise that they truly are the best of humanity. In this state they may smell the fragrance of paradise that emits from the pious just as fever is a breeze of hellfire that can emit form the ill person.

The stations of the Greater stage of Ihsan (Miraj)

- The First Heaven: Adam (as)

In this state the person's view of Paradise becomes like that of Adam (as) who has lived there, so their motivation and want is no longer Paradise but becomes nearness to God. The word Adam means bloodiest, and this implies having much blood meaning progeny, and he is the father of all humanity – the billions of them. He is called this as God created Adam, from nothingness, and not apes as evolutions say. Thus the first point is to recognise the state of nothingness, and this is the state the person wants to enter their ego into.

- The Second Heaven: Jesus and John (as)

In this state the student can experience what is called *gabd* (lit. compression) and *bast* (lit. expansion). When angel Gabriel (as) came to the Prophet (pbuh) in the cave the first time he squeezed and pressed on him three times. The Prophet (pbuh) said **"until I could not bear it any more" (Bukhari).** This was to express to the Prophet (pbuh) the power of Angel Gabriel (as) and the majesty of the Angel as a messenger from God. In this spiritual state the person experiences this compression and it is out of realisation and experience of the Majesty and Power of God – of which the existence and grandeur of the world is testimony of. This *gabd* is then followed by a release and this is called *bast*. In this station the person alternates between the state of *gabd* and *bast*. This state corresponds to the fact that while John (as) was spiritually depressed his maternal cousin Jesus (as) was spiritually euphoric. By knowledge of God's majesty the person is compressed and in knowledge of his mercy his spirits expands.

- The Third Heaven: Joseph(as)

This is a station of appreciation of the beauty of God. The Prophet (pbuh) said **'God is Beautiful and Loves beauty' (Bukhari).** The Prophet (pbuh) said Prophet Joseph (as) was given **'half of beauty' (Bukhari).** The Quran says **'When she heard of their malicious talk, she sent for them and prepared a banquet for them: she gave each of them a knife: and she said to Joseph, "Come out before them." When they saw him, they did extol him, and in their amazement cut their hands:**

they said, "Allah preserve us! no mortal is this! this is none other than a noble angel!'"(12:31)**. This is to relate to us the power of Joseph's beauty that made the ladies cut their hands, and it's the power of God's beauty that cuts the desires of the ego.

- The Fourth Heaven: Enoch (as)

This is a station of spiritual wisdom. The Quran described Prophet Enoch (Idris) (as) as having been raised to a high station. God says **'And We raised him to a high station' (19:57)**. Idris (as) is also said to be the first person to have used the pen to write. The position of Idris (as) is one of realising the greatness and Highness of God beyond all else. The Quran says **"the reward of good is good like it"** (55:60) thus we could assume God raising him to a high station is because he raised God in his belief to a High station. Idris in Arabic comes from a word meaning study, and in this station the person gains love of studying about the religion and about Sufism.

- The Fifth Heaven: Aaron (as)

In the state of Aaron (as) the person appreciates God's name *Al Wahab*, which means to give in great generosity without being asked. Prophet Aaron (as) was given the position of a Prophet without effort from him due to the prayers of his brother Moses (as). In this state the person comes to appreciate the bounties of God, the details that everything is from God. This also included our movements that happen with God's permission and power, and His sustenance that comes to use without much effort from us, including that grains grow just by being watered, and rain falls without our effort. It is in this state that people start to understand how heedless we are of God's working in the world, and how great these workings are.

God says **"it is God who has created people and all their deeds" (37:96)**. The person then becomes spiritually conscious that while they make choice of their movements and actions it is Allah who creates them and *la hawla wa la guwat ila billah* (there is no might nor power except from God). When the student realises this, they enter a very advanced spiritual state of understanding the Greatness and power of God. It is physically experienced by the slave, such that they realise that their own actions are of the creation of their Lord. So that when they move their hands they feel it is Allah who's creating the movement. This state is very intense that it can intoxicate people and lead them to think they are becoming divine but this intoxication can be overcome by repeating '*amantu bellah wa rasulihi*' (my belief is in God and His Messenger). This makes the person remember that these new beliefs contradict the religion and then they can reject them, and so does also remembering the above mentioned verse.

- The Six Heaven: Moses (as)

In this state the student realises the grandeur of becoming nearer to God and witnessing His Vision and want it.

- The Seventh Heaven: Abraham (as)

Abraham (as) is known as *Khalil Allah* (the friend of God), and it is in this state that the student realises God's attribute of Generosity, Kindness, and Mercy that begets the feelings of love and the state of '*walaya*'. But while *walaya* confers formality of allegiance and the following of command, '*khalil*' is the informality of love and companionship.

The state is also of *tawakkul,* reliance and trust in God. When Abraham (as) was thrown into the fire by the disbelievers, he was in certain belief that God is capable of and will help him in his affliction. The Prophet Muhammed (pbuh) said Abraham's (as) prayer in the fire was *hasbi Allah wa nim al wakeel* (God is enough to be relied upon and on Him I put my trust) (Bukhari). This is a feeling that liberates the person from all need and reliance of people and the world, as they come to rely and trust in God, and He is the best to rely upon. This further strengthens their determination to being devoted to God's worship and the desire of His nearness and Vision. The person must come to know God in this stage, which arouses their love to God for the next stage.

- The Vision of God: Mohammed (pbuh)

The state of the Prophet Muhammed (pbuh) is of *mushahada*; witnessing of God. In this state the student witnesses the names of God and His attributes manifesting in the world, and the highest witnessing is the Vision of God.

The last spiritual evolution is the descent of the soul to the earth after vision if it's granted. And this so that the person's soul returns back to earth so the person can worship God complete in a state of slavehood as exemplified by the Prophet Muhammed (pbuh). The state of Slavehood to God is higher than the state of Friendship of God, firstly because it is the state of worship of the seal of Prophets Muhammed (pbuh) but also God says in a *qudsi Hadith* of **'while in paradise Adam (as) used to come to God like kings meeting kings. This was changed so that it is like a slave coming to a king and that is more beloved to God'** (Ibn Al-Gayam).

Some do not experience spiritual descent and become 'stationary saints' in any of the spiritual stations. Those who do experience it increase their knowledge of Allah and His name *Al Khafid* (The Lowerer) as well as gain in spiritual station. Some can become aware of the start of the descending by a dream in which they see himself leave the presence of God. They then do not get intense spiritual feelings from religious activities like they used to. This is due to the change in their spiritual state, from one of spirituality to one of slavehood and physical worship.

After returning to earth the person notices how small and insignificant their self and other humans are and how minute we are compared to the universe, and to God, giving us the first feelings of slavehood and humility to God. In the experience of 'spiritual descending' they increase in love for prostration and prayer (*salah*). This is why the Messenger (pbuh) in his descending after *miraj* was given the prayer. The Messenger (pbuh) said **'the closest the slave can be to his Lord is when they are in prostration. Therefore, make abundant supplication' (Muslim).** Allah commands, **"indeed do not obey them but prostrate in prayer and become near to God"** (96:19). The position of prostration is a position of humility which is truthful of our state as slaves of God, and thus it is the closest and most beloved to God. In this state the nearness of the slave to God becomes no longer in spiritual feeling from witnessing or consciousness of His presence or *zikr*, but a nearness sought in *salah* and prostration. It is important to understand that God is not confined to a certain space, and in the change of the soul's position from the heavens to earth the person does not become farther from God but rather it is a change of spiritual station and a different way of worshiping God and increasing knowledge of Him.

Those who do not experience *khafd* (spiritual descent) find it difficult to guide the slaves as scholars because they do not have knowledge of or experience of the whole path. It is in the middle spiritual stages that the student is most vulnerable to spiritual intoxication, but once *khafd* is experienced and the person returns to a spiritual state of slavehood, it is nearly impossible, as the spiritual highness and ecstasy are replaced with the wish for physical worship. Thus when the prayer becomes the most beloved and a reliever of distress as it brings them closer to God, the person has reached the station of slavehood and their descent is complete. This was the state of the Prophet Muhammed (pbuh) who was unhappy when not in worship of God that he used to hurry Bilal (raa) into making *azan* (the call to prayer) saying *arihna biha ya bilal:* **'Bilal relief us by making the call to prayer' (Abu Dawud).** The experience of the different stations of *miraj* may not be in the order of the heavens and some may even experience some of them during their descent.

CHAPTER TWENTY EIGHT

THE PRESENCE OF GOD

The gaining of audience with God is the aim of the first stage of Ihsan, the greater Ihsan. It is achieved when God discloses to his slave. The Prophet said '**they see Him like the moon uncovered by clouds**'. The Quran describes it by saying "**it's a companionship of Truth**" (54:55), that it does indeed happen and they will know it's truly happening when it takes place. However, God does not admit all His creation to His presence, He has them all veiled. The slave has to beg seriously by bringing what would turn the heart of the begged to giving. This in religious is from '*nafila*' and giving in charity and work dedicated to God as a form of insistent begging until God admits them to his company. The Prophet Muhammed (pbuh) said '**indeed I want the highest companion**' (Bukhari) at the moment of death, since the presence of God after death is uninterrupted by the impurities and needs of survival in this world, so the Prophet Muhammed (pbuh) died for a better view of God.

God is there, it is just a matter of spiritual focus. When this happens we shall see Him for his existence is more certain than all else we enjoy sight of in the world. Spiritual focus is something that will become strong after death, in Judgment Day and Heaven. People will not longer be distracted, and be aware God exists and owner of the passed world as they stand in Judgment Day, and likewise in Heaven, this focus will give them sight of God.

The presence of God has to be made ready for, by struggling against the ego, purification of the spirit, curing of spiritual diseases and learning good character. The presence of God is called "*Hadra Alilahiya*" (Divine Presence) in Arabic.

God says **"those who do not worship God, and neither look forward to the meeting with God in the afterlife, and are contented by the life of this world and pleased by it, and those ignorant of God's signs and revelation, to them is the abode of the hellfire for their sins."** (10:7-8). God is offended for people not to seek Him but instead to rest their pleasures on what he created to nourish believers in this world. Their punishment is a fire, due to the offence it causes God. God says **"on Judgment Day each soul will gain of what is previously did in the world, and they return to God their true Lord, and leaves them all their false believes they believed in this world"** (10:30). In speaking of entering the presence of God, God says their falsehood, their *nafs* will be destroyed, and their ego will be destroyed.

CHAPTER TWENTY NINE

THE VISION OF GOD

The Vision of God is an important element in the practice of Ihsan. There is no excellence in Ihsan without the highest spirituality, and the seeking of and attaining of the vision of God is a spiritual state above which there is none higher. The consideration of the presence of God and its want is the first step in true religiosity. The Quran says "**Unto Allah is the journeying**" (35:18). This is the teachings of Islam; that this world is a place of test and our return to God after death is to be accounted, yet some go to God in this world.

The Possibility of the Vision

The idea that God can be seen is absolute, as His name is *Alnor* (the Light), and this is attributed to that which its existence is apparent and can be seen and through it other things can be seen. However the debate is if humans, in this life or in the hereafter format would be able to see Him. For His name *Alnor* (the light) means He is something that can be seen, and as also the means to seeing other than Him, it means the seeing of else is a proof for his existence. If we can clearly see the room then yes the light is on, likewise the seeing of the world is a proof for the existence of God. God says "**there will be extra giving to the people**

of Ihsan"(2:58) and the Prophet Muhammed (pbuh) said the believers in Heaven will see God in a valley called "extra" (Alfairozabady). The Quran says the vision of God is possible. God says in the Quran **"none really has good deeds to be rewarded except those who seek the face of God, and they will be pleased"** (92:19-21). This is to say those who seek God's face meaning, His vision, will be pleased. Meaning they will be granted their wish of seeing God, even if they are in this world.

The Quran mentions six different types of situations where people seek to see or actually see God. They are:
1. By the children of Israel in mockery, that they won't believe unless they see God first (2:55)
2. By prophet Moses (as) after talking to God as an additional honour to speaking with God (7:143)
3. By Prophet Muhammed (pbuh) during the ascension to the heavens (53:11)
4. By believers on the Day of Judgment (75:23)
5. By believers in Heaven (50:35)
6. By the Prophet Muhammed (pbuh) and saints in this world, those who love God and want to be close to God (6:62). The Prophet Muhammed prayed to see God (Nissai)

Another proof for the possibility of vision is the reporting of the pious, such as Hallaj (raa), and the seeking of Rabia (raa) and other saints. As well as the fact that some scholars of Ihsan declared or alluded it to have happened to them, one of them Sheikh Magzoub son of Sheikh Mohamed son of Sheikh Sadiq (raa) who was also a direct descendant of Prophet Muhammed (pbuh) said in poetic verse:

> If I looked at a barren land it would become green,
> and if I were to transfer my spiritual knowledge to the dead, the dead would raise because of the beautiful melody of my prayer.
> Be mannered and understand,
> my words are not of pride nor empty vanity,

> but I am a God servant who investigated the mercy
> of seeking the presence of Allah
> and a slave who has reached the station of vision of God
> And His manifest Light overwhelmed my presence.
> Sheikh Magzoub of Al Baneya, Sudan (death 1986)

The Prophet (pbuh) in his description of Ihsan said **'And if you see him not'**, meaning some actually see Him, and this alone is proof for its possibility. Nevertheless, there is *ijma'a* (agreement of the scholars) about the possibility of the vision of God, as is stated by the scholars of *Aqida* (creed). This is because the Prophet (pbuh) said it will happen on the Day of Judgment and as a reward for the people of paradise (Bukhari). In the Quran God says **"faces on that day are bright, looking up to their Lord"** (75:22-23). The Prophet (pbuh) said **'You will see your Lord, and you will have no doubt in it'** (Bukhari). He (pbuh) also said in another Hadith **'You will see your Lord and you shall converse with Him' (Nissai)**. The Quran discourages arguing about the vision of God, God says **"do they disagree with Prophet Muhammed about what he sees"**(53:12).

The Prophet (pbuh) saw God whilst alive and in this world (yet in the 7th heaven), which establishes its possibility in this world and that it is not exclusive to the hereafter in *Jennah*. And it is the Islamic principle that what happens to Prophets as miracles can happen to the pious as *karama* (gift from God). This means just like the Prophet (pbuh) saw God in this world, it is also possible for the pious to see Him in this world. God said to the Prophet Muhammed (pbuh) **'And keep your soul content with those who call on their Lord morning and evening, seeking His Face (18:28),** in describing a group of companions who God describes as worshiping Him eagerly in seeking His vision. If it was not possible or in vain, then God would have said it in revelation or the Prophet (pbuh) could have advised them not to have such hope. Also, those who call on God seeking His Face is not for a vision in the next world, for in the next it is general for the people of paradise, but they do specifically for Vision in this world, out of *shog* (yearning) and love for God.

Another proof for people being able to have Vision of God in this world is the *Qudsi* Hadith; that of the angels who visit circles of worship and mention of Allah. When God asks them about the spiritual state of the believers in the *zkir* circles (and God is most knowledgeable of it), He asks if these worshipers have seen God ('*ahum rauni*'), and when the angels say they haven't, God says **"How then would their worship be if they had seen Me" (Bukhari)**. If vision was not possible in this world, then God would not have asked if the worshipers have seen Him or considered the case of their worship if they had.

Some may think that just as the Prophet (pbuh) saw God in the 7th heaven it is only possible there and thus for the slave to see God they too have to journey there. But *miraj* as mentioned in the Quran was not for the purpose of vision of God; it was for God to show His signs (the grander of His creation) to the Prophet (pbuh). God says in the Quran that the reason for the journey was **"so that We might show him some of Our signs" (17:1).** God in the Quran also says that He is nearer to us than our jugular vein (50:16); and He is not in the 7th heaven to require *miraj*. The person must know that God is not like creation, and there is nothing like Him. God is not limited by time or space, they are His creation. He is not limited by time so that people can see Him in a certain time and not another, meaning they can only see Him in the next world and not this, and He is neither limited by space so that people have to travel to a certain place to see Him. God says **"God's chair is as large as the heavens and earth"** (2:255). His Chair as well as being a physical entity located above the heavens is also in this verse a metaphor for His presence and power, meaning that they extend across the heavens and earth. This *aya* (verse) also explains why Moses (as) spoke to God while walking on earth, and Mohammed (pbuh) did in the seventh heaven, supporting that God isn't limited to a certain place and therefore to be in His presence does not require being in a certain place.

The Nature of the Vision

When the Messenger (pbuh) was asked if he saw his Lord, he replied '*nor ini arah*;' **'I see Him as Light' (Muslim)** and in another version **'I saw a Light' (Muslim)**. In his *dua's* the Prophet (pbuh) asked Allah's refuge by **'The light of Your Face' (Muslim)** and used to ask him to give him the **'Pleasure of seeing His face' (Muslim)**. As to the clarity of the vision, the Messenger (pbuh) when describing the vision in the hereafter said it will be **'As clear as the seeing of the moon or the sun when they are not covered by the clouds' (Bukhari)**. In describing the vision of the people of paradise, he also affirmed in some Hadith that vision is with the eyes as apposed to a feeling or a dream. God says in the Quran "**the earth shines with the light of its Lord**"(39:69).

The companions (may Allah be pleased with them) are thought to have differed on if the Messenger (pbuh) saw God in this world. The two main opinions being that of the great scholar of Quran, the cousin of the Prophet (pbuh), Ibn Abass (raa), that the Messenger did see his Lord, while the great scholar Aisha (raa), the beloved wife of the Messenger (raa), and the mother of the believers insisted on the opinion that the Messenger did not see his Lord. These two opinions might appear to be contradictory and then it being a choice between the two. But in fact these two opinions are complementary and must be both accepted and understood for one to have perfect knowledge of the subject and of God. Both their opinions are correct as they both were talking about a different aspect of the vision.

To understand this we must understand the story of Moses (as) mentioned in the Quran. When Moses (as) asked to see God and God replied to this query saying that if the mountain could stand still then he could see Him, and when Allah manifested Himself to the mountain, it trembled. God says "**when Moses came to the meeting of God, and God spoke to Moses, Moses said to God, he wants vision of God. God said to Moses, he will not see Him, but to look at the mountain,** and if it stabilises, Moses will see God, and when God manifested to the mountain, the mountain crumbled and Moses fell down and fainted. When Moses woke up, he said, glory to God, and he repents to God, and is the first believer" (7:143).

We notice that while Moses (as) asked God to allow him to see Him, Muhammed (pbuh) always asked Allah in his prayers specifically the pleasure of seeing His face. The two requests are different; this is because Moses (as) could be said to have asked for the whole, and Muhammed (pbuh) asked in this *duas* for the partial (i.e. face) as is reflected by the words used. The two are different types of visions, and while the first is impossible, the second is. What Aisha (raa) was referring to when she said the Prophet did not see His Lord was the impossible one, and what Ibn Abass (raa) said happened is the second. The face is known to be the site of beauty and that which faces us. In the Arabic language the word face (*wajh*) is used to mean what 'faces', e.g. *wajh al ard* (lit face of the earth meaning the surface of the land). Thus the reference to God's face in the *Quran* and Hadith is not a literal one of eyes, nose and mouth, but a metaphorical one. It is to mean that which faces and thus can be seen. This is not to mean that God is made of parts, a face and hands and neck or sides visible and invisible, but that God can limit what we can see of Him to what He describes as His 'face'. Muhammed (pbuh) knew this and thus asked to see God's face, while Moses (as) asked to see the 'whole' of God, or rather an unlimited vision of God, which is not possible.

In the *sharia* women according to many scholars are allowed to expose two things, the face and hands. This is a metaphor to what we can know and see of God, and while women must do this to be modest and to be safe from others, with God it is for our own safety as if He exposes more, like the mountain we will perish. Also just like the wives of the Messenger (pbuh) were commanded to cover their faces so as not to be seen by immoral men. God's face is veiled from the disbelievers and disobedient believers by their own unspiritual state. We can see God's creation, the heavens and earth which are referred to in the Quran as being in the

Grasp of 'His Hands'. We can also see that which He wishes to show us of Him and thus face us with, i.e. His Light, which is referred to as being 'His Face' in the *Quran* and *Hadith*. The Messenger (pbuh) asked Allah to manifest His light, while Moses (as) asked for the manifestations of all of God's attributes and names, i.e. His essence (*zat*), by not being specific. God's light is referred to as 'His Face' because it is possible for us to have vision of it, and is what He chose to face us. God's essence is that which we know and know not of God. Manifestation of God can be with a single attribute, e.g. His Mercy, or with whole essence, the first is possible for humans to have vision of and the second is impossible. This is why Moses (as) couldn't see God and Muhammed (pbuh) did. The veiling in Islam is not as in some cultures based on shame, shyness or reclusive, but as a formality of protecting identity of expressing belief in a pure God. This is the reason God commanded it, they may be anonymous as not to be harmed, and this is because they were targeted. God likewise is veiled in protection of his identity as a form of majesty like the imperials of china behind a screen, for in the *dunya* there are those who believe and those who disbelieve and those who disbelieve may be abusive towards God if he was apparent, and thus he is in the unseen as a form of avoiding disbelievers to reach this level of insolence towards their creator.

God in Islam is considered to have Attributes and Names that describe Him and His powers. In total at least ninety-nine were communicated to us in the Quran and the Sunnah. Nevertheless, these are considered not to be all there is of God's attributes. This is based on that in one Hadith the Prophet (pbuh) said **'Lord, I ask You by the sake of every name You have, those which you revealed in Your Book, taught to one of Your slaves or kept in Your knowledge' (Al Haithami).** Thus God is considered to be able to *tjala* (manifest or make apparent) His Essence which would be all His attributes, or just one of them like His Light. As Muhammed (pbuh) did not see all God's attributes (His Essence), but His attribute His Light also called 'His face', Aisha's (raa) opinion was correct that Muhammed (pbuh) did not see Allah and that **'whomever** said Muhammed (pbuh) have seen his Lord has said lies against God' (Muslim). This is true, as no one can see God or like the mountain would turn to dust. The manifestation of God's light is God, thus Ibn Abass' (raa) opinion is also correct that Muhammed (pbuh) did see his Lord. Ibn Abass (raa) said in explaining the Prophet's vision of God that **'God manifested His Light which is Him' (Tirmizi)**. In other words the Prophet (pbuh) saw the manifestation of God's attribute of light, and as God's light is Him, he did see God. God's light is God, but it is not everything that is Him. This is because even though a manifestation of one of God's attributes or names is His Essence, His essence is not just that certain attribute. This is the basis of Aisha (raa) opinion; that even though the Messenger (pbuh) saw the manifestation of Allah's Light, he did not see Allah, as Allah's essence is not just that one attribute but there are more. So even though the Messenger (pbuh) did see God as he saw the manifestation of His light, it could also be argued that he did not, as he did not see the manifestation of all of his attributes, which in itself is impossible. The Prophet (pbuh) explains this in the Hadith, which says if Allah were to make visible Himself to us we would perish, just like Moses' (as) mountain turned to dust when God manifested to it.

What Moses (as) asked for is both impossible and possible. It is possible for God to manifest His Essence, but it is impossible for us to have vision of it, as His Grandeur will turn us to dust like it did to the mountain. This is due to the greatness of God. The Messenger (pbuh) when explaining the manifestation of God to the mountain held out the tip of his little finger to imply that God did not manifest Himself totally for the mountain to turn to dust (Al Tirmizi). He (pbuh) was trying to give us an idea of the magnificence of God. For if what would be equal to the tip of the little finger turns mountains to dust, how then could vision be possible for us and how great indeed is God? When Moses (as) asked to see God's Essence, Allah did not say you cannot see Me, as that would then imply vision of God is impossible, but instead God manifested himself to the mountain and allowed Moses (as) to see that he would not be able to stand His vision. This incidence communicated to us that it is allowed for us to ask Allah to give us vision of Himself, but in the religion of Islam it is done in the manner of the Prophet (pbuh) by asking to see *nor wajhihi* (the Light of His Face).

The essence of God (*zat*) is something we cannot comprehend, understand, or have vision of because *laysa kamithlihi shi'a*; **'There is nothing like Him' (Quran 42:11), 'and of knowledge little was communicated to you' (11:85)**. It is also the command of the Messenger (pbuh) that we should not ponder on God's Essence but God's creation. This is due to our limitations and the fact that God is beyond our comprehension. The Prophet (pbuh) said **'His veil is Light and if He were to remove it, the glory of His Countenance would burn everything of His creation, as far as His gaze reaches' (Bukhari)**. This Hadith could be misunderstood if it were taken literally, to say that Allah created a light to veil Himself from His creation. How can The Apparent (one of the name of God) ever be veiled by His creation? This Hadith is metaphorically explaining that we cannot have complete vision of God, but that what we can see is merely a veil compared to His whole essence. And that just like the mountain became dust when Allah manifested to it, we would perish if given complete Vision. In other words we are given little knowledge, and in the case of the Vision it is His Light, which is referred to as His veil in this Hadith. The Messenger (pbuh) in this Hadith told us what is possible for us to see, which is His Light, and that this compared to His Essence is like being faced with a veil and you see only it. So veil here is like face, meaning what faces, as veils face the seer, limiting their vision of what is being veiled. This referring to His Light being a veil or a face, is contradictory if both were to be taken literally, but are not since both were used metaphorically to imply a certain meaning, that our vision of His light is a limited vision compared to the vision of His essence. This understanding of 'His Face' is better understood if there is a firm belief that Allah is not made of parts nor has sides (like His creation –there is nothing like Him), and this is why *face* in the Quran is also translated as Allah's Essence and understood as that. An example is, **"all creation will one day perish and remains the face of the Lord of majesty and beauty"** (55:27). This verse also tells us about the everlastingness of Hell and Heaven, for it tells us that His *Jalal* (Majesty) such as being Just and Vengeful with the inhabitants of Hell is forever, and His *Ikram* (Bounty) of being Merciful and Generous to the inhabitants of Heaven is likewise forever. If the *aya* had said, 'and abide God', then that would have implied that both hell and Heaven would perish and only God will remain.

The vision of His light does not give us complete knowledge of God (complete knowledge of His essence) as **"no vision can grasp God, but God's vision encompasses all. God is the gentle and the informed" (6:103).** Allah said **'none encompasses the protected knowledge of God, without God's permitting it first"** (2:255) and also as creatures we have been given little knowledge **"people are given of knowledge only a little" (17:85).** On the Day of Judgment more of God is going to be shown in Vision. He exposes what He metaphorically referred to as His *sag* (shin). **"The day when exposed is the shin of God, and they are told to prostrate to the Lord but they are incapable" (68:42).** The word '*sag*' (shin) is also used metaphorically like the word 'face', yet unlike 'face' it suggests Might and Power, as the shin holds up the person. The disbelievers as they had not glorified God in the world, the verse says they will have difficulty doing so on the Day of Judgement. This metaphor of sag is to say that the Day of Judgment will reveal a lot to His human creation about His Strength. This is seeing visually the strength of angels and this will only through extrapolation know more about the strength of God.

The confusion some could have regarding the two different visions, of 'face' or essence, is if the person does not understand the difference between when God uses to describe Himself in relation to one of His attributes or to His name, Allah. Allah is the name of the Essence, meaning all of the attributes and names that we know and know not (and thus could be considered *Ism Allah Al A'azam* – God's Greatest Name).

The use of an attribute is to give us understanding of that attribute, e.g. *Alrahman ala al 3arsh istawa*; **"the compassionate established on the throne"** (20:5) is not the same as *Allah ala al Arsh istawa* 'Allah, who is established on the Throne', the second could mean God is established on the throne, but the first is saying that the compassionate God is established on the throne, so the meaning we are trying to be given is not one of God's location, but that God's kingdom is ruled on mercy, and isn't He the one Who said, '*rahmati sabagat gadabi*' **'My Mercy has exceeded My Majesty' (Bukhari).**

The request for the vision of God could be due to different motivations. It can be in wanting knowledge, of wanting to know more about God, as was the case of Moses (as) or out of love and *shog* (yarning) as was the *dua* of the Prophet Muhammed (pbuh). It could also be in mockery as was the request of the disbelievers in the time of Moses (as) who said **"when the people of Israel said to Moses mocking they will not believe in God, except if God exposes Himself for all to see. God punished them in a sudden attack, that dropped them all dead"** (2:55).

In one Hadith it is said on Judgment Day that God will appear in an image not to the description people know and He will say He is God, and the believers will say "**God forbid**" and that they will not leave until the real God comes to them, and if God appears they will know and recognise Him. Then comes God in an image they know to be true and says He is God. The believers will say He is their God and they follow God (Muslim). This Hadith teaches that believers need to know the description of the true God, to be able to identify Him if they gain His Vision.

Seeing The Light

The Prophet (pbuh) in his prayers asked God by **'The light of [His] Face' (Muslim).** The Light is also one of God's names. As to the nature of Light, in Arabic there are two types of light: one is *nor* and the other is *doa*. In the Quran God attributed *nor* to that we see in the moon and *doa* to that we see in the sun. The Quran says **"God made the sun a shinning light and the moon to be a bright light"** (10:5). The word that is used by God in the Quran and by the Messenger (pbuh) in the Hadith to describe the Light of God is *nor,* the one that describes the light of the moon. Rather than this making people think that God is like created light, it must be rather understood that God created light as a metaphor to understand one of His attributes. As the verse says he created this in truth, to mean for a serious purpose to allow people to distinguish light. In fact in modern scientific time, they call some rays ultraviolet light, and in Islam this would be considered inaccurate, that it's '*dia*' and not light; it's not *nor*, only white visible light of the moon is *nor*. Light is the name given to phenomena that makes things possible to see with the eye; it's thus a visual aid, the most basic, because without light there is no vision and things become as if they don't exist. In fact modern science says light is made of small particles; it also has the property of waves as they move from the source of light and hit against the objects of vision and into the eye, after which they change form based on what colour the things they hit is giving this information to the eye and then to the brain, which then plots this into the image we see. However, as any muslim knows the idea of a light messenger is not knew, it is an idea our forefathers heard thousands of years ago, for in Islam Prophet Muhammed (pbuh) is called the Prophet of light, as God called him '*siraj munira*' (a shinning light) as he brought the light of guidance that is the revelation, as well as the fact that one of his miracles is that his body shone light, so that his wife picked a needle from the sand. In fact to teach human absoluteness of faith in that light is how things are seen. God created the night dark, then he created the moon that changes its size throughout the month, and people can see how much light and clarity there is in proportion to the position of the moon. Then when the moon is full on the fourteenth day of the month the night is clear, and the bucket, bed, tent to one side, the goat over there it is all very clear, and thus the glory of the full moon. This is because during the day the light from the sun is so explosive, the person just sees the things but not the light itself, and thus the night is the classroom for studies on light.

As to His *nor* (light), Allah said in the Quran **"God is the light of the heavens and earth, and the parable of His light is like a niche with a lamp and the lamp is in a glass and the glass shines as if a bright star, and the lamp is fuelled by an oil from a blessed olive tree, neither of the west nor east, and its oil could shine even if not touched by fire, it is light upon light, and God guides to His light whom He chooses, and God gives examples to people and God is knowledgable of everything."** (24:35). As God's light is connected to a metaphor we are able to understand what is meant when the word Light is used to describe God and thus appreciate it when we see it. There is something like God's Light; the light of the moon, but there is nothing like God. The Messenger (pbuh) made a similitude of God's mercy to that of a mother. When one of the female companions ran after her toddler to breastfeed him, the Prophet Muhammed (pbuh) described this as mercy and added that the mercy of God is in excess of a Mother's, but in saying that he did not mean that the mother is an equal to God. Thus the Quran did not consider it wrong to follow **'there is none like Him'** by adding and He is The Hearing and The Seeing. Individual attributes of God have examples in the world for us to understand them, but God is One and has no similitude to His essence.

When believers gain vision of God, it is seeing His face, and practically seeing light. Ibn Abass is said to have prayed **"Lord, I ask you by the light of your face, that shine bright the heavens and earth"** (Haithamy). Prophet Muhammed (pbuh) also said **"I seek God's help by the light of His face that shines the darkness, and with it becomes perfect the issues of this world and hereafter"** (Dia Almagdesy)

The Light of God is not a created light nor has its properties; light from the moon can be blocked by objects and comes from a certain direction. The light of God is not blocked by anything, not even our bodies, and has no direction, so that when we have vision of God's Light, it is truly closer to us than our jugular veins. The experience of seeing God's Light not being blocked by our bodies (passing through it), have been misunderstood by spiritually overwhelmed slaves of God (like Al Hallaj), that they are becoming divine, or that humans have a divine nature, but the Quran and Hadith give us clear explanation. The light of God has no limit, so that when a Muslim sees God, they will see light in all directions. The Prophet Muhammed (pbuh) in his prayer to going to the Mosque used to pray for God **"Lord make in my heart light, and in my tongue light, and in my hearing light, and in my sight light, and above me light, and below me light, and to my right light, and to my left light, and in front of me light, and behind me light, and inside me light, and increase my light, and make for me light, and make me light. Lord give me light, and make my nerves light and my flesh light, and my blood light, and in my hair light, and in my skin light"** (Bukhari) and he increased in another Hadith **"and increase me in light (three times)"** (Bukhari) and **"give me light upon light"** (Ibn Hajar) and this is the description of the Vision of God. The person during vision of God will experience as if they are drowning in an ocean of light.

Knowledge of an attribute is knowledge of the essence. A person can claim to know the essence from a knowledge of just an attribute, as the essence is those names and attributes which we know and that which we don't. Thus, as Ibn Abass (raa) explained, the seeing of one of God's Attributes is the seeing of His essence.

The vision of God's Light is with the eyes as is mentioned in some Hadith, and when the Quran says **"the heart did not feel it was false what he saw"** (53:11). This does not mean that the Messenger (pbuh) saw Allah with his heart, but means that the heart believed what the eyes saw (His Light), for 'believing' is exclusively the faculty of the heart. As for saying that Allah can also be seen with the vision of the heart, it is also correct, for some attributes such as Al Rahman (the Merciful) or Al Malik (the King) cannot be seen directly with the eyes, but with the vision and understanding of the heart (mind) alone. The Quran says **"to

God is the east and west, and wherever people direct themselves they will find the face of God, for God is vast and knowledgeable" (2:115). This verse is in support of that **'Allah is the Light of the heavens and the earth'**, and thus that 'wherever you turn' in the heaven or the earth, there is His face. This verse is a reminder of a limitation in our Vision of God. The Quran says 'wherever you turn' as we see by our eyes there is a limited gaze at a time and such the need to turn to see more. It also reminds us that our vision's capacity is limited that it cannot encompass His Face let alone His essence.

The *shahada* (statement of faith) of those with vision is based on *Mushahada* (vision) and no longer *Iman* alone. The knowledge of the existence of God's attributes is no longer based on what was communicated to us by the Messenger (pbuh) alone, but also from personally observing their manifestation. This is the highest state of spirituality, a state of excellence, of Ihsan. It must be remembered that not all supernatural light, is the light of God. For instance the companions of Prophet Muhammed (pbuh) used sticks to emit light at night, as a miracle and this light is not God.

Can the devil take the form of God?

There is a famous story of the great scholar of Ihsan Sheikh Abdalgadir Jailani's (raa) of when the devil tried to trick him. It is said that the sheikh saw a cloud and light which said I am your lord and you no longer need to pray, and when the sheikh damned him, the devil said that he tricked many people but the sheikh's knowledge of God saved him.

The messenger (pbuh) said the devil cannot take his form, this is to affirm that people's vision of him are truthful. This is the same with Allah, even though the devil can come in many forms saying he is God, he can not take the form of the true Allah, as the creation can never be the creator nor take His form. There is nothing like God or can look like God. As the messenger is a creation there is a logical possibility that the devil can take his form. Just like water can take form of the container, or angel can take the form of a human, there is a possibility for the devil to take the physical form of the messenger. To say that the devil can take God's form shows ignorance of God. Nevertheless, the devil can come in many forms to trick those ignorant of the knowledge of God. As mentioned before, knowledge of God by studying *Aqida* is imperative before embarking on the path of Ihsan. This is why the Shafi (raa) said be both a *faqih* (knowledgeable of religion) and *Sufi* (spiritual), for Sufism without knowledge can lead to misguidance.

The Two Heavens

The Prophet (pbuh) said **'God has ninety nine names whoever counts them will enter Heaven' (Bukhari).** Whoever understands Allah's ninety-nine names and experiences them as Allah manifests them, is indeed in Heaven, a Heaven of the lover when witnessing their Beloved. The Quran says **'those who fear their Lord's Majesty to them are two Heavens'** (55:46). Paradise from the pleasure of knowing God and paradise the abode of the pious in the next world and the first is the greater of the two.

Ali (raa) said **'men are asleep when they die *antabahu* (become aware)'**. That is a very deep sleep that required the panic and pain of death to wake a person from it. He said *aware* as Allah is nearer to us than our jugular vein, yet is not totally aware except for those that Allah granted vision. As Sheikh Ibn Attalla (raa) said; 'How can you imagine that something else veils Him, when He is the One with whom there is nothing else?' The scholar meant that only another God would be capable of veiling Him and there is none, and what He created only veils us from being 'aware' and doesn't veil Him from being Apparent, for He is The Apparent before creation and The Apparent after creating creation. The lack of awareness of some of his creation is thus not due to His absence for he is Apparent, but a personal state in them. God says '*agfalna galbhu an zikrna*' (they have closed hearts (18:28)) that make them not conscious of what is near to their neck vein. When God becomes apparent it is not because He changed, for God does not change, but because it is us who have changed, we have gained awareness of His existence.

The Prophet Muhammed (pbuh) said in paradise believers will go to a valley of musk mountains, and they will see their God. This valley is called '*Mazeed*' (The Extra). Perfume symbolises kindness as perfume travels and goes beyond the source, so it represents the spirit of going further from the self and appreciating others. Perfume is sweet to smell so it means kindness, being good to others. The connection of musk and Vision of God is that since musk perfume symbolises kindness, this is utmost good character which is imperative for Vision of God. Just as people must be mannered and curtsy to kings, God is the King of Kings.

In Islam there is no prohibition on seeking Vision of God in this world. Love and want of God is praiseworthy and so should not be discouraged especially by those who limit the Vision of God to be only in the afterlife in Heaven. The Quran says God punishes the disbelievers on the Day of Judgment by being veiled from them. God says **"indeed they are on Judgment Day veiled from seeing their Lord"** (83:15). This says that not seeing God is suffering and hardship to be used as a punishment against the disbelievers. The Prophet Muhammed (pbuh) asked the angel Gabriel if he sees God and the angel replied, **"between the angel and God are seventy veils of light, if the angel were to see their lowest he would burn"** (Asuti). This is to say that the angels are not in configuration to have Vision of God, but the humans are superior and therefore the angels prostrated to Adam (as) in Heaven.

> The vision of God is what we must gain
> In this life and in paradise where we remain
> The vision of God should be why we exist
> It comes from the beauty of God who we can't resist
> The vision of God is the greatest pleasure
> It comes from deep worship and not play and leisure
> The vision of God tells God is the truth

When without God there is pain and no ruth
The vision of God makes a Muslim a saint
Of miracles and spirituality to ecstasy to faint
The vision of God is to see God's light
To see the face of God of majesty and might
The vision of God is the beauty of sight
It is a great pleasure, a bounty a delight
The vision of God is by doing what is right
To purify the spirit and the ego we must fight
The vision of God is when God lifts from His face the veil
Then His presence is gained and His truth prevail

CHAPTER THIRTY

THE PLEASURE OF THE VISION OF GOD

The pleasures of this world only show small resemblance to the pleasure of paradise. About paradise the Prophet (pbuh) said **'God says He prepared in paradise what no eye has seen or ear has heard of and what no one ever imagined' (Bukhari)** as a reward. In Islam paradise does not only provide the pleasures of the body, but also of the mind such as hobbies and other activities people did and enjoyed in the world. The Prophet (pbuh) replied to an avid farmer that he will be able to farm in paradise (Bukhari). God says **"no soul knowns what are hidden to them of pleasure of Heaven, a reward for what they did in the world"** (32:17). But even paradise does not compare to the pleasure of witnessing the Face of Allah, full of Majesty and Glory. The Prophet (pbuh) said **'When the people of paradise see God, they will forget all the pleasures of paradise in that instant of looking at God' (Ahmed),** such is the great pleasure of vision of God. And in another Hadith the Prophet (pbuh) said **'there will be nothing of paradise that is more loved or pleasurable to its inhabitants than seeing their Lord'** (Tirmizi).

The pleasure of seeing God is merely the extrapolation of *halawat al iman*; sweetness or pleasure of belief. The pleasure of belief comes from knowing that God really does exist, as the person's *Iman* increases. The Prophet (pbuh) **'Whoever possesses three attributes will experience the sweetness of belief: that he loves Allah and His Messenger more than anything else; that he loves another person for the sake of Allah alone; and he hates returning to disbelief as much as he would hate being thrown into a fire' (Bukhari).** Seeing God is the greatest strengthener of belief, and thus the pleasure of belief dramatically increases. The pleasure of God is also due to His Beauty and Bounty. God is great, glorified, and majestic; to be accepted to His presence, and for God to lift the veil and for a person to then see God is a great honour and one of intense pleasure. In the *Sunnah* and example of the Messenger (pbuh) we should ask Allah to give us the pleasure of seeing His face. The Prophet Muhammed (pbuh) used to pray **'I ask you Lord to give me the pleasure of looking at Your face, and the yearning to Your meeting'** (Nissai).

> Lord, give me the pleasure of seeing Your Face
> So that I become blessed, full of grace
> It's because I love you, I swear it is the case
> You said compete towards God, so make me win the race
> You are not a physical entity, so I can't ask You for an embrace
> But I will forever seek Your Face, in every time and place

CHAPTER THIRTY ONE

AFTER THE VISION

The increase in knowledge of God and sincere worship as the person gets better in *Jihadul-nafs* and increase in *tazzkiya* gets the person into a state of longing for their Lord, of arduous worship for God's sake and continued yearning for a glimpse of His Diving Face. Like the Messenger (pbuh) they eagerly ask Allah for His vision. This occurs as their desires become one, just like their belief becomes more monotheistic; from the diverse desires of the body to a single desire of seeing God. This is the greatest worship and praise of God, for it reveals an understanding of and belief in God.

The slave then craves the death of their ego that is hassling and keeping them busy from contemplating their beloved. An ego that keeps them away from Him by its demands and sins, how could they let such a thing live? As long as the ego is alive and the person is under its command and care, God does not grant vision (rather their ego distracts them from Him) nor can they worship and obey Him alone. He is the One who said if a slave shows partnership in their worship He leaves them to that partner (Muslim). He is in no need of partners, even if a person's own ego. The Quran says **"is God not enough for His worshipers"** (39:36). Can't the slave trust that God's orders and commands take care of them well if not more than their own egos and desires? Are not God's commands and their following for the benefit of the slave, in this world and the next?

The death of the ego which is the fruit and success of *Jihadul-nafs* is a struggle of love and power for command and control. It occurs as one takes the authority and command it has on the mind and body, and gives it to God so that nothing of its commands is obeyed and only that of God. Death of it occurs by ignoring its presence and commands, and becomes oblivious of it as the person concentrates on contemplating the Greatness of God and their want to see Him. The knowledge and love of God when they intensify makes the student enter a state of *fana fi Allah* (intense love and attention to God that makes them oblivious to all else) and this state leads to the *nafs* to be annihilated in a way it cannot recover (unlike the other types of *fana*) so that it could be said to have died, hence called *mot-ul-nafs* (death of the ego).

After death of the ego the person changes from being a self-centred being into an obedient slave of God. The person becomes a God centred person who accepts that all goodness is from Him and all harm happens with His permission and for the slave's benefit. They change from one who is in constant awareness of their self and desires and controlled by them, into someone who is God conscious and subservient to Him only. This is true slavehood and absolute worship. This is what is ideal, what is excellent; what is Ihsan.

As the slave performs *Jihadul-nafs* and allows their ego to die, with His generosity Allah is capable of giving His slaves the pleasure of seeing the Light of His Face full of Majesty and Beauty. Yet this is not guaranteed in *Jihadul-nafs*; what is guaranteed is by making good worship and *nafila* the person's *dua* is accepted, and for those in this high spiritual state their *dua* is indeed His vision.

God says "**among the believers are men who have been true to their covenant with Allah. Some of them have completed their vow, and some still wait, but they have never changed their determination in the least**" (33:23). Those who fulfil their *bay'a* of Ihsan have fulfilled their promise and obeyed their commands and this is most evident if they reach the state of *fanaul nafs fi Allah and Mot al nafs*. *Jihadul-nafs* is a struggle that is in parallel to that of war, and just as those who do not abandon their army have fulfilled their promise so do those who continue on their study of the branch of Ihsan. These are the *Awlya* (saints), those who *walu* (gave allegiance) to Allah against His enemies including their egos out of their love and worship for Him, and thus He can choose to gives them vision out of His love and acceptance of them and to honour their request and answer their prayer. If the slave has been graced with Vision of God they have been granted a great bounty indeed.

If the slave is granted vision and feels overwhelmed spiritually by high spiritual state, and thoughts contrary to Islamic creed enter their mind, they should repeat '*Amantu bellah wa rasulihi*' (I believe in Allah and His Prophet – a prayer prescribed by the Prophet (pbuh) to combat doubt in belief) to prevent them from entering into a state of spiritual intoxication and to maintain the pure belief of the religion. In this state they experience the truthfulness of Allah's name The Peace, as peace and safety enters their heart, so that they do not become frightened of that which frighten people nor become sad by that which brings sadness to people. The Quran says **"is it not in the mention of God that hearts find peace and contentment?"**(13:28) Imagine then if His mention gives content and peace, how about His presence, or to a greater extent His vision? The peace from His presence or vision and the sweetness of *iman* that accompanies them brings a spiritually euphoric state.

Death of the ego does not prevent the person from sins as they do not become angels after annihilating their *nafs*, they remain human. The Messenger (pbuh) said, **'all sons of Adam sin but the best amongst sinners are those who repent' (Ibn Hajr)**. This is because *Jihadul-nafs* does not make people infallible but gives them discipline and makes them sin less as the main cause of sin –the ego– dies. People do not become infallible if their egos die, rather they become perfect slaves who remember Allah and are sure to ask God's forgiveness if they do fall into sin. And they gain discipline in being able to restrain from sin and perform good deeds.

After death of the ego the great restrain from luxury of *Jihadul-nafs* is eased, for it was for a purpose and it has been fulfilled. If this wasn't the case then Jesus (as) and his discipline would have not indulged by asking for a banquet from Heaven and neither would God provide the luxury of grapes for an imprisoned companion of the Prophet (pbuh) or Mary (as). This is the case as during *Jihadul-nafs* the student should and do restrain from luxuries as they work hard to fulfil what is important. Then the slave can return to normal level of living as by doing so they are in constant remembrance of the bounties of God and thus can better praise Him. As well as being able to refrain from sin, death of the ego allows the person to have spiritual desires of great worship and an ability to perform them, allowing them to perform great number of night prayer, charity and a lot of *zikr* that a normal person wouldn't be able to do as they would be discouraged by their egos.

God tests His slaves according to their capabilities and capacities and this increases as when their spiritual state and religious knowledge increase. Thus those of high spiritual states are the utmost tested. The Prophet (pbuh) said the most tested are the Prophets then the pious in a level according to their religion (Tirmizi). Allah said **"do people think they will be left to say they believe and not be trialled with hardship"** (29:2). This is because the person is tested as long as they are alive and are in this world, even if their *nafs* is dead. This is because during disobedience it is a form of encouragement and punishment but tests to the pious are confirmations of their belief by their patience and steadfastness to God during hardship. The Quran says, **"worship God in devotion until comes death"** (15:99) i.e. follow the commands of God in worship until death. This confirms that the person will be tested up to that time and that nothing stops worship even high spiritual station. This is further proven by the example of the Prophet (pbuh) and his companions whose worship never decreased but was only on the increase.

The Prophet (pbuh) made the *dua* given by the Quran **"Lord, lay not on us a burden greater than we have strength to bear.' (2:286).**

With knowledge of the religion and increase in spiritual station the slave's only fear becomes being cut from their lord and worse fear is to lose faith. God says **"God made belief beloved to them and beautiful it in their hearts, and made hateful to them disbelief and becoming disbelievers, and they are the wise" (49:7).**

The Prophet (pbuh) said: **'Whoever possesses three things will find the sweetness of *iman*. For Allah and His Messenger (pbuh) to be more beloved to him than anything else. To be able to love a person for Allah's sake alone. To hate to return to disbelief the way he hates to be thrown into the fire.'(Bukhari).** Then their love becomes what God commands and their detest is what is forbidden. The Prophet (pbuh) said **'no one is a complete believer until their desires concur with God's message' (Al Nawawi).**

In the Hadith of the angels that visit circles of knowledge and group *zikr*, the angels said to God, **'if they saw You they would be even more worshiping of You, more praising of You, and more glorifying' (Bukhari).** A slave who has been graced with vision has been through spiritual stations and purification from diseases that make them inclined to worship more intensely and perfectly. Their capacity for worship increases and it should be filled. The worship at different spiritual stations is different, and after reaching the station of slavehood the emphasis should be in making prayer, especially night prayer, reading the Quran and making great amounts of *zikr*. Nevertheless, they still must fulfil the rights of their bodies, families and other obligations, and thus not go into excess beyond their spiritual capacity as they may then neglect other responsibilities. However, the measure of the amount of worship required of us by God must be honoured and kept to the limit decided by Him.

After cleaning the Prophet's (pbuh) heart in the start of the Prophet's journey to God, the Prophet (pbuh) said **"Gabriel then brought a**

container of gold filled with wisdom and belief and he poured it into my heart" (Bukhari). When the person performs *tazzkiya* as their diseases are erased they are replaced with wisdom and belief, and it is then no wonder that the people of Ihsan are famed for their great wisdom. And who is wiser than he who recognises God and worships Him? Most importantly after the Vision the slave is then able to worship God on a level of consciousness and belief as if they see him even when they are not and thus complete the highest stage of Ihsan. In this way they have perfected their practice of their religion.

CHAPTER THIRTY TWO

SAINTHOOD IN ISLAM

Sainthood is to become accepted by God, as a close worshiper, an ally and friend of God. The Quran says about the saints **"the saints of God have nothing to fear and they shall not become sad" (10:62)**. The saints are those who are distinguished from other believers by their miracles even if it's as simple as a dream that became true. All saints of God in Islam have been practitioners of Sufism (Ihsan), as how can a person be considered a saint if they haven't perfected their worship in their practice of the branch of Ihsan. The Vision of God is the highest level of Sainthood in Islam, as it expresses God's love and acceptance of the Saint by God.

Being a saint doesn't make a person infallible however close they come to being so due to their strict worship and much devotion. We are the sons of Adam (as), the sons of a sinner. We are not infallible angels. The greatest of sin is not the performing of sins, as we are created to sin, but the sin is lack of acknowledgement that a sin is a sin and asking for forgiveness for it. All saints are sinners, but not all sinners are saints. It is a spiritual disease to not appreciate what you are: a human who will sin, and not infallible angels. If a person sins, they should repent and ask Allah's forgiveness. Know that humans were created in a way that predisposes them to sinning and thus be able to understand Allah's mercy and also His names *Algafar* (The Forgiver) and Alafu (The Pardoner), which can never be truly understood by angels as they don't sin and thus our higher status to them. This is why the angels said to God **"angels said people would destroy earth and shed blood, while they praise and glorify God in worship. God said He knows what the angels do not know"** (2:30). Allah told them that they had limited knowledge, for their disposition that doesn't allow them to sin doesn't allow them to know that Allah is The forgiving, and thus mentioned the human mischief. If a person does a mistake in secret then they should ask forgiveness for it in secret, and if they do it in public then ask for forgiveness for it in public, and if it is done in the company of someone then to tell them that they admit it's wrong and ask God to forgive for it. The Prophet said that God said **"whoever shows enmity to a saint God declares war on them. My slave does not near to me with something loved to me than obligatory worship. My slaves continues to do voluntary worship until I love them. Then when I love them I become their hearing, their sight, their hand which hits and their foot which he walks, and I accept their prayer. I do not hesitate at anything like I hesitate at giving a believer death, knowing they hate death."** (Bukhari). This means that the saints are under the protection of God, and that people should be careful with them and respect them. Anything that becomes associated to God should be respected. God says in the Quran **"respect the symbols of God, it is from piety of the heart" (22:32),** respect for the saints, their admiration and following is not worship as claimed by the Wahhabis.

In Islam there is the idea of blessing, that God's mention is blessed, and those who mention God, love God, and teach and spread the religion are blessed alive and dead. The Prophet Muhammed (pbuh) taught a blind man to ask God by the sake of Muhammed (pbuh) and he became seeing (Munzri). Wahhabism, an enemy sect to Sufism (Ihsan) consider seeking help from living or dead saints to be polytheism (disbelief) as they consider it giving the saint a power independent and in conjunction with God. However, Sufis are firm that when they seek help of saints it is out of knowing that God is merciful and recognises their desperation and that they are only using all means to elevate suffering. God says in the Quran **"the believers should fear God, and seek all means and struggle in the way of God as to perhaps succeed"**(5:35). God says in the Quran **"when it is said to them to give in charity, the disbelievers say to the believers why give to the poor when if God wanted them to be given God would have gave them directly"** (36:47) this verse shows that sometimes going to God directly can be wrong especially when other people can help. For a person to believe they are a high station with God as to believe all their prayers will be answered to the point that they need no saints or prophets help or prayer is a lie against God. This is because they assume to themselves a high station with God that they don't have. The Quran says **"the Beduins say they believe and the Prophet should tell them, they have not reaches the station of true belief but have merely submitted to God"** (49:14). No good person will belittle going directly to God in prayer, but because average believers are not confident they will be answered, they intercede. It is based on the superiority of the saints compared to general believers, the saints are near to God and their prayers are more likely to be accepted and answered. The Quran says **"and they said to Moses to pray for them because he is closer to God than them and they will stop disbelieving"** (43:49) and this verse gives example of asking prophets and saints to pray on people's behalf since they are closer to God and more likely to be answered. Being told not to seek help for problems from saints is what severe criminals do, telling people not to tell anyone so their victim suffers in secret.

The idea of prohibiting people from seeking the help of prophets and saints, is lack of mercy and shows little understanding of the suffering people experience in hardship. To say that only God can help, is the definition of a curse or damnation, since the average person is less likely to be answered by God. It also limits help and mercy, like when a man prayed in front of Prophet Muhammed (pbuh) that God should have mercy on him and Muhammed only, the Prophet Muhammed (pbuh) said to him not to constrict the vast. To believe that people should only approach God with prayer, is to believe they have a high station with God so that God will promptly answer their prayer. It is arrogance. God says **"Do no praise yourselves, God knows the truly pious"** (53:32)

Saints traditionally have domes over their graves, to protect their graves from rain water, bird droppings and to beautify their mausoleum.

Over the years a lot of misunderstanding about this important branch has risen due to the misunderstanding of the complex states of some of it scholars. This has led it to suffer from much attack and and the emotions of some have led them to condemn the branch as a whole. Nevertheless, their attacks do not change the fact that Ihsan is a branch of the religion. Unfortunately, the existence of much confusion and misunderstanding has hindered many people from appreciating and fulfilling an important branch of their religion. We should respect all the past Ihsan scholars and their works. When they were right they teach us what is right and when they are wrong they teach us what is wrong. Every part of their additions is a lesson well needed.

ABOUT THE AUTHOR

Mysa Elsheikh is a Muslim Arab Queen (Um-fugara or Mother of the Poor) from Sudan. Her full name is: Mysa daughter of Mohamed Elgasim son of Elsheikh Almagzoub. Mysa is the 61 direct descendant from Prophet Muhammed (pbuh) on her father's side and number 62 from her mother's side. She is also a descendant of Abdullah ibn Abass (raa), Prophet Muhammed's cousin and great Quran scholar. Mysa learned Arabic and the Quran in Sudan as a child, and she attended her grandfather's Quran School (*khalwa*) with her brother. Mysa once qualified for a high IQ society when she was young, and she did her GCSE Maths and Arabic a year earlier studying for both on her own, and she received A* on both, she also received an A* on Religion Education. Mysa studied Medicine at St George's University of London, she graduated early in the course by leaving in the third year with a diploma in Medical Studies. She left Medicine mainly because she wanted to finish her book Ihsan, and pursue a career in writing Islamic books and calling people to God and Islam. She studied a Medical summer course at Magdalen College University of Oxford. She also studied a year of Psychology and Creative Writing at Bolton University. In 2019 she decided to return back to Medicine and returned to Sudan, where she studied 4th and 5th year of Medicine at Ahfad University for Women in Sudan. She again left before finishing the course to pursue her career in inviting to Islam.

Inspired by a dream of Prophet Muhammed (pbuh) in the Christmas holiday of 2003, she was guided to study Sufism (Ihsan) with her paternal uncle, King Sheikh Jaily son of Elsheikh Almagzoub of Albaneya, Sudan. In the summer of 2004 she took a formal pact and became initiated into Sammaniya Sufi Path. Four months later at the age of 19 years old, Mysa has a vision of God walking down Longmead Road, in south London, Britain. In the Vision of God, Mysa saw God, Allah, the God of Islam. She reports seeing an ocean of light, that there was light to her right, and light to her left, and light above her and light below her, and light in front of her and light behind her and even light inside her. The light penetrated everything hard and solid, and it was as if she was drowning in an ocean of light. Before the vision, Mysa was for months begging God to give her His vision, and this was out of her great love for God and in seeking the divine beauty of God. Mysa comes from a family of Sufi (Ihsan) scholars, and her grandfathers and forefathers called Magazeeb of Damer were all Sufi scholars and Saints in Sudan for more than 500 years. Mysa was the favourite granddaughter of the great Sufi saint, King Sheikh Magzoub of Albaneya, Sudan (died 1986). In May 2022 she married her first cousin to fulfil verse (33:50) of the Quran and after another dream of Prophet Muhammed (pbuh), Sheikh Hamza son of Sheikh Awadallah son of Elsheikh Almagzoub. In November 2022 she accepted her first Ihsan Student. Mysa is a famous influencer in Sudan and as of December 2022 she has over 40,000 followers on TikTok alone and many viral videos watched by millions. Mysa wrote the first draft of Ihsan in a month, in February of 2006. Then writing on and off through the years until the book became over 1200 pages, which were cut down to form this book, which was published in March 2022 and updated in early 2023. When Mysa was a teenager she had a dream that she asked her uncle King Sheikh Jaily who is a Sufi scholar to give her the "secrets of the sufis", which she believes to be the knowledge of the book Ihsan. The book Ihsan was written to answer Wahhabism, and give proof for Sufism from the Quran and Sunnah, and so to defend Sufism and Sufis as a legitimate part of Islam. It is also meant to educate all people on Sufism and Islam, and introduce non-Muslims to the beauty of Islam.

Mysa is fortunate to be a descendant of Prophet Muhammed (pbuh) and her Genealogy to Prophet Muhammed (pbuh):

Mysa daughter of Sharif Mohammed Algasim, son of Sharif Magzoub, son of Sharifiya Sakeena, daughter of Sharif Fadul is the son of Sharif Hussain, son of Sharif Ibrahim, son of Sharif Muhammed, son of Sharif

Hamad, son of Sharif Muahmmed Zumrawi, son of Sharif Muhammed Ahmed Al Bagir, son of Sharif Mahmoud, son of Sharif Hamad, son of Sharif Abdalkareem, son of Sharif Hassaballah Abu Khuf, son of Sharif Muhammed Almadani, son of Sharif Jabal, son of Sharif Abdullah, son of Sharif Barakat, son of Sharif Gasim, son of Sharif Rattib, son of Sharif Shahwan, son of Sharif Messaya, son of Sharif Taglab, son of Sharif Hober, son of Sharif Zakir, son of Sharif Sirajaldeen, son of Sharif Ja Alnaser, son of Sharif Gais, son of Sharif Shafi, son of Sharif Fayed, son of Sharif Umayra, son of Sharif Umran, son of Sharif Ali Noraldeen Ameel Murij, son of Sharif Hussain, son of Sharif Hassan Alakbar, son of Sharif Ali Albadri, son of Sharif Ibrahim, son of Sharif Muhammed, son of Sharif Abi Baker, son of Sharif Ismael, son of Sharif Umar, son of Sharif Ali, son of Sharif Usman, son of Sharif Hassan, son of Sharif Muhammed, son of Sharif Mosa, son of Sharif Yahya, son of Sharif Essa, son of Sharif Ali, son of Imam Muhammed Altagi, son of Imam Hassan Alaskari, son of Imam Muhammed Alhadi, son of Imam Muhammed Aljawad, son of Imam Ali Alrida, son of Imam Mosa Alkazim, son of Imam Jafer Alsadig, son of Imam Muhammed Albagir, son of Imam Ali zain Alabdeen, son of Imam Hussain, son of Imam Ali and son of Fatimah daughter of Muhammed (pbuh) the Prophet of Islam.

Scholars chain of Sammanyah Sufi path:

Mysa took the Sufi path from Sheikh Jaily (her uncle) from Sheikh Magzoub (her grandfather) from Sheikh Awadallah son of Nimir from Sheikh Muhamed Birair son of Hussain, from Sheikh Tom son of Banaga, from Sheikh Ahmed-Altayeb son of Bashir, from Sheikh Muhammed son of Abdalkareem Alsaman, from Muhamed Altahir Almadany, from Muhammed Aqila Alhanafi Almaky, from Muhammed Alsadig, from Gassim son of Muhammed Albagdady, from Aez Alfatah, from Ali Alhadady, from Gariballah Alsaeh, from Sheikh Abdalgadir Aljailani, from Muhammed Algadi Almubarak, from Ali son of Ahmed son of Yousuf Alhakary, from Abu Alfarj Altarsosy, from Abu Nasser Bishr son of Alharith Alhafy, from Abubakr Dalf son of Jahdar Alshibly, from Aljunaid ibn Muhammed Albagdady, from Alsary son of Almuglis Alsagdy, from Marouf son of Fairoz Alkarakhy, from Dawud son of Nissair Altai, from Habib Alajamy from Hassan Albisry, from Ali son of Abi Taleb from Prophet Muhammed (peace be upon him).

www.ingramcontent.com/pod-product-compliance
Lightning Source LLC
Chambersburg PA
CBHW071858290426
44110CB00013B/1198